Tweaks

How to Fix and Fine Tune Your Volunteer Organization

Tim Bongard

FTB Press, LLC.
Chandler, AZ USA
Printed in the USA.

ISBN-13: 978-0692742969 (FTB Press)
ISBN-10: 0692742964

Foreword

Change means different things to different people. In some instances, change comes from within and manifests as behaviors or choices toward balance in the everyday. In other instances, change can mean the ability to tangibly alter the state or being of a physical space whether that be landscaping a garden, picking up litter in a local park or volunteering at a local hospital or food bank. And what of those instances where change means both? For those of us for whom life has provided favor of productivity, we might find ourselves in a moment of pause wondering how we might share of that life's work in a meaningful way... but how? That seems the most obvious of questions and yet we find ourselves in the same position as the chef or scientist: what do I cook and what do I research? Moreover, how do I organize myself and my resources? How much time do I have and what resources do I need!?! Pretty soon we might find the questions so overwhelming we might forget why we started asking questions in the first place and walk away from the endeavor!!

Something to keep in mind: change and change-agency need not be so overwhelming and Tim Bongard offers us a way to view our agency in a different way. Drawing on experiences and conversations as diverse as higher education, vintage car collecting and leading Boy Scout troops, Tim opens the conversation with just that - conversation...

If it is change we are after, in whatever shape or form; sometimes the best answers are found not in pure direction, but honest and authentic dialogue with friends or family and *Tweaks* offers us a bit of both in an accessible manner.

As Tim suggests, assumption breeds convention; the mother of invention, change or innovation, is curiosity and question; knowing where to look and what to ask is the real key!

I think you'll find in the following pages as I did, a welcoming space in which discussion of sometimes uncomfortable areas of address (when to support and when to cut ties with individuals for instance) are presented not as directives but reminders of what is possible if we equip ourselves with the necessary information and tools of engagement.

Seanan Kelly, Ed.D.

Higher and Postsecondary Education

Acknowledgements

No work such as *TWEAKS* is ever a solo act. It is a collaboration of a lifetime's worth of events, life-lessons, observations, and memories, but none of *that* would count if it weren't for the players and individuals that brought each and every one to life. I have been blest by having a wonderful cadre of people throughout time who have made this book possible.

My father and paternal grandfather set the stage for me, teaching me to observe and absorb and to savor everything that life has to offer even when the going gets rough.

I have also had a number of mentors who have come into my life during different seasons and I am so grateful for everyone one. Ma & Pa Farley for helping to keep the wheels on in my rebellious youth. Roland Polhem, Billy Prendergast, Skip Cohen, Neil Taft, and Tom Slavicek were all tremendous business and leadership mentors that brought alive what it is to lead well and with the right kind of heart.

I owe a special thanks to Joe Stanley who has been my professor, friend, confidant, encourager, and spiritual mentor for years. Joe has that ability to see things in people that they themselves can't see. I first met Joe in a leadership course he taught at Grand Canyon University and he has always been there to encourage, prod, and even cajole when needed. His belief in me as a leader has helped me through some pretty rough times when my belief in myself was poised to crumble. I am John Mark to his St. Barnabas, and Joe, I thank you for always being there and believing in me.

There are so many others who have had a pivotal influence on my life and have contributed directly to this book. Folks from the various groups I've belonged to, but especially several outstanding volunteer leaders who made all this possible. Charlie Jackson – I will always admire you. Thanks for all you have done! And to the rest of the Grumpy

Old Bears and volunteers at Camp Acahela and GPSR, my deepest thanks.

Thanks also to Scott Lange, my friend and publisher – wow, what a trip this has been! Thanks for your support and friendship. And to Cynthia Staats, our editor, who did the final polishing of the manuscript and corrected all my grammatical travesties and idiosyncrasies while leaving the spirit and soul of the work intact – *many* thanks! (Italics deliberate... ☺).

Our Beta-readers are owed a special thanks too. I am indebted to all of you, but I need to give special acknowledgement to Joe Stanley, Jerry Lupien, and John Papp for all their encouragement *and* clear critiques. Special thanks to my daughter Amande for her razor sharp and insightful advice. Thanks for all the time you spend and your input – you really are the other half of my brain and provided very valuable dialog and feedback! And a special thanks to Dan White, a young colleague I admire and trust who read every word of the early transcript and not only gave his honest appraisal, but provided several bumps of encouragement at just the right time – I might have given up on this without you, young man. Own that.

Finally, thanks to my wife Maureen who did all the initial edits and my kids Kate, Mary, Amande, Abby, and Joe. You all have endured the endless conversations about leadership and volunteer groups, have watched and encouraged and been so patient as I lived the experiences and then put all of that into words and tried to pull this project together. It was years in the making, I could not have done it without your patient and enduring love and support.

Finally, to the author of my life and faith – Father, Lord Jesus, Holy Spirit, Three in One, the Great I Am – thank you.

Soli Deo Gloria
Tim

Contents

Warning to
SPEED READERS

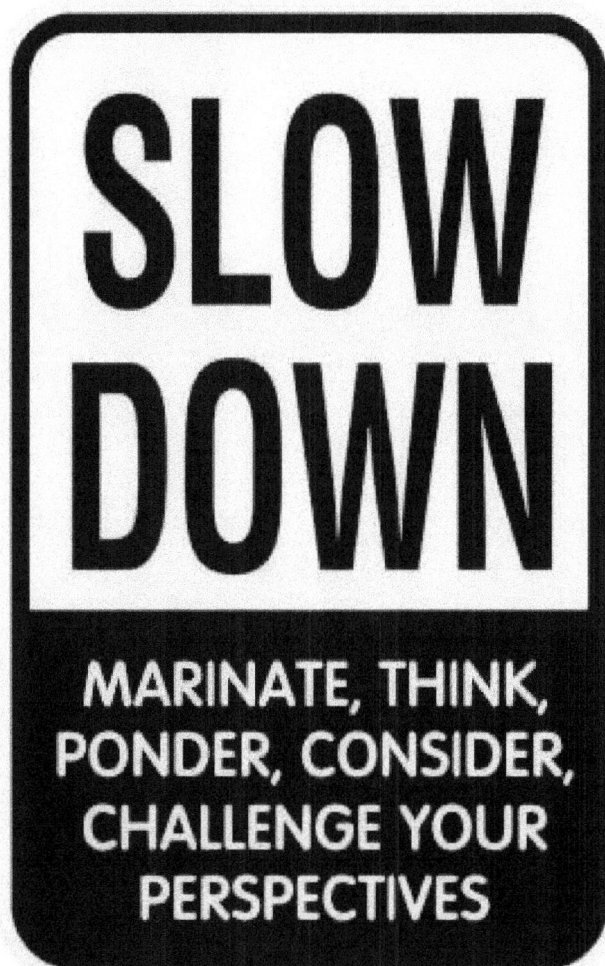

SLOW
DOWN

MARINATE, THINK, PONDER, CONSIDER, CHALLENGE YOUR PERSPECTIVES

You will get far more out of this book if you take your time.

Introduction

A Practical Handbook for Leading Volunteers and Volunteer Groups

"Infuse the right spirit; as powder is to the shot, so is spirit to action."

Lord Robert Baden-Powell

DNA of the Handbook

When I was a kid growing up in New Jersey, I used to love to watch as contractors built homes in the area. I was fascinated by the process and would stop and watch as the footers for the foundations were poured, or the platforms were assembled on each successive floor, or as the carpenters first assembled and then raised a wall into place. Whether it was site preparation, masonry, carpentry, plumbing, electrical, even roofing – it didn't matter – I was curious and wanted to understand how it all worked.

I always had a good eye for detail, so while a home was built I watched and was able to pick-up on *how* things were done and *the order* in which things were done. However, there was some critical information missing that I couldn't get from just watching or from getting an occasional quick answer from a contractor. When I was eighteen, I bumped across a book by Richard J. De Cristoforo that has been one of my favorites ever since, though I think it may be a book only a contracting nerd could love. *De Cristoforo's Housebuilding Illustrated* is a beautifully and lavishly illustrated book, chock full of drawings and photos showing how buildings are constructed. But what really got me then were the plain and simple explanations as to why things are done the way I had seen them done over the years. It was *so* cool to fully understand the process. It only added to the respect that I still feel for contractors of all types. It is truly a beautiful dance that is done when building a well-crafted home.

I not only thought the concepts were cool, but De Cristoforo's book was so inspiring, I couldn't help but want to *build* something. I didn't have the place, money, or resources to build even a full-sized shed, but I had built models for years, so I decided to try and follow his precise instructions. I built a cabin in 1/12th scale and replicated the process of building a house using balsawood and cardstock as scale substitutes for 2x4s, plywood, and sheetrock. It was one of the best learning experiences I ever gave myself, and one that I thoroughly enjoyed. The biggest takeaway from the book was the realization that the book itself was so good and so engaging that I simply had to try out what was written – and I never regretted a moment of it.

A similar experience happened a few years prior with a slightly different kind of book. A few of my buddies had joined a local Boy Scout Troop and would vanish once a month when they went on one of their camping trips. I was not all that keen on camping, but it was a major annoyance to be the only guy left in my Sunday school class at church. Gradually, it sunk in that the Saturdays on those same weekends were pretty dull too, having to occupy myself while the rest of my buddies were away. The worst part was enduring the tales and stories of all the fun they were having, and after about a half a year of this, I finally surrendered and said I would consider joining.

There was only one hitch: I was already 13 going on 14 and would be almost two and a half years older than most other kids entering the troop. For those of you who may not know it, Scouting is an achievement-oriented activity where your rank is determined by your accomplishments. To

14

accomplish things you have to know stuff. Lots of *stuff*. Outdoor stuff, safety stuff, and even citizenship stuff. Stuff like tying knots, setting up tents, knowing how to pack a backpack, knowing first aid, and things like the Scout Law and the Scout Oath (*stuff* we were supposed to be about and believe in as Scouts). Back in the early seventies the norm was to join Scouting at 11 years old and, as a rankless newbie, earn the rank of Tenderfoot and then advance to Second Class, and then First Class. (Beyond that is Star, Life, and Eagle.) The idea of being a rankless newbie at 13 made me cringe and I realized I had a lot of catching up to do, but I wasn't sure how to do it or *what* I even needed to do.

Finally, I broke down and asked one of my buddies what I would have to do to join and he showed me his *Boy Scout Handbook*. It not only had the lists of the stuff you needed to *know* in order to earn the various ranks, but it told you *how* to do the things you needed to *do*. Gaining or earning rank in Scouting has four essential components: What you *know*, what you *do*, *time in*, and *experience*. Being so old, I wanted to be sure I flew up the ranks to catch up to my pals – there was no way I was going to be a 14 year old Tenderfoot! So I asked my buddy, Gary, if I could borrow a manual and he lent me his older brother's copy. Once I had it, I simply couldn't put it down.

The 1960s editions of the *Boy Scout Handbook* were without a doubt some of the best versions ever written. This is not just my personal opinion - even the Boy Scouts of America (BSA) has come to that conclusion. They were written in a way that captured your imagination, provided you with great information, showed you how to do all kinds of *stuff*, and did it in a way that you would keep referring back to it time and again. It was really the first reference book I ever had that I wore out. Each section gave background on a topic, showed you how to do the things you needed to know, and then had you practice them so you understood, what we now call, "best practices." If that wasn't enough, there was a companion book called the *Boy Scout Fieldbook*. It took the concepts to an even higher level and was frequently used to underpin the skills needed for high adventure outdoor activities such as canoeing, survival skills, lashing, winter camping and the like. It was frequently used as the handbook for older Scouts in, what was then called, the Explorer program.

I studied the handbook Gary loaned me for about two weeks and practiced everything needed so that I could pass the Tenderfoot test. I memorized the citizenship questions, oaths, and learned how to tie my basic knots. To everyone's shock and amusement (my own included), I actually passed all of the Tenderfoot requirements the first night. One of two keys to my success was the Scout book because it was so good at illustrating each part of what I needed to know and do that I could pass the Tenderfoot tests all on the first night. The second key was *being driven enough to want to apply what the book said*. You can read almost anything, but it doesn't become transformational until you do something about it and apply it. Many managers and leaders fail at this point. They read something really good about leadership, chew on it for a while and then fail to apply it. I mean *really* apply it – as in *I tried it so much I nearly wore myself out trying to do it – apply* it. Like your kid glued to his or her latest video game.

The same goes for many Christians or other persons of faith who read their Bibles or holy books and fail to apply – *really apply* – *what* those sacred writings say. Many take short cuts and just listen to their preachers, ministers, or leaders and only take away a particular twist or part of their faith, missing the point entirely that their faith isn't as much about *listening* to a good message as it is about the *application* of the message and finding a personal relationship with your Maker in the process. Being devoted to the *application* is what sets apart those who bump, bounce, and stumble through life like they are careening downhill in an old push cart on the edge of crashing at any moment from those who are sailing along the Interstate in a muscle car, well on their way to their destination. The difference is *that* profound.

This goes a long way in explaining the final piece of the learning puzzle, which came to me by way of my faith. In my late teens I rediscovered my Christian faith and began to read more of the Bible, especially the Gospels. I was fascinated by the way Jesus taught. He had this marvelous way of saying, "See this over here? Well, God is like that," or, "Heaven is like this," or, "this is what God is looking for from you." Analogies and stories were how He taught, putting a handle on things that made the lessons easy to remember and repeat, and easy to apply as well. Something in me keenly responded to that. Not only me, but many others over the course of time have also enthusiastically embraced His way of teaching and have made it their own. Abraham Lincoln is perhaps one of the best noted in history to do this and readily admitted that the teachings of Christ and the way Christ taught profoundly influenced how Lincoln himself chose to teach and share. Lincoln's homespun stories and anecdotes made him very accessible. However, as Doris Kearns Goodwin points out in *A Team of Rivals,* it tended to drive men, like Secretary of War Edwin Stanton, crazy. Still, we learn from our experiences and when they are shared, they really can keep others from making the same mistakes or help them solve their problems faster.

This is why so many native cultures are so rich in storytelling and embrace it as so important. It is not so much a point of accuracy as it is a handle on how to remember things. For example, many eastern native tribes thought of North America as a great island on the back of a gigantic, living turtle (*Turtle Island)*, and as *Mother Earth.* That kind of viewpoint is far more likely to cultivate respect for the land in terms of thinking about what we should do with it and where it came from. The way most of us think about the property we own, I'm surprised it doesn't end up figuratively stuffed into the garage like one of our other neglected possessions.

The point is that a mental or emotional *handle* created from a good story often leads to an improved *mindset* – a way of understanding something, which in turn, leads to a better way of applying the lesson, and thus yields more focused *actions* and better *results.* This is essentially the same conclusion that John Wesley, the founder of the Methodist movement, came to when he wrote his famous *Quadrilateral*, the underpinnings of Methodist thought and practice. *What* we have heard and *how* we think about it ultimately produces *what we do and how we do it.*

Why TWEAKs

Tweaks may seem like a very odd title for a book, but I think it immediately frames a very simple but profound concept about the way we live and think of things. Especially the organizations we are a part of.

Half a lifetime ago, Robert Fulghum penned a wonderful little book called, *"All I Really Need to Know I Learned in Kindergarten."* It is a delightful and insightful book loaded with an abundance of truths that hit most of us at a level that makes us nod with a wry smile that says, "Yeah. Ain't that the truth?" I remember reading it for the first time and, for all the professional knowledge and adult skills I had developed up to that point, Fulghum's message was one that went back to things I really *had* learned as a kid and knew at my deepest core *worked.*

Much of this was confirmed later in life when I was a full grown adult and found myself in charge of two Boy Scout camps in the heart of the Pocono Mountains in Eastern Pennsylvania. This second kindergarten took all my professional executive and managerial experience and stood it on its head as I re-learned management, leadership, and organizational development from a *volunteer's* perspective. My classmates and playmates this time around were the wonderful volunteer Scouters (adult members) and Scouts (youth members) of the Northeastern Pennsylvania Council of the Boy Scouts of America. It was my experience as a Council Ranger that brought into sharp focus something that I had observed as a truth throughout a host of other volunteer clubs and organizations I had belonged to in my lifetime, and one that many leaders of volunteers learn themselves. The simple truth is this: *Leading volunteers and managing volunteer organizations is **very** different from leading employees and managing professional organizations.*

Anyone who has actual field experience leading volunteers knows this. It is an experiential thing. If you've actually done it, you know the experience is far more like herding cats or rounding up butterflies than it is leading employees. Employees are easy and far more predictable by comparison – the key words there being *by comparison* – but it is an experiential and undeniable truth that can only be learned by doing it. The difference is like dancing. Corporate leadership and management is complicated, fast paced, and geared towards production or output. In dancing terms, it's the Charleston with all the fancy steps, splash, and glitz. That is not a criticism but an honest observation. It takes skill, a ton of practice, focus of energy, and an ability to maintain the rhythm to do the Charleston well, if at all, and you have to be courageous to do it to boot!

The dance you do with and as a volunteer is very different! It's a community affair that has to come from the heart, with the rhythm and purpose coming from deep within. The motivations for participating and diving in are as different as the energy and time invested. The steps are more varied, more individualized, and more of an expression of personal fulfillment. The dance a volunteer organization does is more like the ritual dances done by our indigenous tribes celebrating a particular feast or festival than a Charleston done at a lively party. Both are full of energy and expression, but they are clearly different. Assuming you can easily translate the steps from the corporate dance to the volunteer dance is very likely to leave you looking a bit foolish, like Corporal Agarn from the old 1960s TV comedy *F Troop* attempting to dance with his native friends.

The reason why this book is called *Tweaks* is that, while the dances are different, it is entirely possible to master *both* sets of steps and *know when* to apply them. The trick is understanding how the steps are different, what works, and why. The reason why so many people with high levels of corporate leadership and management skills fail at leading and managing volunteers is either, not being aware of the nuances and differences between the two groups, or assuming it doesn't matter. They assume that their corporate skill and expertise trumps what might be needed in volunteer scenarios, and that is as foolish as a vascular surgeon assuming his knowledge and expertise trumps that of his plumber. Best of luck with that one Doc! Sail into a volunteer scenario with no volunteer experience, but armed with only your corporate expertise and all-knowing, "I can handle this, I do this all the time at work," approach, and the volunteers will probably be exchanging those glances that say, "Oh boy," as they step back to watch yet another corporate "expert" crash and burn.

This book is designed to help you understand the difference between the dance steps of corporate leadership and volunteer leadership, and to help you master the two. In the process I will attempt to help you understand a number of myths and misunderstandings, and to bring some honest clarity to how volunteers *should* be lead, what makes them tick, and how to help volunteer organizations thrive. In the end it's all about learning the rules of a new sandbox and learning how to "play nice" with the other kids.

But there is one other thing that this project has driven home to me and it goes back to Fulghum, kindergarten, and a lot of the things we have all learned when we were a lot younger.

I think more than anything else, this book will help you dust off and uncover some good, old-fashioned and underused *common sense*. There is a lot we learn when we are younger that gets crowded out by other stuff as life becomes more complicated and sophisticated. When it comes to running businesses and organizations, we seem to set aside some of the basic things that probably qualify as common sense and chase after things that can get pretty complicated pretty quickly. This only makes trying to accomplish your goals harder.

The goal of this book is to walk you through the processes and tools needed to lead individual volunteers, volunteer organizations, not-for-profit organizations, community groups, clubs, Scout units, or fellowships successfully and at a higher level than what you may be experiencing now. If you have been frustrated by leading volunteers or your group needs a serious reboot, this book is for you. My hope is that this little book will be one that you will add to your list of favorites and use like a well-worn handbook that you go back to again and again as you lead those around you.

KEY TWEAKS TO GO

- *THIS BOOK IS DESIGNED TO BE A HANDBOOK THAT YOU CAN USE TO HELP GUIDE YOU THROUGH VARIOUS SITUATIONS WHILE LEADING VOLUNTEERS.*
- *LEADING VOLUNTEERS IS OFTEN MORE CHALLENGING THAN LEADING EMPLOYEES.*
- *OFTEN, A TWEAK TO A CURRENT SITUATION IS ALL THAT IS NEEDED TO SET IT RIGHT.*

PART I

Personal Mindset – What YOU Need From the Start

"Very little is needed to make a happy life: it is all within yourself, in your way of thinking."

Marcus Aurelius

In this first section we are going to take a closer look at several pivotal concepts that form the foundation needed to lead volunteer organizations well, whether it is out of a crisis or into a solid future. You have probably heard it said, "Attitude is everything," and that certainly is true when it comes to leadership, but there are also some very important distinctions within leadership itself and differences between leadership and management.

Some think or assume that it's all the same, but in these next few chapters we will not only show you the kind of attitude needed to be a successful and productive leader, but the best way to lead *people* and manage *things* – an important distinction that many overlook.

In a nutshell, the leadership/management equation can be boiled down to these lowest possible denominators: Leadership is all about getting your people involved and management is all about staging your assets.

Marinate on that.

It's so elemental, it makes a lot of things really obvious, like the number one focus in leadership has to be on your *people* and what they need and how to provide it. In management, staging means that you have prepared stuff ahead of time and it is there waiting for what is going to happen, not constantly playing catch-up. When this takes place in a volunteer environment, having leadership and management skills that are people, or member, focused will make or break what you do.

These chapters will go into much greater detail on the mindsets, attitudes, and practices you will need in order to insure you are leading and managing in the best possible ways, right down to the very roots of what each demands. *This* is where *traction* begins!

Chapter 1

Hope in Numbers and Death by Assumption: The Truth About ORGS and Volunteers

"We all make basic assumptions about things in life, but sometimes those assumptions are wrong. We must never trust in what we assume, only in what we know."

Darren Shan

Hope in Numbers

The Pew Research Center did a study in 2011 that revealed some pretty interesting statistics on how many people actually participate in small groups that cater to mutual interests and skills. Actually, "interesting" would be a gross understatement. "Shocking" would probably be far more accurate. While examining the social side of the Internet, the Pew Center looked at the state of groups and voluntary organizations in America and found that three out of four Americans are active in these groups with a full 14% belonging to at least *eight* groups or more.

Stop and think about that for a moment.

That is a *huge* number of people, and those statistics represent an equally *huge* number of groups. Yet, it's important to point out that the vast majority of the kind of groups the Pew Center was looking at were *not* the larger non-profit organizations that have been the focus of all kinds of management and academic studies. For the most part, Pew looked at groups like the local Little League, the Church or

Synagogue down the street, a Boy Scout Troop or Cub Scout Pack, a barbershop or Sweet Adeline chorus, or nearby wing of the Commemorative Air Force or Civil Air Patrol. It could be a reading club, sewing circle, motorcycle gang, or hot rod cruising club. The fact of the matter is that small organizations that cater to our interests, groups that are run by volunteers for volunteers, are alive and well in America and elsewhere. And that, for me as a volunteer leader, is good news and gives me hope. I hope it does the same for you.

With so many folks belonging to groups, the numbers reported in the Pew study call to question a belief that was popularized by books like *Bowling Alone* and reinforced by all kinds of social examples such as hordes of cell users who seem to be completely unaware of the rest of society around them. Over the course of the last decade and a half, there has been a growing belief that our society has changed and that we are no longer as social a society as we once were. Robert Putnam, the author of *Bowling Alone*, and others have presented compelling evidence to reinforce this point and, as a result, most reasonable people now take it for granted that our society is becoming increasingly isolationist and the days of old-style comradery and group activities is long gone. I wouldn't necessarily call this an Internet myth.

There is no denying that many old-time organizations have been experiencing serious declines over the last few decades, and there is equally no denying that the landscape of our culture has changed. We *don't* tend to socialize the way we did 30, 40 or even 50 years ago, *but few societies ever have*. A quick look back in time will bring to light an ever-changing social dynamic where the way we communicate and interact with each other is fluid and in a constant state of change with new paradigms and new genres of communication and interaction under constant change and evolution. Most of us take it now as fact that, in general, people don't care enough to belong, or participate, or be involved in small groups any more. But is that really the case?

The Pew Center's studies seem to fly in the face of the current beliefs we have about our neighbors and friends. It's *really* hard to claim you are being reasonably sane when you say, "Yep, people just don't care enough to participate anymore," when the numbers show that *three out of four* of us participate in clubs and groups and apparently *still do* care. It's equally crazy to conclude with those numbers that small volunteer organizations are *dead*. These kinds of assumptions are the mindsets that *kill* – they kill enthusiasm, they kill hope, and they kill participation. It's death by assumption.

It is not that people do not care or that society is becoming increasingly isolationist. I think it is more likely that small volunteer organizations are *grossly* misunderstood, as are the volunteers who make up the wonderful and vast array of organizations that are alive and well and those that are still being created even today.

What if we actually have it upside down? What if the corporate models of leadership not only don't work well in volunteer settings but will never work well in volunteer organizations?

What If
But, we have a problem. A *big* problem.

After forty plus years of intense scrutiny, study, research, deep academic thought, and hundreds and hundreds of published books and articles on leadership, management, organizations, communication, and motivation, most of our organizations are a mess. With so much concentrated effort, you would think that all of our organizations, from our companies to our local hobby clubs, would be humming along at top efficiency, but they aren't.

In fact, our smaller organizations are generally more of a mess than most of their bigger corporate cousins. Churches, clubs, interest groups, and all kinds of small social organizations that we belong to in many cases are just hobbling along or are flat out on life support.

Why is that?

When you take a hard look at volunteer organizations today, the picture is not a pretty one. Stories about the difficulties of dwindling membership, lack of interest, and members who simply don't seem to care anymore are so rampant, individual disinterest is now a commonly assumed member state of mind. Human Resource experts and other business leaders look at situations like this and shake their heads saying things like, "Well, if they would only apply a more professional, business-like approach, these small groups would solve all their problems." But that doesn't seem to work as well as it should. As a leader in small organizations, I have seen that approach fail fairly often. Even more frequently, I have seen experienced corporate leaders, and managers, crash and burn in spectacular fashion when trying to manage Johnny's Little League Team or Mary's Girl Scout Troop. Why is that?

What if, when it comes to our volunteer organizations, we have it all wrong?

What if we actually have it upside down? What if the corporate models of leadership not only *don't* work well in volunteer organizations but *will never* work well in volunteer organizations? What if it's a different kind of wiring, like DC electrical systems compared to AC electrical systems – similar, but not the same?

What if the models we use here in the US for classifying organizations are really becoming anachronisms and are doing more harm than good? Does it really make sense to classify our organizations based on their *tax status* as a corporation or non-profit organizations (NPOs)? You would think from the bulk of academic studies that there are no other kinds of organizations. But what if that isn't entirely right? There is a big difference between Arizona State University and the local International Plastic Modeling Society chapter I belong to or the church I attend. They are all NPOs, but is tax status the *wisest* way to classify our organizations and gain an understanding of how and why volunteers or members function the way they do? What if there were a better, more precise way?

What if there were a far more efficient way to communicate with members? Would that change the dynamics in our organizations? What if the ways we communicate in most volunteer organizations are just assumptions based on what we do in our companies? What if the struggles to gain member enthusiasm isn't a global problem of member disinterest, but a matter of misaligned internal communications?

What if, in our haste to find the newer, better, and catchier technique or management trend, we have abandoned or forgotten our roots, or some of the basic, foundational principles that make things work well together regardless of the size of the group or the type of group? What if working up a scale to constantly improve is a better approach than looking for perfect answers and solutions right out of the box? What if improving as you go is a *necessary* component of organizational life because you can't truly see what you will need until you are actually there? What if plan *and adjust* is the *best* way to go?

I wonder what would happen if we were really courageous enough to ask hard and honest questions about our organizations and the roles we play in them, as well as how we go about doing things. I wonder if the results would be far better than what many of us are experiencing today.

KEY TWEAKS TO GO

- *A STUDY BY THE PEW FOUNDATION SHOWS THAT AMERICANS ARE STILL VOLUNTEERING AND PARTICIPATING IN VOLUNTEER ORGANIZATIONS IN HUGE NUMBERS.*
- *THERE IS A WIDE VARIETY OF ORGANIZATIONS IN OUR SOCIETY AND CATEGORIZING THEM BY TAX STATUS ALONE MAY NOT HELP US FIND WAYS TO RUN THEM BETTER.*
- *THE "NEWER, BETTER" WAY OF LEADING VOLUNTEER GROUPS MAY HAVE MORE TO DO WITH REDISCOVERING SOME BASIC, OLD-TIME COMMON SENSE ABOUT GOOD LEADERSHIP AND GOOD COMMUNITY INTERACTION.*

Chapter 2

Where to Start

*"The purpose in life is to contribute in some way
to making things better."*

Bobby Kennedy

Imagine waking up and wondering where, in God's name, you are and what the heck has happened. You look around and things are in shambles. There is fire and smoke, and the ship you are on is sinking – you can tell that because the deck you were lying on is awash, and the seawater splashing on your face is what revived you. Through the smoke you hear yelling and moans of pain, but there is also an uneasy stillness. The ship is dead in the water and you realize this is the aftermath. You need to figure out what's going on so that you know what to do next, but *that* is not going to come easy. You need to look around, get your bearings, wrap your mind around what's going on so you know what to do next and help get things right.

That is exactly the situation my Uncle Charlie found himself in on the morning of May 11, 1945, on the USS *Hugh W. Hadley* (DD-774) off Okinawa. He was a 20mm gunner on the fantail – the very back end of the ship. His station was literally on the tip of the tail of the dog. *Hadley* was an *Allen M. Sumner*-class destroyer that had been on radar picket duty at Picket Station 11, about 75 miles northwest of Okinawa, when it and her consort, the USS *Robley D. Evans* (DD-552), were attacked at just after 8 a.m. local time by over 100 Japanese airplanes in a massed suicide attack. Both *Evans* and *Hadley* were badly mauled – *Evans* taking five hits and going dead in the water at about 9 a.m. while *Hadley* fought on alone for another 25 minutes –

an eternity as any of the survivors would tell you – eventually setting a record by shooting down 26 Japanese airplanes, but at a terrible price. The intrepid crew worked feverishly to save their badly damaged ship, find the rest of their shipmates, and get things back under control.

After the Kamikazes stopped coming and the attack ended, the Captain of *Hadley*, Commander Baron Mullaney, looked over his battered ship and realized she was in real danger of sinking and gave the order to abandon ship. However, he asked for volunteers to assist the damage control party to try and save her. The attack had left *Hadley* without any power except for what was coming from an auxiliary generator, with no propulsion, and taking on enough water from battle damage that she was listing and slowly settling at the stern – the back of the ship. Fires needed to be put out, the wounded needed to be attended to and evacuated, live ammunition and excess weight had to be dumped over the side, and the flooding needed to be stopped. The smaller landing craft on station at RP15 that morning came alongside both *Hadley* and *Evans* to assist and provide power, pumping, and help evacuate the wounded. Charlie initially went over the side with the rest of the crew but, after a while, he began to get a handle on how bad things were and wondered if he could be more help on board the ship than bobbing in the ocean waiting to be picked up. It was an event that shaped the rest of my uncle's life.

In a strange way his stories of that fateful day, and what I have learned since of that engagement at Radar Picket Station 11, have had a profound impact on my life. While never as cataclysmic as what Charlie went through, there have been a number of times when I've stepped into situations that left me feeling a little like how Charlie felt in those initial moments after the battle, when the seawater splashed him awake. This is especially true with some of the organizations I've belonged to. More than a few organizations I've stepped into have left me wondering what happened, how could things have gotten this bad, and what in heavens name do we do next? And like Charlie, I've had to make the decision to either abandon ship or climb back on board to see if the old girl can be saved. Decisions like that are risky and never easy. There are no guarantees of success, it may take a huge investment of personal effort, and it is something that you have to prepare yourself emotionally. That is hard, because in many cases, like Charlie, you've just been through the battle. Sticking around to clean up the aftermath is usually the last thing you want to do. But, that is when the sense of higher duty, responsibility, and a need to do your part ultimately kicks in. There can be great reward in being part of the damage control party and helping to save the ship.

It is important to understand that it often isn't *one* thing that drives an organization into the ground or sends everyone over the side to escape the sinking ship. It is usually a combination of things that compound on top of one another that make bad situations thoroughly rotten. Problems become *interrelated*. That's what gives organizational problems the knot-like quality that can make solving the problems so complex or exasperating. Most accident investigators will tell you that it wasn't one single thing that caused an accident, but a series of things that combined all at the right time that turned simple mistakes into catastrophes. Airline and rail accidents investigated by the National Transportation Safety Board, shipping and boating accidents documented by the Coast Guard, and even local auto accidents usually reveal that several things were going on at the same time which, when combined, turned a little wiggle into a wreck.

The Great Chicago Fire is a case in point. Regardless of how the fire started – either a cow kicking over a lantern or men gambling and knocking over a lantern – the fire started in a barn and by the time it was over two days later, over three square miles of Chicago had been reduced to charred rubble. What were the co-joined factors? Most of the buildings in 1871 in Chicago were built of wood, as were the sidewalks. Most of the buildings were also topped with flammable tar roofing. Chicago was in the middle of a bad drought, and the winds that night were strong enough to fan the flames, feed the fires, and send burning embers everywhere. Those were the factors that greeted the Chicago Fire Department which, at the time, had only 17 horse-drawn pumpers in the entire city and the small force was already worn out from fighting several other fires from the week prior. If all of this wasn't bad enough, the initial engine companies were sent to the wrong address, and a fault in the communications system failed to catch the error. Even as the firefighters scrambled in an effort to make a rapid response, they were delayed long enough that a simple barn fire quickly evolved into one of the biggest conflagrations in US

Combine a program that doesn't have a clear plan with a lack of universally understood vision, add in late communication of events sent out by a method two-thirds of the members don't routinely use, and mix it with a fair dose of ego that inhibits creative thinking, and you have the makings of an organization that is about to implode.

history.

      This kind of thing happens in organizations all the time. It is usually not just one thing that is going wrong, being neglected, or not being given enough attention. Typically, it's a number of things that are not being done well or not being done at all. And while this can happen in corporations and larger non-profits, it is the unfortunate hallmark of many of our volunteer organizations, associations, chapters, and churches. Combine a program that doesn't have a clear plan with a lack of universally understood vision, add in late communication of events sent out by a method two-thirds of the members don't routinely use, and mix it with a fair dose of ego that inhibits creative thinking, and you have the makings of an organization that is about to implode. The match to this powder keg can be as simple as a motion to do something relatively or seemingly easy. The debate suddenly gets complicated, other issues are dragged off the shelf like a bad fight with your spouse, and, voila! You have flames and a sinking ship with the crew wondering what went wrong. Such is the life cycle of many of our volunteer organizations.

Simply put, small things can have a great impact. They can pile up fast and combine in the worst possible fashion to create a complete disaster, or just gum up the works bad enough that the organization never comes close to its full potential. Yet, this can also be a point of real, genuine hope. Small things *do* have an impact – and that can also be to the positive. If small things can make a real mess, then the right small things and the right simple things at the right time can be the tug on the thread that untangles the entire knot. History and experience have shown that getting organizations turned around usually does not require groundbreaking, new, wiz bang technologies. It is usually the application of a simple concept or two that leads to the installation of a few more simple ideas that gets real synergy and teamwork going. Organizations are rarely instantaneously teleported from shipwreck to star performer. It requires a progression of steps – simple steps – and as that momentum builds, things gradually get better and better.

So how *do* you fix a broken or ailing ORG?

The Boy Scouts of America and Scouting worldwide has one of the most comprehensive training programs ever created. Aside from the basic mission of training youth members in a staggering array of skills, interests, and abilities, there are a bewildering number of leadership, safety, and program execution trainings available to both youth and adult members. There are trainings for *everything.*

There are even trainings to train trainers. Yet with all the Scouting tradition and all the knowledge passed on to everyone in the organization through all the training programs available, we still have all kinds of Scouting organizations – Councils, Districts, packs, troops, crews, ships, lodges, camp maintenance corps, committees, and other groups designed to assist other Scouting functions – that are struggling to survive. With all of this practical knowledge, Scouting *should* be the shining star of how organizations can and should be run by volunteers for volunteers but, all too frequently, they all are suffering from the ills that befall many of the volunteer and corporate organizations around us.

What's wrong? Where is the disconnect?

Some would immediately point to a decline in interest or how our society has changed, but if that were really true then every unit and group in Scouting would be in the tank and the fact is that there are some *outstanding* groups out there who are *thriving*.

Some would say that we are simply too busy, or that we are all – youth and adults – too distracted in today's world with all the media, stimulation, and choices we have before us. But, then again, how do you explain the units that *are* thriving and seem to have plenty of participants and gangbuster programs?

Some would say that thriving organizations require a more "professional" approach, but if you have been an adult leader for anything longer than a month you already know that leading volunteers is an exercise in herding cats – and these cats very much have a mind of their own and are very likely to tell you to take a hike the first time you treat them like an employee. There is something uniquely different about leading volunteers well and in a way that inspires action and creates synergy. It goes beyond the usual stuff you may find at work if you are lucky enough to work in one of those places where you can't wait to get there. Others would point to the wealth of academic research showing how NPOs should be run. However, that is a bit misleading. In a few cases that *might* help with some ailing Councils or Districts, but for the most part much of the academic research that is out there focuses on NPOs that treat volunteers as *human capital*, free labor to achieve their goals while keeping the machine of the NPO going, and that isn't what Baden-Powell had in mind at all. Yes, there are some realities that apply, but at the local unit level where the vast majority of us toil away in the Scouting Program, there isn't much there that provides practical, down-to-earth help in getting our groups to thrive.

So what is it? What's going wrong? Again, how do we fix it?

The really good news is that the series of things you need to do amount to tweaks – hence the title of this book. None of them are really complicated, none take years of practice to master, and most can be put into place very quickly.

I spent several wonderful years as the Ranger of Camp Acahela and Goose Pond Scout Reservation in Northeastern Pennsylvania while earning my Bachelor and Master's degrees in Leadership. At the same time, my youngest son and daughter were just the right age to participate in the Scouting program, and of course, I ended up also acting as a unit level volunteer. All of this proved to be a fantastic combination where I got to see how the theories of leadership actually played out first hand in the realities of the Scouting program. I not only got a chance to see in great detail what works and what doesn't, but *why*.

The other thing I finally comprehended through a long series of experiences, is that there is not just one thing that will make it all click. There's not one single magic bullet to use or pill to take that is going to suddenly make it all work. The bad news is that it is a series of things you need to be doing in order to help set the stage to make it all work and work well. But again, the *really* good news is that the series of things you need to do amount to *tweaks* – hence the title of this book. None of them are really complicated, none take years of practice to master, and most can be put into place very quickly. The results, if you are already trying to use most of what Scouting offers in the way of leadership and programming training, are like lighting an afterburner on a jet engine or using higher octane fuel – you are going to get a heckuva lot more bang for your buck.

So what are these *tweaks* I speak of?

First, as strange as it may sound, and as simple and "street" as it is, the root principle and solution to most of the things that ail all of our various groups, is simply this:

"Ya gotta reach 'em where they is, not where they ain't."

Every other solution needed to get our organizations thriving, regardless of what they are, is all based on that simple little axiom. This will be a recurring theme throughout the book, but when I finally wrapped my own head around the idea, leading volunteers got a whole lot easier. They didn't need to come to me – I needed to go to them. In the kind of volunteerism that makes the vast majority of volunteer organizations run well, this is the golden rule of leadership and organizational management. We will show just how many ways this is applied as we work through the rest of the tweaks, but if you are looking for the best way to start changing your organization into a high performing and thriving organization that is exciting and fun to be a part of, *this* is the place to start and plant your flag.

So what are the rest of the *Tweaks?*

There are a number of things you need to know and practice that we discuss here in this book. If you do these things, your organization will be well-led, focused, and capable of navigating any of the troubles that will come its way. They break into four groups, so this book will also break into four sections that follow four basic themes: What *you* need to practice, understanding your group, understanding ORGs, and pulling together.

The first three have to do with you and your mindset. How you approach leadership and organizing is *firmly* rooted in how *you* think and perceive things. We'll wrestle with why initiatives get bogged down and master a fresh way to look at making progress – it's a practice I call UPGBB or *Ugly, Poor, Good, Better, Best.* We'll also discuss the very important concepts of *authentic leadership* and *servant leadership* and the roles these play in leading members and volunteers. There is an awful lot of assumption that goes along with both of these concepts, so it is important that you take a look at these afresh and how they apply as *Tweaks.*

The next set deals with knowing your members. Let me restate that. It has to do with *really knowing* your members. Good – that's better. It amazes me that we frequently plow ahead in leadership without any real intelligence, as in the kind of intelligence that is gathered to help you know what to do or when to do it. We *think* we know our members, but this section will help you understand just how blind most of us usually are. There are a few habits to get into that will transform your leadership skills so that you get the maximum amount of traction.

The third set has to do with organizations and how they grow. This is another form of very important intelligence and a lot like a handbook for a very sophisticated piece of tech equipment you may have recently purchased. Not that the information is high tech – it isn't – it's just that it is different from what you might expect and there are some important nuances you will want to know if you are going to get your ORG to run at maximum potential or fix whatever ails it.

The last section pulls it all together and ties it back to some of the great practices, but it also comes with a number of healthy warnings. Great organizations don't just happen, it usually takes a bit of hard and deliberate work to make it all come together. Once the formula is found, keeping things going can get easier, but still it isn't easy. This may sound like a contradiction, but it actually is not and we will get into that in more detail. The trick to continued success is making sure you build *legacy* into the program, and this is fairly easy to do – that's the good news. The bad news is that the synergy created by a great program with great leaders at the helm who are engaging their members in a rewarding program is a rare and delicate thing, and one that can come unglued in a dazzling variety of ways. More frustrating and heartbreaking then trying to get that struggling ORG off the ground and seeing it die is watching a successful, champion level program implode either from a series of uninformed moves or willful personalities – usually both are present in the ugly math that adds up to destruction. The bottom line is that an ORG is a lot like a pet that needs to be well taken care of. The rewards of good care are manifold, but so are the penalties for neglect.

I have also seen the huge difference between authentic leadership that was well-grounded and coming from the best places within an individual and what happens when people *act out* leadership, and when leadership and organizational practice come from places that are fairly well adrift of "*Trustworthy, Loyal, Helpful, Friendly, Courteous,*

Kind, Obedient, Cheerful, Thrifty, Brave, Clean, and Reverent." That's the great part about Scouting. They have this built-in checklist that should be screaming in every leader's head to let them know when they are acting like the kind of leaders they should be and when they are not living up to a standard by which *every* act should be measured. They may not get it right all the time, but at least they *have* a code. It is something many other ORGS should try to develop and implement.

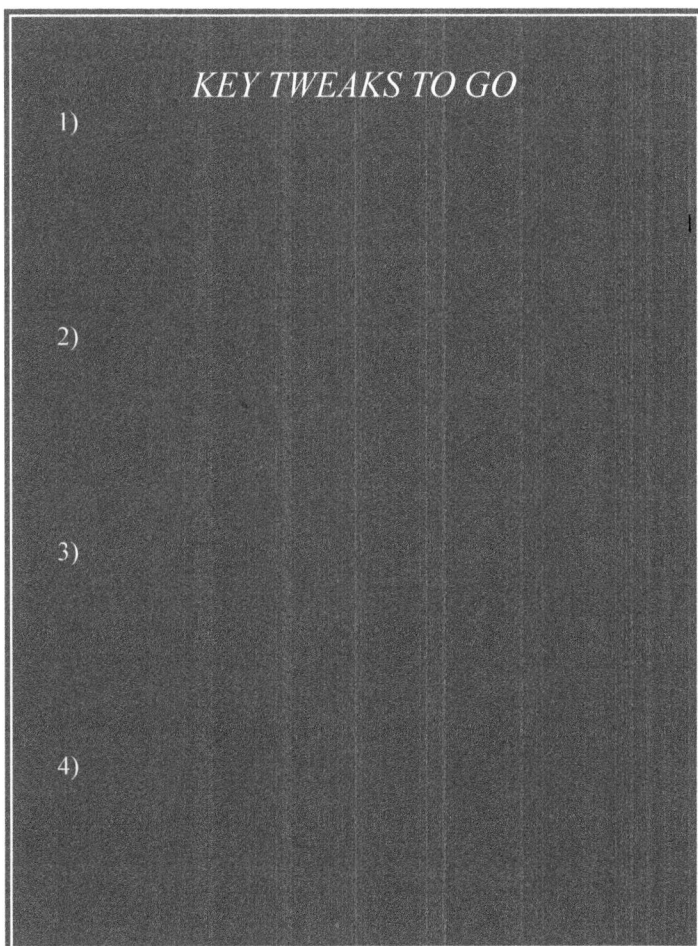

KEY TWEAKS TO GO

1)

2)

3)

4)

Chapter 3

Ugly, Poor, Good, Better, Best and a Gunther Frame of Mind

"How you approach the problem is more important than what you actually do because it sets the tone with everything else that follows."

Opa

A Gunther Frame of Mind

As I hunted around for a really good place to start when talking about leading volunteers, I wrestled with trying to find *the* leadership concept that was clearly *the* most important concept, idea, or practice above any other. As I was closing in on completing my graduate studies in leadership it seemed that every week we focused on one aspect of leadership or another that was hawked as *the thing* that you needed in order to have a thriving and vibrant organization, but often times that was measured by ways of thrashing the competition or making wads of cash in the process. It was a little frustrating because from my own experience in leading volunteers, making wads of cash usually wasn't the goal and simply keeping your charges motivated and pointed in the right direction was challenging enough. It was clear to me that there are a *lot* of things you need to make *any* leadership model or formula work, but putting your finger on *one* thing, especially in volunteer-based organizations? Hmmm…*That* was the question I wrestled with for quite a while. There are so many great concepts and ideas. Which one tops them all?

As time went on, I realized that good leadership and

43

having a good organization both require a lot of things to be done well. As I've mentioned before, no one thing is the magic silver bullet, but there are a few things that seem to really matter and a good part of this book is devoted to those ideas and practices. There is one that I think trumps most of the others and I did not learn it in college, on the job, or in another organization I belonged to. The most important thing I learned about good leadership and management I learned from watching my grandfather and my dad.

My grandfather was a German immigrant who came to the US in the early 1920s. He was a very creative and artistic guy, about as handy as they come. Like many immigrants from that time, he worked very hard to make a good life for the family. By trade, he was a photoengraver. Photoengravers used to be the guys that would convert photographs to a complex set of tiny dots on metal plates – all by hand no less – so that the images could be printed in magazines, newspapers, and other publications. This was the process used *before* the offset and xerographic printing processes used today. He was an artisan and first-class craftsman to say the least. He was very eclectic and had a pile of interests. Therefore, as I grew up, I was shown how to paint with oil paints, cast and fire ceramics and china, woodworking and carpentry, and how to repair classic German cuckoo clocks.

One of my favorite memories was when he showed me how to develop black and white prints in his darkroom. Watching the images magically appear on the photographic paper as we rocked them back and forth in developer and fixer was simply amazing. Under his tutelage, I learned the wildest collection of skills any kid growing up in the late sixties and early seventies could ever hope to learn, and as I learned from him, it became clear to me that he *never* stopped learning, but was always looking for the next thing *to teach himself.*

There was one incident in particular that I remember

as clear as a bell and it was one of those pivotal lessons. As artistic and talented as he obviously was, he stunned me one time when I asked him to teach me how to draw. He said he would love to, but couldn't, that he himself never learned to free-hand draw. Mind you, he was an accomplished painter, did beautiful landscapes and still lifes, and this bit of news came as a complete shock and I had a hard time believing it.

"How you approach the problem is more important than what you actually do because it sets the tone with everything that follows."

He went on to explain that he was unable to just look at something and draw it – *that* skill eluded him. But he also explained that he learned to compensate by using a system where he would grid a photo and then grid a canvas, essentially upscaling the picture block by block. In showing me how he did it, he explained that some people have the raw talent to be able to free-hand sketch a large drawing – but that he did not. He went onto explain that tools and other helps can often make up for the raw talent that we may lack *or have yet to develop*. To underscore the point, he then free-hand drew an almost a perfect circle, critiqued its flaws, then grabbed a cup, inverted it, and traced a perfect circle. **Improvise.** *That* was the lesson, and he went on to explain that life itself was full of these adaptations. "How you approach the problem is more important than what you actually do because it sets the tone with everything that follows," is what he lived by.

As time went on after that, I watched him and realized that a good deal of what he did – regardless of what it was – he did by carefully thinking it through and then either teaching himself how to do it or adapting something else so that he could get the job done. He lived the lesson of, "there are more ways than one to skin a cat," and

45

improvising and creative thinking are at the heart of problem solving – *any* kind of problem solving. Opa – the German slang for grandfather – taught me that lesson and the mindset that went with it. He then went on to craft all kinds of beautiful things as if to demonstrate the lesson in an endless variety of ways.

That *should* be enough, but there is more. One of the other lessons Opa taught me was that the best thing a parent can do is to teach and encourage his or her children so that they are capable of exceeding everything the parent has done. In some cases this may not be precisely practical, but the idea that making it possible for my kids to do what I have done, and do it better, is a pretty good goal for a parent to have. When it came to this idea that there are more ways than one to skin a cat and that improvising and creativity are at the heart of problem solving, Dad trumped him by taking the lesson to the max.

You see, Dad was born with hydrocephalus, or water on the brain. Most children back in the early 20th century born with this condition rarely lived through childhood, but Dad somehow survived it. A side-effect of this condition, however, was that his eyesight was never great. He gradually lost his vision over time and by age fifty, it was pretty much gone all together. Eventually, it forced him into an early retirement first as an offset pressman and then later from owning our neighborhood hardware store.

The first month or so after giving up the store was tough, and he and Mom had decided he should go to the School for the Blind so he could learn some new skills. He wasn't thrilled to say the least. He acted like a kid headed to first grade and dug in his heals, grumbling the whole way as he went on that first day. Some guy was introduced to him when he arrived and gave Dad a tour of the place, asking him what he liked to do. At this point Dad wasn't *totally* blind, but he was well past *legally* blind and told the guide that he used to like to do woodworking, to which the guide enthusiastically responded he did too and immediately walked them both to the School's woodshop. They spent a while going over a bunch of things, showing Dad how the tools could be safely used *without* eyesight, and then Dad was given a Click-O-Matic – a handmade tool that he could use to measure more accurately than I could fully sighted. At the end of the tour the guy tells Dad that he would be one of his instructors and Dad was thrilled. It was only when they went to shake hands that Dad even realized that his guide was *totally* blind. Needless to say, he came home far more excited and enthusiastic than when he had left that first morning. After that, it was as if Opa's lessons on improvising became Dad's life mission and watchwords.

Over the course of the next decade Dad took a hobby he had done while he could still see and honed it to a fine degree of craftsmanship *even as he continued to lose more and more of his eyesight!* He cranked out some truly amazing pieces in his time and he spent most of his later years applying that craft to making wooden toys for children. When I became a firefighter with the Ogdensburg Volunteer Fire Department, Dad made me a wooden firetruck complete with removable ladders and it was all done from scratch – it wasn't a kit. The firetruck model is a tour de force of Dad's determination and proof that, "where there's a will, there's a way."

By the time he built this for me, he was *completely* blind. He had no plans other than those in his head, a lesson well learned from the Jimmy Stewart movie *Carbine Williams*. The move was one of his favorites and we watched it together a couple of times. In the movie, Marshall Williams is placed in solitary confinement and, in order to keep from going crazy, he starts designing the mechanism that eventually ends up as the guts of the M-1 Carbine. Dad took that lesson and figured if Williams could do it in his head, so could he. So, he designed the entire truck and kept the plans in his head. Each part is highly detailed such as the wheels and placement of the holes in the rims or the rungs on the ladders. He not only built it from a variety of wood species, but he put a beautiful finish on it too. It took me until just recently to be able to replicate that same level of craftsmanship, and I can see!

None of this was easy for him. It took several tries on each piece before he was able to get it to look right. And because he couldn't see it, he relied on his sense of touch and the verbal feedback of others. I asked him how he knew to put intake and discharge outlets on the truck and he told me he had asked someone about the truck, if anything might be missing, and then took the advice and added them. He *listened*, a skill many of us do not use frequently. All of this so far speaks to the level of tenaciousness he had. He just simply wouldn't give up. He might back up, take a deep breath and rethink a problem, but I don't think he ever really gave up on anything. That's *tenacity*, but there was something more and it's something every one of us can use, and that's *an unrestrained, nearly crazy level of creative thinking*.

It also helped that he had a really good sense of humor, which is probably one of the best weapons anyone can have when facing adversity. When the School for the Blind issued him his folding cane, he promptly named it Seymour, as in see-more. He always understood the severity of what he was dealing with and had a very realistic handle on the seriousness of life, but he realized humor went a long way towards making things better and never took himself so seriously that he couldn't poke fun at himself. This kind of modesty kept his ego in check and helped him understand things could be a lot worse.

One time he walked three miles one way to get flowers for my mother as a gift. At one point near his destination in downtown Cranford he stumbled on the edge of a raised piece of sidewalk. He managed to stay upright and avoided falling altogether, but, unknown to him, he was no longer pointed down the center of the sidewalk. After collecting himself, he took a step or two forward and immediately collided with a signpost. Not at all sure of what it was, he thought he was being attacked, took a step back, and in the spirit of Don Quixote, defended himself with several quick slaps of the cane like a Jedi knight wielding a light saber. It would have made Luke Skywalker proud, except that his quarry didn't go down or yelp in pain. Dad later told me in fits of laughter that his first though was, "Oh nuts, this guy must be *huge!*" and then braced himself for a beating that didn't come. He then reached back out with his cane and gently tapped his foe, slowly tracing the shape of the signpost and sign. He realized what it was just as a beat cop came over to ask him if he was okay. Dad told him yes, other than being a bit embarrassed and the cop laughed with him saying it was one of the most impressive defensive actions he had ever seen. Afterwards, he frequently told that story as a humorous and self-effacing lesson on how to keep from getting an overblown ego. Dad's sense of humor gave value to an otherwise discouraging and hurtful experience. That's what attitude can do.

Creative thinking counts for a lot as well. In the early nineties my folks moved from New Jersey to a new home in Delaware where Dad was finally able to set up the wood shop of his dreams. To Mom's chagrin – though she took it extraordinarily well – Dad claimed the two-car garage and quickly set-up a beautiful and practical workshop where he would spend endless hours working on several projects at once. The outer walls of the garage were lined with workbenches that held a wide variety of hand tools and power tools. He set up a second ring of tables and benches in the center of the garage so that he ended up with four wide aisles with benches and tools on either side.

Now keep in mind that Dad was not only blind but also had this propensity for working on multiple projects at one time, each in various stages of development. The trick was how to set up the shop up so that he could find things, so that he could remember where he left various parts, and be able to navigate around a shop that most of us would find challenging even with the ability to see.

To solve this, Dad and an engineering friend of his, came up with a set of strings that they ran down the center of each aisle at about seven feet above the floor. The lines obviously crossed where the aisles met, like intersections on a street, and then they also tied knots halfway down each aisle to mark the center length of each aisle. This gave Dad some distinct "markers" so that he knew quite accurately where he was at any one time. Next, Dad visualized each aisle as a street and named each one after streets in our neighborhood. So, in order to keep track of things, he knew that his drill press was at the corner of First and Amsterdam and that his sander was at Liberto's house on Aldene Road. By mapping "the neighborhood" in this way, he could catalog all of his projects and their various parts and know exactly where he left them. It became so second nature to him after a while that he could buzz around the shop like he was sighted and knew where everything was or at least have an excellent idea of where to search when something was missing. Sounds pretty amazing, huh?

When Dad passed away, I asked my Mom and my brother if I could keep those guidelines of his. I carefully took down those well-worn cords, carefully rolled them up, and put them in a quart-sized zip-lock that now hangs in my shop. The coiled up cords are a constant reminder of what someone can do when they joyfully and creatively put their mind to it.

I have faced some really tough organizational problems in my time and the basic idea of working up the scale always works. Ugly, Poor, Good, Better, Best. The trick is to get a handle on what you are dealing with.

The foundation Opa and Dad laid for me was *all about attitude*. One demonstrated the concept of creative problem solving and creative thinking while the other demonstrated power of the concept when put into action and did it to the max. In both cases, they worked the idea of making things *better*. This kind of attitude not only creates an atmosphere where possibilities can be tried out and new solutions found, but also sets the stage for both a willingness to keep trying and the creation of contingencies. The old adage, "If at first you don't succeed, try, try again," needs to be applied far more often than it is. It amazes me how willing kids are to play video games and practice this, yet most often kids, or even young executives and workers of all kinds, often give up if something doesn't work for them immediately. We seem to gear all our efforts towards instant success and often times it simply takes longer than that. When trying to solve problems in volunteer organizations, often the long haul is the solution; but few leaders have the patience to cultivate the solutions and work up the scale from Ugly to Best.

Likewise, I've seen far too many instances where a plan is created and given a try, but there are no contingencies in place or developed along the way. So as a program starts to fail, the leaders keep hammering without thinking through any adjustments that might be necessary or even obvious. Sometimes when you are in a fight for survival it helps to have a "Plan B," or even a "Plan C" or "D." Sir Ernest Shackleton experienced this very dynamic when trying to save his crew on the Imperial Trans-Antarctic Expedition of 1914-16. In his book *South: The ENDURANCE Expedition*, Shackleton details the ordeals of the crew as they first tried to land in Antarctica at the old base previously used by Robert Falcon Scott, only to have the *Endurance* get caught in the ice. The ship was then dragged by the moving ice flows over 1500 miles away from their landing spot. In the process *Endurance* was slowly crushed and sunk, forcing the crew to first live on the ice flows and then into the open water, eventually ending up on a barren rock in the South Atlantic called Elephant Island. When Shackleton and several others went to get help, they further endured huge storms, landing on the wrong side of the South Atlantic island of South Georgia, and had to hike across an uncharted mountain chain before reaching a whaling station. From there, it took four concerted tries to get back to the men on Elephant Island. He eventually succeeded and all of his men were rescued, but the entire exercise was one of plan and adapt, plan and adapt. Shackleton never succeeded in completing the goals of that expedition, but the lessons learned and the story of his crew's survival is now well known in business and leadership circles as a story of determination and flexibility in the face of adversity, just like what Dad did on a personal level.

Now stop and think about this: We seem to live in an age of unbelievable polarization. So much of our lives have become part of trying to find solutions, but they are always framed as "the right way" or "the wrong way" and the idea of doing the "best" thing means doing something perfectly or not bothering at all. The thing that eats all of us up is, either silently or by default or by a paralysis brought on by groups that can't agree on anything, that unless we can find the perfect way to do something, nothing changes and we are stuck.

I really do believe that when it comes to questions of ethics and morals it is important to try and "get it right" or "to do the right thing," however, most of the situations that come up in our lives, be it personal, professional, or otherwise, cannot be measured simply in terms of right or wrong, but on a continuum of Ugly, Poor, Good, Better, and Best. Few things in life are perfectly good and few things in life are perfectly bad. Most fall somewhere between Ugly and Best. And if that is true, then the trick is to work at

---

Working up the scale ALWAYS works!

---

moving things up the scale.

Opa couldn't draw, but he kept working the problem and eventually came up with a solution that helped him compensate, moving his skill level from Ugly up the scale so that his paintings and other artwork are well above Ugly. Dad faced decaying vision and continued to find ways to compensate. In doing so, his woodworking skill, which was Good when he could see, *improved* to Best by the time he was completely blind. In other words, the ground shifted beneath him to the negative and he *still* improved. The coolest thing is this: I have faced some really tough organizational problems in my time and the basic idea of working up the scale *always works*. Ugly, Poor, Good, Better, Best. The trick is to get a handle on what you are dealing with. Confront it. Study it. Get to know it. Then *think* about it, mull it over, and consider the ways it can be *improved* if it cannot be fixed right away.

Many of the problems we face are so apparently complex or have so many variables that any immediate solution is impossible. Take New York City or Newark, New Jersey in the seventies and the task of making either city safe seemed impossible. Yet here we are, years later and both cities are far better off than they were before. Are they perfect? No. But are they better? Yes! Ugly, Poor, Good, Better, Best. *You have to work the scale*.

True craftsmanship takes looking at each piece with total quality in mind – and if that means adjusting things here and there as you go or using different approaches as the situation demands (as it will with dealing with human members), then one-size-fits-all should be banished and every situation addressed with a tool box filled with strategies aimed at handling every situation possible.

> ## KEY TWEAKS TO GO
>
> 1)
>
> 2)
>
> 3)

Chapter 4

Leading Well – The Heart of a Real Leader

"The true test of a man's character is what he does when no one is watching."

John Wooden

Authentic Leadership

Jacob Needleman, a modern American philosopher who could actually get me to enjoy philosophy made, what I think, is an astounding observation about Abraham Lincoln in his book, *The American Soul.* Needleman has a way of getting you to think deeper, but he does it in a way that is completely accessible or "street" as you have heard me refer to it. His observation about Lincoln has to do with the photographs that exist of Lincoln and many of his contemporaries, and it has a direct application that gets right at the heart of authentic leadership.

In the 1860s, photography was still in its infancy and taking a picture was no easy matter. Taking a clear, sharp image required the subject to sit very still for several seconds, so photographers learned quickly to suggest to their subjects to strike a pose they could hold. As odd or presumptuous as this may sound now, this was not so unusual back then – portrait painters used the same technique since the idea wasn't just to capture an image, but some sense of the character of the subject. If you look at many of Lincoln's contemporaries, the poses they strike tend to give away who they are, or more accurately, how they wanted to be seen.

The most obvious perhaps is George B. McClellan who served as the General in Chief of the Union Army. In his famous portrait, he struck a pose that projected complete authority, but it now seems to be very much as Needleman calls it, "a mask."

Likewise, General William Tecumseh Sherman's portrait displays an angry fierceness. In photo after photo in that time period, you can clearly see "masks" of all kinds, but as Needleman deftly points out, when you get to the many photos of Lincoln it's as if there is really no mask at all. In several famous portraits,

Lincoln looks right into the lens and is so completely devoid of any mask or pretense, your eyes are immediately drawn to meet his gaze. It's like you are being allowed to look right into the man's soul, like he's saying, "Here I am. This is me."

The first time I read this idea in *The American Soul* the idea simply blew me away. It was so spot on and I could, not only immediately sense the projection of this in Lincoln's photograph, but also see that quality in the photographs of other leaders I respected and admired. I realized I did this almost routinely with leaders I have met face to face. They say, *"There is something in the eyes,"* and I think Needleman may be right when he points us towards the *thing* being someone's genuine or *authentic* character, the *real* essence of who they are.

So what has this got to do with leadership? *Everything.*

In the quest, over the last three decades, to distill what makes a great leader and to find the formula that people can use to replicate it, is the idea that the best leaders are those who have integrity, are authentic, and know how to treat the people they lead in a way that gets the most out of them. As simple as this sounds, all three are a little more complex than saying, "OK, honest, real, and courteous. Got it." All three give most leaders fits in corporate settings and in the crucible that is *real* volunteer leadership – in the thick of cat herding – nailing integrity, authentic leadership, and servant leadership is harder than just replicating a formula or acting in a particular way. It's something a little more elusive than that, something harder to define, and yet, when we see it in the face of someone like Lincoln it is immediately recognizable *and we are drawn to it.* Leaders like that evoke a level of devotion and loyalty from their followers that makes them willing to march to Hell and back if that's what the boss wants. When it comes right down to it, *every* leader wants to inspire *that* kind of devotion. The trick is that some, like Lincoln, seem to do it without even trying while others desperately try and fail miserably.

Why?

Because authenticity is not something you put on like a coat or wear like a uniform. It isn't a temporary state, but a permanent part of your being. It isn't a series of best practices or a procedure to follow. It is your flesh and blood and spirit and being. If you aren't really authentic to the bone, if it isn't really WHO you are, people will eventually figure it out.

Humans seem to know, almost innately, and have an uncanny ability to identify, with little or no training, who is a lousy leader not worth following and who is a great leader worthy of our every devotion. How is this possible? How can the least educated and least trained of our people *know* what bosses are worth listening to and which ones should be shipped on a very slow boat to the Bermuda Triangle? The immediate, simple answer is "decent treatment." How is it that even in our darkest chapters of history that slaves and servants have been devoted to certain masters, fiefs to certain Lords, and peasants to certain Kings? That people in the lowliest of stations *loved,* with genuine affection, those who lorded over them? Again, the simple, quick answer is "decent treatment." It takes *caring* to treat people decently. It takes time, awareness, and involvement. It takes a will to make things better, not make them "make do."

I had a boss that continually and deliberately made me "make do" to the point that my personal safety was frequently compromised because he was so cheap and cared so little for my welfare. As my complaints about this bias grew louder, his willingness to care actually, but not surprisingly, *shrank.* Some leaders are so appallingly bad that it isn't hard to identify them. They don't even attempt to hide the disdain they have for people in general or for those they are supposed to be looking after as they lead them. But a more difficult brand of leader is one who is very common in today's world – the poser.

Right after Thanksgiving each year, the church I attend hosts a spectacular Christmas display. There is a huge celebration the first time they throw the switch to turn on all the lights and displays. It is an event that is a highpoint for the entire church and the surrounding neighborhood. It takes weeks to set up all the lights, the displays, and the computer animation used to run the lights and sounds, and it takes dozens of volunteers and hundreds of man hours to set up and run the event.

As impressive as all the preparation and hard work is to set-up the displays, decorate the entire campus, and then orchestrate the month-long series of events, what floors me and leaves me completely slack-jawed is how quickly it all comes down. The transformation into a beautiful Christmas display takes weeks. Taking it all down takes all of two *days*, and because it happens over the New Year's holiday, it seems as if it happens instantaneously. One day the decorations are all in place and a day or so later, there is not a Christmas decoration to be found. The transition is so fast it can take your breath away.

The sad thing is, I know some leaders and managers who act the same way when it comes to practicing their leadership. When it is time for them to *act* like a leader, it's as if they put on a certain suit of clothes or put on a certain persona as if getting ready for a performance – it really *is*, for them anyway, an *act*. The leader you see out in front of the people is not the same person you see in private or, worse still, the leader you see in private is a wicked alter-ego of the publicly seen leader.

The first time I smacked headlong into this was at a camera company I worked for right out of college. One of the senior managers was a wonderful man who eventually became one of my most treasured mentors. He was a great guy. He was courteous and made you feel like you mattered, he looked for the best in people, and was as steady as a rock. Another guy joined us as a senior manager and took over some of the first guy's workload. He, too, seemed like a great guy. In fact, he seemed a bit more outgoing and was a real "hard charger." But there was something about him that didn't immediately convey that you could really trust the guy. Something seemed "off," but I couldn't put my finger on it.

Two or three months into his tenure, my wife and I were walking along the beach at the Jersey shore when a man walking towards us with his family called out to me and walked up, slapped me on the shoulder and greeted me warmly. To be honest, I was taken aback – shocked really. I was a lowly manager and suddenly this guy is enthusiastically introducing me to his wife and family. I was completely taken in and thought I had really misjudged the

59

guy – that was until I saw him back at the office in the week that followed. I expected that the congeniality would continue at work, but he was back to his aloof, albeit, charming self. I wondered if I had done or said anything wrong until finally a week or so later there was another event that left me even more stunned than the first. In a conversation he ventured to let me know his philosophy of what made a great leader and he said that you really can't afford to have any friends in business and relationships with people were only temporary. When he saw my puzzled look, he said that our meeting at the shore was more for the benefit of our families – all for show – and that it was nothing *personal*. I'll say! I know that at the time, this was a fairly common perception in business, but the calculating nature of it made me want to wretch and I had a flash of *never* wanting to be *that* false or *that* calculating.

Oddly enough, later that day I ran into the first leader I mentioned in this story. He asked me how I was doing and then asked about my family, knowing my dad was having some health issues. I filled him in and he seemed genuinely concerned. He told me to wish my dad his best and then walked way and I stood there transfixed by the all too apparent differences between the two. For one, caring was real, personal, and went beyond the job. It was who Roland was. On the other hand, for Tom, it was simply a tool used as a means to get to an end. In the end it wasn't Tom who I would go *anywhere* or do *anything* for, it was Roland.

Roland understood that it is *authenticity* that creates *bonds,* not status or position. And when your leadership is creating bonds, it's functioning at a level that the average leader simply doesn't get – let alone *practice.* Nevertheless, if you want to be a truly successful leader of *volunteers*, you had better not only understand this, but be able to do it, because volunteers will not tolerate anything less for very long.

So how exactly does an *authentic leader* act? What do they do that is so different? How do you learn how to do it?

Well, it isn't like learning how to parallel park or learning the ins and outs of managing a project. It isn't so much *what* to do as it is *how* you do it. Here's the acid test: When everything is going wrong, and the pressure is at its worst, and no one is around to see what you do or don't do, to see how willing you are to get it done even when no one is watching, or will know, or ever find out what you did – that will be one of those moments when you will get a chance to see the *real* you and see how *authentic* you really are. You have to get to a point where it comes *automatically.* That ethics, sound leadership, and integrity are there, *regardless.*

A decade or so after the story I told above, I was at work and some other managers were upset with a situation and proposed doing something that rubbed up against the wicked edge of being unethical. After a few moments of discussion and seeing that they were actually serious, I voiced my objections. One of the participants looked at me and said in a very derogatory fashion, "What are you, some kind of Boy Scout?" It was one of the rare times in my life that I was not actually in a unit or participating in the Scouting program, but something welled up inside me. I stood and smiled, leaned right at her and said, "Yeah, as a matter of fact I am," and then walked out. Nothing ever came of their hairball scheme – it thankfully died on the vine – but it made me realize something about myself that I hadn't fully realized up to that point: You *are* something deep down inside, and *that* is the home of *authentic leadership.*

At its core, authentic leadership is the code you live and work by. It guides *everything* you do. For me, the Scout Law ("*A Scout is trustworthy, loyal, helpful, friendly, courteous, kind, obedient, cheerful, thrifty, brave, clean, and reverent."*) and the Scout Oath (*"On my Honor, I will do my best, to do my duty…"*) are part of a set of standards that I have come to learn and have tried to practice over a lifetime. I haven't always been successful at it and can painfully cite failures and lapses more easily than successes. But the code is ingrained deeply enough that if I have only enough time to *react* and not necessarily *think* about it first, I think I stand a pretty good chance at coming close to the code. In leadership, sometimes all you have time to do is *react* and *that* will be your telling moment.

Authenticity is not something you put on like a coat or wear like a uniform. It isn't a temporary state, but a permanent part of your being. It isn't a series of best practices or a procedure to follow. It is your flesh and blood and spirit and being. And if you aren't really authentic to the bone, if it isn't really WHO you are, people will eventually figure it out.

Authentic leaders are *anchored* leaders. They may not parade it around all the time – and beware those that do – but they know where they stand, they know what they are about, they know what they stand for, what is acceptable to them and what isn't. They have that internal compass and they pay attention to it. That sense of direction and the construct of their internal code can trace its source to any number of things, but it is usually an accumulation of lessons, experiences, and ideas. For example, my code is not just the Scout Law and Scout Oath, but things I learned from my dad and grandfather and from mentors like Roland, and from a host of writings and sayings like Teddy Roosevelt's *Man in the Arena*. Most of all, a good deal of it is grounded in my faith and belief in the teachings of Christ. Talk about authentic leaders, Jesus represents the *most* authentic leader that ever lived. But none of that would matter if I were to put the whole package on and take it off like a pair of pajamas or coat. It has to be *ingrained* to the point where people see it in you, even when you aren't trying to show it – *like what you see in Lincoln's eyes*.

So what is the big deal about authentic leadership? Simply this: the cornerstone for being a true, servant leader is to be *authentic*. You simply can't be a genuine servant leader, a true leader who practices stewardship at the highest level, if you aren't *authentic* or don't understand how to be authentic when leading, especially when leading volunteers and members. If leadership is just a show for you, a well-practiced act and that those you lead matter little in the arithmetic in what you are doing, then stop reading, close this book, *and walk away*. You are really doing more harm than good. But if you want to learn what the *real* nature of servant leadership is, to lead in a way that makes you an outstanding steward of your organization, and help your organization to become the best it can be for the benefit of *all* its members and the members to come, then read on. Mr. Greenleaf's concept is just for you.

Servant Leadership

One of the funnier and perhaps more tragic routines that Jay Leno used to do on *The Tonight Show* was when he would go out onto the street and ask folks to answer questions that should be easily answered by most of us. Common knowledge kind of things like the names of state capitals or lyrics to well-known songs. Perhaps the most painful is when he would ask folks to recite the lyrics of our national anthem, *The Star Spangled Banner*. The tangled up replies replete with wrong words and phrases are enough to make anyone who grew up before 1970 cringe in pain. Worse still is if you ask the average person on the street things like: "What is *The Star Spangled Banner* all about?", "What is the Star Spangled Banner?", or "What were the events surrounding the writing of the original lyrics or, more accurately, poem?" You would think that everyone should know these things, but when pressed, what we know is sometimes a mangled, muddled mess and far from an accurate truth.

It's funny what we assume, isn't it? By now, I think you are starting to get the idea that the dangers of assuming things or the logical errors that follow from assumptions, *attribution error* being chief among them, is a recurring theme of this book. Mangled lyrics, tangled history, and Internet myths and legends are all wonderful examples of how we all participate in this to one degree or another.

One example of this in leadership circles is the tangled, muddled, and largely assumed understanding of what *servant leadership* really is. Like a lot of things in modern business and organizational studies, at the turn of the millennium, *servant leadership* was a hot topic and nearly fad-like method that was written about to a point where some universities stopped accepting dissertations on the topic – too *over*done they would say. It took nearly twenty years for Robert Greenleaf's concept to catch on and for folks to be able to look back through history and see that many of our most successful and powerful leaders were actually *servant leaders*. Very recently I had a conversation with a dear friend who stunned me by saying he would *never* aspire to be a servant leader. I was stunned because he clearly had many of the traits of a servant leader, but he flat out said he hated the concept. "No way will I ever allow myself to be a wussy leader," he said. I asked him what he read to get the kind of impression that servant leadership is a "wussy" way to lead and he replied that he didn't read it anywhere, he just knew that, "rolling over and giving your followers whatever they wanted wasn't leadership at all." I agreed with that, but it also *isn't* what servant leadership *is*.

Many of our police departments across our nation live by the motto, "To protect and *serve*," and I don't think there is a firefighter alive, either professional or volunteer,

64

who's routine selflessness can be seen as anything other than acting on the behalf of others – clearly a servant attitude. The only way I could approach the time I spent as a Ranger was with the clear understanding that in everything I was doing, I was acting as a servant. Likewise, pastors, doctors, nurses, paramedics, our military, civil *servants* of all kinds, and a host of other jobs can all be seen as *serving* others – and *none* of that should ever be seen as wussy acts. It often takes guts and determination to do these jobs and do them well.

Part of the problem may be that Christ is often cited as the ultimate example of what it takes to be a servant leader. And the mental picture of Jesus that many have is one of a gentle, quiet man who walked this earth in passive humility. That may be one point of view and Jesus certainly had all those attributes, but the Gospels also record several incidents such as when He cleared the temple of the money changers where the terms "gentle" and "passive" hardly apply. The Jesus I believe in and follow could be fearsomely forceful when it was *appropriate* to do so, He just had a better handle on that skill than the rest of us.

Over time, the real meaning of what it is to be a servant leader has become diluted by our muddled assumptions and one of my hopes is that this chapter will help set the understanding straight for those who read it. So let me be clear about this.

Servant leadership *is not* wussy leadership. Servant leadership *is not* leadership that rolls over and allows followers to do whatever they want. Nor is servant leadership a style of leadership where the followers are free to dictate a wish list to the leader like he or she is Santa Claus and will grant every wish. Servant leadership *is not* weak leadership. As Robert Greenleaf pointed out in his original essay on servant leadership, it is a style of leadership that is marked by *where it comes from*, and again, as Greenleaf pointed out, it has to be grounded in one's character.

Perhaps the best way to encapsulate what a servant leader is, especially for our purposes here in dealing with volunteer organizations, is this: *A servant leader is one who grasps the common good in the context of his or her situation with such clarity and force that the only plausible, sensible, and most natural expression of it is to serve those they lead **for the common good***. To with confidence say, "Follow me! This is the way *we* want to go!*" with the understanding that the common good is the first, middle, and end goal. All other motivations for the servant leader are side games and subservient to that.

Servant Leaders as Shepherds

Since the definition of the term "Servant Leader" now comes loaded with so much inferred or assumed baggage, I want to change up the dialog about what it really means to be a servant leader. The primary reason for this is that once a term like this enters very common use, especially in business or leadership circles, it eventually gets *over*used and becomes a catchphrase that people *kinda* understand, but may not *really* understand at the intended level. This is especially important when it comes to volunteer leadership because of two important factors: it is imperative that volunteer leaders think in terms along the line of servant leadership in order to stay true to the most valued leaderships a volunteer leader can have, but it also is the style of leadership that members and followers – *volunteer* members and followers – will respond to the best.

Robert Greenleaf observed that Jesus of Nazareth is the ultimate example of what it means to be a servant leader. Greenleaf coined the term "servant leader" and Jesus never really called himself that, though His behavior clearly demonstrated the concept. Christ *did,* however, refer to Himself as "the good shepherd" and on several occasions used the analogy of being a shepherd to describe the relationship He felt He shared with his followers.

Relationship. Did you catch that?

Shepherds have a *relationship* with their flock. Shepherds care about their flocks, protect them, provide for them, give them food and shelter, lead them to safe places, watch over them, keep predators away, and often retrieve those of the flock that get lost or wander away. They care for the wide variety of needs their flock may encounter and keep a watchful eye on them.

Do you see yourself and what *you* do for your followers and members in the description above?

The key to all of this – leading like a *shepherd* – is to *have a relationship with your followers* and that you see yourself more focused on them and their needs and the needs of the flock, than in thinking about your own welfare. Jesus makes a point about this when he points out the differences between the shepherd and a hired hand (John 10:12). Jesus rightly points out that someone who acts just like a hired hand, who is in it for what the hired hand can gain, will abandon the flock when real threats occur, where the shepherd will stand his or her ground and fight for the sheep. Few things in life disgust me more than "bus chuckers" and at the head of that list is the poser that quickly throws his own membership under the bus when things fall apart or threats come from outside.

Look, let me make this clear: If you are into leading a volunteer group because it gives you prestige, power, authority, a cool uniform, a fancy title, or the admiration of the community and *all that* is what makes you do what you do, *go find something else to do.* Hand the reins over to someone who *really* cares and does so *first* and probably would do so even if he or she never received a word or credit or any acknowledgement. *Get out of the way of the **real** shepherd.*

Real shepherds are not afraid to sacrifice and do not make a big deal out of it. They are willing to make the sacrifices, not just for themselves, but routinely for others.

The *flock* comes first. If it doesn't, go find something else to do until you gain the right kind of heart.

Take a historic look at those who might be considered real servant leaders and every one of them can be seen as shepherds. Christ certainly acted like a shepherd for his flock and set the tone for how every pastor and church leader should act since. The comparison is *especially* stark when you compare how He acted and the compassion He had towards people versus the other religious leaders of the day. Some of the most scathing criticisms Jesus uttered were aimed squarely at the leaders of the day and how they only added to the burden of those who tried to be faithful while they themselves were corrupt to the core.

Lincoln is regarded as one of the best examples of a servant leader in the way he managed all the complexities of the presidency while struggling to hold our nation together. He is widely known for his personal approach to leadership, how he managed from the front, paid frequent visits to the front and to all kinds of places where getting firsthand information while providing a bit of intimate or personal encouragement was badly needed. His humor in dealing with situations, and patience when dealing with subordinates makes it easy to not only see him as a servant leader, but certainly as a shepherd.

Likewise, if you read the book *South* by Sir Ernest Shackleton and then several other books about Shackleton's leadership style, again, it will be easy to see that, "The Boss," as his crew affectionately called him, was a lot of things and again, "shepherd" could easily be applied. The crew of *Endurance* owed their lives to the fact that he took the stewardship role of shepherd seriously. In fact, many of our best leaders have been outstanding shepherds with a personal touch that brought uplifting encouragement, inspirational strength, and abundant wisdom to all around them.

Another common thread of all the best servant/shepherds leaders is that they just can't help being *mentors*. They have the kind of personalities and character attributes that others want to emulate. I'm not saying that these examples or others that we could cite as historic servant/shepherd leaders were without fault – we all fail and possess a healthy pile of dirt others can dig into with relish. Failings and failure are one of the few constants and assured things that we all will possess before we pass from this world – even the best of us. But what an individual *tries* to be because it has become part of his or her character is what ultimately marks them in the way they lead.

You too should be able to see this in the places you work. Have you ever seen the kind of boss who *really* got to know his or her people? Knew the names of the worker's kids, walked the floor to see how things were going, took the time to ask questions and then *actually* listened? *That* is a servant/shepherd leader. They don't keep themselves closed in behind a desk or door, rarely interact or really hear what the regular employees are concerned about, and are so self-impressed that the shallowness of their leadership leaves you with a really creepy feeling.

Now if you have seen how either of those play out at work with employees, how much *more* important do you think *any* of those things are in a *volunteer setting* with *members*?

The bottom line is this: If you are going to try to lead volunteers, then learn how to lead from a very personal, engaged, and ethical centering. **Lead like a shepherd**. Recognize the great stewardship that is involved when people give freely of their time and devotion. Lead in a way where you *serve* them well.

KEY TWEAKS TO GO

1)

2)

3)

Chapter 5

Managing Well - Be Prepared

"By failing to prepare you are preparing to fail."
Benjamin Franklin

It is very easy to slip into the belief that if you have leadership honed to a fine degree, then great management follows, but in reality *leadership* and *management* are two distinctly different skill sets that overlap to a certain degree like a Venn diagram, and each need to be worked separately to insure the best possible results. At the core of this is the difference between people and things. One of the failings of modern business is that we often fail to differentiate between the two and treat them much in the same way. This dehumanizes how we deal with people and in *any* volunteer environment this simply should not be. It would be far better if we used the analogy of the woodworker, his tools, and the heirloom he or she creates.

Good *management* and the things you do to manage well are like the tools a woodworker uses to create the heirloom (and by heirloom, I intend you to understand the word its original meaning of an object worth passing on from generation to generation). *Leadership* is like the raw materials and the craftsmanship and care applied to the materials to turn ordinary lumber into something beautiful, useful, and worth keeping. In order to do craftsman-like work, you can't just throw the materials around without a care in the world. If you bang up the materials as you go, the end results are not going to be anything like what you envision. Likewise, if you bang up and abuse your people as you strive to complete your objectives, the outcome is *not* going to be what anyone hoped for – again, *especially* in volunteer organizations. It takes both good *leadership* and good *management* to create an organization worth keeping, and the two have to work together, like two opposite hands picking up a bulky item – the hands are opposites but similar, and their differences have to be used together to get the job done.

In the last chapter, we learned the value of leadership and how authentic character and a stewardship mindset are the ideal mindset to have on the *leadership* side of the equation. In this chapter, we are going to look more closely at the kind of *management* practices that are specifically needed in most volunteer organizations but most often overlooked or not practiced well. And this is where I would like to make an observation about one of the quirkier things about ORGs. The smaller the ORG, the more critical good *management* is to its survival. The physical *work* can be more demanding on a few because it is harder to spread out the responsibilities. Here's the rub: When faced with this conundrum, instead of working on developing the teamwork needed to spread out the responsibilities, small ORG leaders/managers often absorb all the responsibility into one or two key people who are then saddled with, or saddle themselves with, everything to make the ORG go. As you will see, this is dangerous and unnecessary.

We live by a harsh reality of management that can be applied to just about any part of our lives and it is this: *Whatever YOU don't manage will end up managing YOU.*

Let's get into what *management* is all about. I'm going to start with a story that illustrates the differences between leadership and management and how one can impact the other.

There once was a wealthy man who one day decided that the time had come for him to prepare for his later life. The time when his health might start to fail or when he would not be able to care for himself. He carefully organized all his finances, created all the accounts he needed, purchased insurance for his care, and then named one of his young relatives to oversee his affairs when the right time came. He had carefully managed to arrange many of the *things* of his life.

All of this sounds great, but the flaw was that he was a widower and a stubborn man who wanted his own way. He was so private that he jealously guarded his affairs to the point that even the young man he wanted to attend to his affairs knew very little about the substance of the man's daily living. Years passed, and he finally had an event that triggered the intervention of his steward. When this happened, one fact became abundantly clear – many of the preparations that he had made were inadequate, obsolete, or had changed over time and his young steward, friends, and loved ones were left to scramble to catch up with a surprising number of details that had not been managed. Because of his own personal management approach to his own affairs, once the original arrangements were planned, no further maintenance was done. As he began to decline, instead of trusting his steward, he hid his condition and resisted the very plans he created for his own benefit. The result was entirely unfair to the steward and all the neighbors and friends who cared deeply about the old man, and is an illustration of what happens when management becomes a passive activity and it isn't connected with leadership. When that happens, plans are not really plans at all – it is all disconnected fiction.

We live by the harsh reality of management that can be applied to just about any part of our lives and it is this: *Whatever YOU don't manage will end up managing YOU.* If you use the tools of management at hand proactively, you can stay ahead of the curve and manage the situations you will be confronted with. But if you don't use the tools proactively and don't *really* think ahead, then the situations will ultimately manage *you*, and that can get pretty ugly. And it's a sliding curve too. To whatever degree you don't plan ahead and don't think proactively, will determine how much you will always be playing catch up. Dealing with this reality is where good leadership and good management converge. If you are leading well, foresight is a practiced skill that feeds into proactive engagement and planning. With proactive engagement and planning, you can *manage* well enough that you minimize the reactive scrambles when a crisis occurs – and crises *will* occur.

So what are the essential steps and what is the necessary mindset needed to really manage well as seen from a practical, street-level approach? There are essentially eleven steps in the process.

1. Planning
2. Staging
3. Timing
4. Executing
5. Re-applying What you Learn
6. Gaining Purchase and Leverage
7. Getting your Second Wind
8. Mopping up
9. Following up
10. Incorporating your Gains
11. Catching your Next Vision

As we have discussed already, your attitude and how you approach things is a foundational ingredient to insuring your success. An Emergency Management Coordinator who goes into a disaster scene with a bad attitude is already lost. The same goes for anyone confronting a personal problem – go in thinking all is lost and in short order *it will be*. It is essential to go into a situation with an open enough mind to believe that you have a running chance at making things better or improving the situation. This isn't blind optimism – its determined realism that you have to grasp hold of, but the only way you can do that is to start working through the steps outlined below.

Again, *leadership* and the steps you follow in a crisis, and *management* and the steps you follow in a crisis, are like your right and left hands – similar, but with some significant differences. Ever try to open a jar that has a lid that simply won't budge? It takes two strong hands doing two entirely different but similar things in order to get the jar open without spilling the contents all over the place. So if you *think* you have this covered because you are a *solid leader*, keep reading - there are some differences.

Probably one of the best approaches to *management* is at the heart of the Boy Scout motto, *"Be Prepared."* Lots of folks in recent years have found reasons to criticize the Scouting program for one reason or another, but the program and how it trains young men and women around the world is thoroughly grounded in two simple words, *Be Prepared.* The phrase sounds deceptively simple but there is an awful lot that goes into it and as kids go through the Scouting program, one of the lessons taught in a variety of ways is the idea we mentioned above – what you don't manage and stay on top of is very likely to end up managing you. But it also teaches that preparation is a set of interlocking and interconnected activities that require thought, planning, preparation, and determined execution.

PLANNING - Thinking it through

A practice that may illustrate the best approach to preparing by planning appropriately and the level of detail you should strive for is one provided by C.S. Forrester's character Horatio Hornblower in Forrester's famous series of nautical novels. Hornblower is the central character in a set of stories about the rise of a young British naval officer and follows his career through the years which also coincides with the Napoleonic Wars in the late 18th century and early 19th century. In the books, when faced with a complex situation or opportunity, Hornblower would take to pacing his quarterdeck and thinking through every possible detail of an operation, from beginning to end, and then comparing this to different variations of solving the problem. Every possible avenue was carefully considered, thought through, played out, and weighed before he would decide which plan to execute and the contingencies he would have available in case something when amiss. Contingencies were not options, but necessary variables in the plans he created. By going to these levels of detail, he could anticipate problems before they occurred, figuring out what he needed to find out before executing the plan, or determining which plan had the best possible chance of success.

Similarly, Sherlock Holmes, both in the original Arthur Conan Doyle stories and in the BBC television series, talk about Holmes using a "mind palace" where he could retreat for deep contemplation and play through facts and information that he had absorbed through various sources. Though fictional, this process is valid and it works. A case in point is how Marshall Williams dreamed up the original design for the mechanism at the heart of the M-1 Carbine. Williams was in prison in solitary confinement when, to keep himself from going crazy in the cramped dark cell, he began designing and building the mechanism in his mind. He *imagineered* the entire device from start to finish so that when he finally got out, he was able to commit it all to paper and then proceeded to build a prototype –first secretly and then with the Warden's consent. (A rare film, Jimmy Stewart plays this whole thing out beautifully in *Carbine Williams*, one of his first films after serving in World War II. So rare in fact, it doesn't appear on many of Stewart's filmographies. It is definitely worth watching.)

Thoroughly playing a situation through in your mind is the key to not overdoing it when it comes to planning or putting anything else in place. Leaders in emergency management will tell you that it is possible to inadvertently *over* prepare and that can be as counterproductive as not preparing at all. It can help you see things that otherwise get overlooked. You will never catch them all, but getting as many of them as you can *before* you start anything – or while you are walking through something to insure you have everything covered – is the best way to avoid being blindsided by something else down the pike.

STAGING – Putting the pieces in place

Staging is putting into place the essential parts that are needed to pull off the plan. Think of it as the plan's shopping spree and packing for the trip.

In volunteer ORGs, this is one part of the process that is rarely done well, if at all. Those who are more *leadership minded* and less *management oriented* will tend to skip over this part not realizing that this can seriously inhibit, if not cripple, any initiative if the stuff needed isn't ready to go. It is simply amazing how something obvious like this can so thoroughly gum up the works or derail a project.

I saw this firsthand as a Ranger when we would have outsiders come in for a special work day. The United Way hosts a "Day of Caring" event in many places throughout the US where companies and groups can donate a workday doing something for a worthy cause, charity, or non-profit. Every year we held a Day of Caring at the two camps I cared for. The trick was to find a number of projects that could be accomplished or significantly impacted in a single day, and were simple enough for the groups to attend. This was complicated enough – I had some groups that did not know one end of a paint brush from another, and other groups were highly skilled, such as a faithful crew from Williams, the natural gas pipeline company.

The first time I staged materials and tasks for this event I wasn't sure how to do it and didn't find out enough to really think it through. I took it at face value and used a one-size-fits-all approach. That was obviously a mistake and

I heard about it from both ends. The tasks I set up were too complicated for the office folks and way too simple for the Williams crew, but I quickly learned from that mistake and the next year I significantly ratcheted up my approach. I made sure I had more materials ready for use, saved really simply projects for the Day of Caring, and then met ahead of time with one of the managers from Williams to get his input on my array of project ideas. We consulted about what might be appropriate for the level of skill, the kind of tools they could bring, and their abundant willingness. I made a point of tapping into their knowledge and once we had agreed on what things they were willing to tackle, I set about getting everything that might be needed. With them, it was still a challenge to stay ahead of them – sometimes I succeeded, but in a lot of cases their enthusiasm kicked what they did for us up another notch or two. They were simply *awesome* and went well beyond the scope of what the Day of Caring was about and we formed some great friendships from working together in the years that followed.

Now understand the nuance here. For the majority of the volunteers, I had a set of simple tasks set up and usually had a list or chart prepared with an estimated number of people needed to complete a task. That was the low end of staging for this kind of event. On the other end of the spectrum, I met with the Williams gang ahead of time, talked over and negotiated the tasks they would do for me. I then created an illustrated set of instructions using a program like PowerPoint that I printed and was able to forward to them ahead of time or have ready for when they arrived. With all the materials and instructions ready, I only needed to check on them every so often, but this helped teach me a lesson too. In something complex like a Day of Caring with multiple things going on, I couldn't be everywhere at once. I ran myself ragged the first time running around getting people where they needed to be and then continuing to supply them. After the first year, I started assigning team leaders or crew chiefs to each team to help keep things rolling, but eventually I also got one of my camp volunteers to come up and act as a quartermaster who could get materials to folks if they needed something. In the last year, we even incorporated a runner who would take things to folks as they were needed. Each improvement made the process work better and there was still plenty of room to get the process to work even better. We incorporated what we learned at the Day of Caring events into other camp-wide activities.

The simple truth about staging is that the better staged you are, the easier it is to get started and keep moving. However, herein is another aspect that is often missed: Don't just stage for the start. *Stage for the whole project or event –* start to finish. When your workers get to stage two of whatever they are doing, have it good and ready. Then plan out how to finish, clean up, and follow-up.

TIMING – *Picking the optimal time to go*

You've heard the old adage, "Timing is everything," and so it is. You can have the best plans in the world, have everything staged in the best possible way but if you get the timing of the execution wrong, it can sink you in a heartbeat or wreck you before you even get a few steps out of the starting gate. I *really* learned the lesson the hard way on this one and it was a lesson that eventually prompted my education in leadership and the desire to want to learn more so I would *never* make the mistake I made again and could teach others to avoid the same pitfalls.

Back in the early 1990s, I had been writing for several hobby magazines and was developing a real passion for writing how-to material. I worked for several years developing an idea for a new model building magazine, *In Scale Illustrated,* that was fun to read, lavishly illustrated, and slick in its presentation. The plans and preparation took a long time, but eventually I couldn't stand it any longer and decided to make the jump and start the business. In hindsight, it was too soon and I moved way too fast. Impatient to be successful, I made decisions that were not as well thought out as I thought they were, and after just a couple of issues of *In Scale Illustrated* the company folded. Actually, augured in with a spectacular crash and burn is probably more accurate, at least from the pain and anguish it caused on a personal and professional level. I see now that I should have waited a bit more, planned a bit more, staged a bit more, and should have been far more conservative in how we grew the company. My impatience and lack of respect for timing and deeper preparation cost us everything, and Walker P. Stephens & Company died an untimely death because of it.

True, there were some things I could not have seen coming that might have killed the company and magazine even if we had been more conservative or careful. The model hobby industry made a dramatic, nearly tectonic shift around the same time that moved model kits towards simpler, pre-painted models and away from the super-detailing that was the editorial core of *In Scale Illustrated*. However, I'm not the only leader in history to have faced bad timing. Some bad timing is bad timing *you* create, and some bad timing simply befalls you.

As mentioned earlier, Sir Ernest Shackleton faced terrible timing in 1914 when he and his crew of the ship *Endurance* sailed for Antarctica on what was supposed to be the first transcontinental trek across the frozen continent. Roald Amundsen had already reached the South Pole several years earlier, but that was a run in and out meant just to get to the South Pole. What Shackleton had planned to do was something a magnitude or two harder by going all the way across the continent. You see, a team going to the Pole could only take so much equipment. Taking everything they needed for the entire trip would be like a backpacker trying to hike the 2160 mile Appalachian Trail (AT) and bringing everything needed right from the start – the backpacker would need to drag a trailer behind him or her to make it work. Instead, AT hikers usually ship supplies to handy post offices near the trail so they can pick-up supplies as they go.

AT hikers use post offices the way Interstate travelers use rest stops. To fuel up and get food on long trips down an Interstate, it's the same basic idea.

Shackleton, however, did not have the benefit of post offices or Interstate rest stops. He had to make his own. He stashed supplies along the planned route by going in, setting up supply caches and having the supply crews retrace their steps back out. To make that work, supplies had to be staged along the planned route going to and from the South Pole, so *two* ships, *Endurance* and *Aurora,* were sent with plans to stage supplies to and from the South Pole. *Endurance* approached from the Weddell Sea and *Aurora* from the Ross Ice Shelf on the other side of Antarctica. This would eventually allow the transcontinental team to travel quickly and efficiently to each supply depot along the way and dash across the entire continent from one ship to the other. At least that was the plan.

Unfortunately, Mother Nature conspired against Shackleton and his crew. The annual freeze in the Weddell Sea came early that year and the ship was frozen in the ice several miles from the spot where they were supposed to disembark. They never made it to their initial landfall or even set foot on Antarctica. Yet Shackleton's failed mission has become a legendary illustration of adapting to circumstances and determined survival and leadership.

Choosing the right time can be *very* complicated – sometimes more a matter of Ugly, Poor, Good, Better, Best – than of right or wrong. That certainly is true of Eisenhower's decision of when to start the D-Day invasion. Eisenhower faced a number of conflicting challenges; from the heights of the tides, to getting men in the right places, to a host of other mind-boggling and complex issues that had the potential to wreck the invasion. Thankfully, he chose the *best* he could and history vindicated that decision.

EXECUTING – Put the plans in gear

This one is pretty obvious – just put the plan in play. Well, actually *it is* a little more complicated than that. This is also the one where management and leadership have to work hand-in-hand, side-by-side, in absolute cooperation and coordination. No rivalry, just teamwork. This is where understanding the person/things division of labor between the two is actually an overlapping Venn diagram.

Good execution is not pulling the trigger or saying, "make it so." Execution is where a manager can really excel by providing everything needed to keep the initiative going.

What this means is keeping a sharp eye out for *things* that *people* may need, thus keeping the supply chain going to the troops. Materials, information, announcements, clarification of instructions, a form that makes registrations easier – anything that helps the *people* in the effort do the job or do it more efficiently – that is what represents your supply chain, either figuratively or literally.

It also means making sure that there are enough people present to do the job. This is one area that can be the most challenging for a volunteer organization. Lots of folks may want to benefit from the activity, but it can happen that few are willing to help *run* the event. In situations like this, it is necessary to make sure your organizational culture is adapted to *sharing the load*. Frequently, this is a result of not training folks how to do some of the simple jobs that need to be done, and *shadowing* can often be the best solution for this. Just get new folks to *watch* what someone is doing to learn the job. Half the time, you'll find that they won't be shadowing when you come back, but actually sharing the job with their instructor. This can have tremendous benefits and prevents members from burning out.

Whatever you do, be sure there are enough members on hand to share the load. If you can't recruit them, then things need to be cut back, or the group as a whole has to come to a collective understanding that responsibilities need to be shared. That may be hard to take at first, but in the long run, it will benefit the entire group. Be sure *not* to berate your members to get them to do things. *Appeal* instead.

Understand that part of managing well is knowing when to shift to a contingency, or to improvise one, if things begin to bog down. A timely shift from "Plan A" to "Plan B" can save an effort, but be sure not to panic and change too quickly or be so stunned by the problems that you make changes too late. Adjust as you go, just be careful not to overdo it. Think of this warning in terms of a small airplane flying into the wind. The forward progress of the plane may not be all that you hoped for, but you *are* still in the air and climbing, if ever so slowly. If grasped by a fit of impatience, you might be tempted to put the tail to the wind and therefore increase your forward motion, but it doesn't really work that way. If you actually try that maneuver, the wind over the wings *vanishes,* as does lift, and the plane will surely pick up speed as it falls from the sky! I know it sounds counter-intuitive, but it is true nevertheless. Think all changes through and make them carefully.

That having been said, history, both global and probably in your own experience (you wouldn't be reading this otherwise), is full of shocking examples of groups that construct great plans, fire the starter's pistol and then... anything BUT what was planned happens! It's like being in a team huddle, lining up, and at the snap of the ball the plan evaporates faster than dew in the desert. You get back to the huddle and want to slap the quarterback on the back of the head and say something like, "What the heck was *that?*"

This phenomenon is initially hard to understand. But when you look at it, there are usually one of several reasons why it happens. The most common is that the leader says one thing and then habitually does as he or she pleases with little or no consideration of the team or the plan. On the other end of the spectrum, is the leader who freezes at the precise moment you need them most – fear does that; fear of failing, fear of not being sure what to do. In either case, this is born out of people who have learned how to say the right things, act the right ways, or have the right postures, but the smoke and mirrors fail to deliver the genuine goods when the time comes.

Another way this can happen is when the plan meets the first point of resistance or runs into the first or second thing that goes wrong and the crew is ill-prepared with back-up contingencies. Any plan worth its salt needs to have back-ups at each point, especially critical things. You don't host a campfire with only one pack of matches being the only way to light the fire. If you want to study leadership and management to gain a greater understanding of this, read histories of great battles or disasters and it will become clear that failures are often rooted in giving up too easily or having only one plan or contingency and that ultimately leads to failure. *Redundancy* and *resiliency* are key assets needed – one being a thing and the other being a character trait of people – that can help keep an initiative going at the start. And that leads us to…

RE-APPLYING WHAT YOU LEARN – *Adapting to realities*

Plan as well as you might, things probably will go wrong or may not work or unfold as you expect, even if you have imagineered the project at a high level. When bad things happen, it takes a really clear and objective head to stand back, look at the problem, and find a way to fix it in a way that can keep the operation going or at least hanging together. Improvising is part of the game. Yet, it isn't always bad stuff that bubbles to the surface as you execute a plan. If you pay close attention as things unfold you will discover things that happen as a result of what you are doing that are *unpredicted benefits* – perhaps a way of doing something, a mindset, or an improvement of some kind that yields some outsized or very welcome paybacks.

For example, when I was trying to get the crew of volunteers restarted at Camp Acahela, I was having a devil of a time getting in touch with those who might be interested.

(You will hear more of this in Chapter 8 in the section on communication.) One of the things that became clear was that I needed to let some folks know by sending out old fashioned postcards. This came as a bit of a surprise, but there was real promise to making that accommodation, so I did it. In the process, I realized I needed to plan and announce events a couple of weeks earlier than I had been in order to get the postcards to those who wanted them in time for them to plan to attend. It never occurred to me that this extra bit of time had the added and unforeseen benefit of helping the electronic media crowd as well. I had more of the postal crowd showing up, but additional "modern media" members had more time to plan and save the date, and it is something I have incorporated in every volunteer operation since.

Volunteers are a crafty bunch and this can play itself out to the negative *and* to the positive. Give a group a set of instructions and you have to be careful how they might be interpreted or what they will come up with in order to get the task done. I know of a fellow Ranger who asked a very skilled construction crew to repair a rotted corner of his primary shower house two weeks before the start of summer camp. The Ranger had some other important task to attend to during most of that day, but he left the task to his crew, confident in their skills, and he uttered these fateful parting words, "Just tear out everything that is bad and we'll replace it." He returned hours later to find a pile of lumber, a pile of tubing and fixtures, a collection of hot water heaters, and *no* shower house. The Ranger was beside himself and was so angry he could have swallowed his tongue. I think he said he simply kicked his truck and stamped on his ball cap like a baseball manager throwing a fit over a bad call. The guy acting as the crew chief faced this display of frustration and fury by shrugging and saying something like, "What? You told us we'd replace anything that was bad, and it was all bad." From that point on, the Ranger learned to be *far* more specific of his intentions and *a lot less* casual with his instructions, regardless of how skilled the group.

On the other side of the equation, my experience with the United Way Days of Caring, and setting up detailed punch lists with the Williams Pipeline crew, taught me a few things about how to set up a detailed, *illustrated* plan and relay instructions to execute a complex or large project. To be sure the Williams crew knew where to go and what to do, I created a PowerPoint presentation complete with photos and plans. PowerPoint was perfect for this situation because the program was simple, quick, and allowed me to include text, photos, and other things that made the intentions clear. Instead of projecting it at some meeting, I simply printed out copies and handed them to the crews. It also allowed the Williams crew to provide their headquarters, or anyone else who needed to know, what they had accomplished on the donated day. I also realized I could use the same idea for a project that might require multiple crews to come in on multiple days. We had a clean-up project at our Maintenance Yard that was complex and required just that kind of division of labor. This kind of printed presentation allowed groups to come in and accomplish part of it, and then to hand off the project to the next group coming in after them.

It could be that what you learn may seem like just a small thing, but they tend to have a big impact or can connect several dots that can supercharge an effort in unexpected ways. So, watch for these little gifts and find ways to add them to your bag of tricks.

GAINING PURCHASE & LEVERAGE – *The handle and applied force*

A fresh and tighter grip, a better leverage point, a bigger tool, or more bodies. By the time you get into the middle of a project, you may discover that the inertia starts to ebb or the forward progress begins to stall. On an individual basis, especially when using tools and applying effort to something, it is helpful to stop, back-up, get a better grip on the stubborn item, and go at it anew. Perhaps a bigger tool is required, a better leverage point, lubricant, or some more bodies need to be applied to the problem, but in the middle of what you are trying to accomplish, you also need to be aware of adjustments that may be needed to keep the plan on track, get it back on track, or keep it from stalling.

The only difference between a project that stalls and one that overcomes obstacles is *intelligent* persistence. That not only means adjusting as you go, but understanding the subtle reality of taking a breather and then attacking the issue with renewed application of effort. This goes hand in hand with...

GETTING YOUR SECOND WIND – Sustaining the effort

The battle is often won on the second, third, or fourth surge, not on the first assault. Overrunning the enemy on the first try is rare, and the problem most volunteer organizations face is that if the first effort to try something isn't a rousing success, folks are quick to throw in the towel. In any effort that involves volunteers, it is the *sustained* effort that gains their attention, loyalty, devotion, and dedication. The difference between a flash-in-the-pan and the group experiencing ongoing success is that the latter has had the guts and will to stick it out, to keep trying and adjusting, and doing all the things we have discussed here, in order to make the plan succeed.

At some point in this process, weariness gives way to finding the groove and the most effective way of getting things done. Additional help will come. More volunteers will want to participate and a synergy can start to develop that will energize even the most tattered and worn out of souls. The trick is to persist – keep calling for help and keep working to improve things as it goes forward. *Progress* is the real measure of accomplishment here. Celebrate *every* little success.

MOPPING UP – Ending well part 1

Before you know it, your plan will be well on its way and your project will either be close to completion or ready to make that transition into becoming a regular part of your operations. This is where ending well becomes critical. Ending well has two components: mopping up and following up. There is a big difference between the two. Mopping up is the finishing of the details. Following up is making sure the gains you have fought for are not lost, nor will they deteriorate.

Mopping up looks at what the ultimate goals were and combines that information with additional items that may have made themselves known in the course of the project – like combining what you *thought* you knew with what you *learned* along the way to create a more comprehensive punch list or more detailed set of goals. Armed with that *revised* knowledge, you can then start working through what has been completed and what details still need to be addressed. Having said that, resist the temptation to let the little things go with the false belief that they will take care of themselves as a matter of course. Not so! You need to keep repeating the mantra that the detail you ignore today will be a much bigger issue that may come back to bite you in the days to come.

As a case in point, I know of one club that was so eager to get a website up and running that they contracted with a service provider who offered to get them their web domain, set up the site, and then host it on the Internet for a set fee and a monthly maintenance fee. The club did not realize two key parts of the deal. First, that the provider actually owned all the administrative rights to the domain – it was never put in the name of one of the club members or the club itself – and second, the domain needed to be renewed after five years. Five years represented three significant personnel changes on the Board of Directors and collective knowledge of these details ebbed away. One day the website quit working. The domain renewal fees had not been paid. It was later determined that the notices probably went to a former member who had been involved with this at the start but now was long gone. When the club tried to renew the domain, the service provider wanted the maximum possible cost to renew or obtain the domain – as in hundreds of dollars. What should have been a detail attended to in mopping up after the domain was established, and could have been reduced to a simple annual renewal that could have cost less than $20, ended up turning into a major issue resulting in a fiasco that significantly cost the club, and not just from a financial aspect.

Hopefully, doing that little bit of engaged management thinking, of what things still need to be attended to, based on what we have learned along the way will catch situations like this and prevent these things from happening, but it takes going through these extra steps to be sure that you have "crossed every t" and "dotted every i" before the job is *really* finished.

FOLLOWING UP – Ending well part 2
Following up differs from mopping up in that it looks at all the things that need attention *as a result of* what you have just accomplished. Once you have accomplished a major gain, project, or program, you need to take a hard look at what kind of maintenance may need to be done to keep all of it from coming unglued at some point down the road.

Say for example, you are some kind of flying club and after a long search you have found an ideal piece of property for the club to use for monthly events. Just because you have signed a lease or sent a check doesn't necessarily mean all the maintenance is finished and nothing else needs to be done. *Relationships* require as much maintenance as *things* do (and this may be one of those overlapping areas between *leadership* and *management*). The *best* thing to do (going back to UPGBB as discussed earlier) is to make sure that the club is reaching out to the property owner in a proactive way, welcoming them to see what the group does or offering benefits in some way that the owners might find useful. Not that they would ever take advantage of any offer, but staying on the plus side and having active contact is always much better than no contact for long stretches of time.

There is an old southern adage that really applies here: *It is better to leave them beholden to you than for you to be beholden to them.* In other words, in all your dealings with others, it's always wise for you to be on the plus side of the ledger in indebtedness to others. This mindset is a lost art among most leaders and managers and one that leaders and managers of *volunteers* and *members* would be wise to rediscover and wholeheartedly embrace.

Again, as an example of a failure in this regard, a similar type of club lost their connection with the real property owners over time. When the property suddenly was no longer available it was discovered that the contact they had been using was not an owner or a direct part of the ownership group at all. The property deal eroded over time from a lack of care and proper maintenance resulting in the loss of the use of the property and a protracted search for a suitable replacement. When it happened, it struck like a thunderbolt. In reality it was a train on the tracks that should have been seen *long* before the day of reckoning arrived. I'm of a firm belief that had the right kind of relational maintenance taken place, they would still be flying there today or at some similar property through the same owners.

Follow-up is *so* important and in volunteer organizations it can make the difference between a vibrant healthy ORG and one scrambling to survive.

INCORPORATING YOUR GAINS – Folding in your successes

With your project complete, one final aspect needs to be considered. Think through what you have gained and how to add it to the regular array of things you do. This may seem obvious, but sometimes some careful thought will reveal possibilities that again might *not* have been so obvious at the start. As I mentioned earlier, I discovered that a fair number of my older volunteers in my camp maintenance group wanted postcards instead of e-mails and that pushed me to announce events sooner rather than later. It was a little thing, but it worked so well that pushing out the announcement dates and preparing further ahead became standard operating procedure because it yielded terrific results. I made it a part of everything I did.

There is a great practice that you should consider using if you don't use it or something like it already. It is called, "Stop, Start, Continue," and the idea is to meet regularly and evaluate how your operations are actually working. You look at what things you need to *stop* doing right away or as soon as possible. Some things are just plain bad and need to be gotten rid of as quickly as possible. Then again, it could be apparent that something needs to be *added* to the mix or *started.* Finally, there should be a number of things you should be able to say that you need to *continue* doing, and some of these things should be celebrated as things the group is doing and may be doing especially well. When you find something that works, incorporate it and try to replicate it as often as possible.

CATCHING YOUR NEXT VISION – The view from the high ground

Once you have reached the end of the project and have attended to all the details of ending well, there is still one more thing to do that can be incredibly helpful to you and your organization. Now is the time to not only look back and review, but to try to catch a glimpse of the *next* thing. You are on the high ground at this point and there is no better place to get a good look at what has been accomplished, but also what *can be* accomplished next. Robert Schuller, the preacher famous for his sermons on positive thinking and positive outlook, wrote a little, inspirational book called *The*

Peak to Peek Principle. It focuses precisely on this dynamic. The idea is that once you have climbed to the top of your challenge and gotten to the *peak*, one of the benefits and rewards is that it will give you a chance to *peek* at other possibilities on the horizon that you may not have been able to see while working on the now completed project. In order to do this at the highest and most productive level, the *best* approach should include thinking about a number of different things about the past, the present, and the future.

First, you have to consider what was just accomplished. In many business and professional circles this kind of review is called a "post mortem," but getting together with your leadership team and key players to review what everyone has just gone through is a wonderful practice. You need to *honestly* review not only what was accomplished, but what went wrong, what went right, what you learned and what you would do differently in the future knowing what you know now. There is *always* room for improvement and this kind of review will show you what you did right and probably highlight a few close calls. Sometimes you realize that you weren't so smart, just incredibly lucky and that the hand of God spared you from a potential disaster. The key to this, however, is real, genuine, selfless *honesty* – the guts to call a spade a spade and see what you have done warts and all.

One of the most tragic leadership experiences I have ever had was watching first hand a leadership training course become an exercise in unadulterated groupthink. I know it didn't start that way, but it certainly evolved into something the nearly twenty years later strikes me with profound sadness and disappointment. The course was run entirely by volunteers and followed a curriculum established by the national office of our organization. But in the leader's zeal to excel and deliver a course that was equal to or exceeded all previous performance markers for courses like this, there developed a mindset that obliterated any thought or consideration to opposing views. By the time that week long course reached its end, every one of the staff members was expected to see and agree that the course had been an outstanding, mountaintop experience for staff and participants alike. Absolutely *no* sentiment to the contrary was either considered or even allowed. You either felt this was the best event ever or your career in future events was over – and for quite a number it was their *last* event for precisely that reason. It accomplished nothing and left a lot of bitter feelings in its wake, and I think the organization as a whole suffered for it in the years that followed. Stubborn pride is a cowardly and blind way to lead or manage and has no legitimate place in the volunteer universe. If you do not have the guts to look hard at yourself and your potential failings and call them what they are, you lack the essential credential needed to be a legitimate leader or manager. Get out before you hurt someone or your organization and go find something else to do.

If you have done an honest and good job in looking over what you did, then take the next step and apply it! Then take a look at what can be accomplished in light of what has just *been* accomplished. What's next? What can be solved based on what you have learned? Look around from the heights and see what you couldn't see before. This is the benefit of arriving at the top and being on the high ground. Sure, you should celebrate, but take advantage of where you are and catch a fresh vision for the future and start the process all over again. *That* is what drives great organizations forward and keeps them growing.

KEY TWEAKS TO GO

1)

2)

3)

4)

PART II

The Volunteer Mindset – What Makes ORG Members Tick

"First seek to understand, then to be understood."
Stephen Covey

In racing, if you have a great car and a good driver, there are still several other things you need aside from a healthy dose of luck in order to win races. One of them is an intimate knowledge of the track you are racing on. Tracks are not just paved plots of land or wandering streets in the middle of nowhere, but complex combinations of turns, banking, straight runs, and, on occasion, the rise and fall of the roadway itself. Not all tracks are level – many, deliberately, rise and fall.

Roger Penske's old Nazareth Speedway, also known as the Pennsylvania International Raceway, is a case in point. The D-shaped oval was just over a mile long, and while it looked a lot like the bigger Daytona's high-banked superspeedway, Penske's little track would give NASCAR racers fits trying to get their cars hooked up and dialed in to handle the different turns *and* the rise and fall of the track. If your car had the *best* possible set-up, it was said to drive like it had only three turns. But if your set-up was off, or the driver couldn't get the rhythm and shape of the track right in his or her mind, then the track drove like it had five, six, or even seven turns – a driver's nightmare in a short mile.

That is why getting to know the track is *so* important and why NASCAR drivers practice and practice and practice on tracks they have been to dozens of times. You have to know the track in and out because conditions will change and drivers need to constantly adapt.

It is the same with volunteers.

This section will, not only help you to better understand your volunteers and members, but will help you run the race laid out before you as a leader with the knowledge of *how* to apply the skills and concepts discussed in the previous chapters.

Chapter 6

Understanding Volunteers

"Alone we can do so little;
together we can do so much."

Helen Keller

A Different Dance

There are three things that make our small organizations different from their larger corporate and non-profit cousins: The volunteers who make up these groups, the steps needed to lead them effectively, and the way these organizations need to be structured in order to meet their unique operational needs and demands. The differences are not huge, but they are significant enough that not addressing the specifics will lead to sub-par performances. Despite the fact that I am a big fan of small organizations, I have to admit that most clubs and small organizations drive me, and a lot of their members, *crazy*. Most small volunteer organizations are poorly run and few have lived up to their true potential. In most cases it is not that the organizations have outlived their usefulness, but that the folks trying to run them do not realize the subtle ways these groups are *radically* different from any other form of organization on the planet.

That is not hyperbole, but fact. Volunteers respond

Needing a paycheck, and what you might be coaxed to do or tolerate as an employee, is very different from what drives a volunteer.

---

differently, work by a different set of rules, and have an entirely different set of motivations than employees do.

Volunteers participate at *their* will, on *their* time, and with a dizzying array of commitment levels that can befuddle the best manager and confound the best operations or program director. Leaders and managers often suspect these differences but make the mistake of believing these will be easy to overcome and harness, bringing the volunteer around to the leader's way of thinking or to the management's agenda. In doing so, they fail to realize a simple, pivotal point: the *agenda always belongs to the volunteers*. When it ceases to be their agenda, they are no longer volunteers, and upon this nuance is built every other success strategy one can use regarding volunteer members.

This means that leading a volunteer organization is *very* different from leading a corporation or even a large non-profit. Leadership is never easy and it is a complicated dance at best. In recent years transformational leadership practices such as servant leadership have become more and more accepted as the best way to energize and lead employees to greater heights of performance, but even knowing and practicing these techniques does not guarantee success at the *volunteer* level. Needing a paycheck, and what you might be coaxed to do or tolerate as an *employee*, is very different from what drives a *volunteer*. If you give orders or try using the same leverage on volunteers that you do with your employees, they will very likely hand you their cup of coffee and leave you with a smile as they walk out the door.

There is a well-known saying among those who have led volunteers that trying to lead volunteers is like trying the herd cats, and it's true. If you have never truly done it before, you will be in for a big surprise. It is harder than you might think and takes a special, nuanced feel that can leave experienced corporate leaders floundering. The dance steps used when leading volunteers are *very* different than those used elsewhere. The trick, when thrust into the arena of leading volunteer members, is to find the different beat, master the different steps, and flow with a different rhythm.

Aside from the leadership dance being different, the

way small volunteer organizations work is different as well. To use a computer analogy, the problem is simply this: Corporations, and everything else, run on an operating system like Microsoft Windows. Volunteers are running Apple OS. Similar, but *very* different, right down to the very core. The way your members act and how they respond to your leadership is only the start of how these groups differ from all other organizations. These facts alone would mandate a different approach to *organizing* how the group is supposed to establish and accomplish its vision, mission, and goals, but there are some other significant points that make *operations* different. Internal communications is one of the key ways these small organizations differ from their bigger cousins. If, as a leader or organizer, you fail to understand the nuance of *how* these groups communicate, and even more importantly *why*, you are likely to run an event and not have anyone show up and swear that no one cares any more. However, as the Pew study showed, that should not be the case.

I've used the term *nuance* three times now and with deliberate and significant reason. Successful small volunteer organizations are populated by, run by, and operate on a set of rules and guidelines that are different from those used in most other leadership and organization scenarios. The differences are not huge, they are nuances. They are adjustments to what many think of as the norm – in essence, *tweaks*. However, if they are ignored, they pile up and cause nothing but grief and heartache to the members, leaders, and other benefactors of the group. But if they are applied to *each* part of the organization, if those at the front understand themselves, their members, and how these organizations *really* work and what makes them tick, the organization will hum like a well-oiled machine and reach heights that its founding members only dreamed of.

Why Business Leaders Frequently Fail at Leading Volunteers

I have seen time and again some of the best corporate leaders fail miserably and in spectacular fashion when it comes to leading volunteers. Corporate leaders simply can't get volunteers to respond or move like they can their employees at work. I actually had one of our professional Council leaders, in the Boy Scout Council where I worked, say in a conversation about trying to get a particular project done, "You just can't trust them. They are undependable and just won't follow through." In his mind, volunteers were lazy, unmotivated, and lacked drive to accomplish anything. He never realized that the problem wasn't their dependability, but *his* leadership as he applied it to them. He was treating them like they were employees by applying the same expectations and metrics of performance to them as he would to me or any of the rest of the professional staff. Volunteers respond to a completely different set of motivating points and pressures.

Leading volunteers *is* like herding cats – and you frequently get the same looks from volunteers that you get from your household tabby. There is a huge gulf of differences between leading employees and leading volunteers. It is not that one is any better than the other, it's simply different. The same way dogs and cats are different as pets. It is as different as being an auto mechanic and a diesel mechanic, or driving a car and driving an eighteen wheeler. These pairs are similar but different. Each requires a bit of a twist on the basic theme in order to truly understand the nuances and dramatic differences that can lead to success or failure. You simply need to understand how leading volunteers is different in order to up your game if you want to lead volunteers successfully and make your volunteer organizations thrive.

Taking the mechanic or driver analogies a step further, if the biggest thing you have ever driven is a small sedan and never towed anything, you would have to be out of your mind to try and climb into a cab of a big eighteen wheeler and take it out on the road. There are some vital bits of information you will need just to get rolling, and a healthy amount of training to keep from crashing. The same applies for trying to fix a diesel if you have no experience with that kind of engine. You might get away with following some instructions, but it really is far more helpful and productive if you have someone with experience with diesels showing you how to do it. Diving into leading volunteers without understanding *how it differs* from leading professionals is just as crazy. Of course you can adapt, but learning the ground rules and basics from someone who has done it is a *huge* benefit.

So how exactly are volunteers different from professionals?

There are a lot of ways they are different from your employees. Here's how:

- Volunteers don't earn pay. They *give* their time.
- They *lend* their expertise.
- They have *other commitments* that may take them away from what they do for you.
- They will work or not work *based on how motivated they are* about your mission or goals.
- They *won't* bend to the same pressure points as your employees.
- They are not beyond telling you to "pound salt" or give you a piece of their minds if crossed. They don't *need* to put up with you and they won't.
- They will show up or not show up at *their* will, not *yours*.
- Their training is usually what they *bring* with them. Try treating their expertise like the asset it is.

- They *expect* a visible result or, at least, positive affirmation of their efforts.
- If their enthusiasm drops off, they go away.
- If criticized, especially unduly, they won't come back.
- If you screw up with one, you very likely will lose the *whole crew*.

In fact, I think the whole professional/volunteer paradigm may be upside down. I think if you can learn to lead volunteers and make a volunteer organization thrive, you can lead *anyone* and make *any* organization grow, but not the other way around. I'm not the only one that thinks this way. Tony Dungy mentions a similar sentiment in his book, *The Mentor Leader,* when it comes to leading like you are leading volunteers.

It usually is not a lack of synergy that chokes an organization, but a form of anti-synergy that leaves a handful of people doing most or all of the work and the rest acting like an unwilling, demotivated, and grumbling mass.

Why Volunteers Fail at Leading Themselves

This question of *who* is actually doing the work also lies at the heart of why so many community organizations, clubs, church groups, fire companies, first aid squads, or other volunteer organizations are failing and deserve to be on life support. Volunteer organizations do not run themselves; there has to be a strong framework in place with a vision, mission, and a set of operative goals in place that everyone knows, understands, embraces, and acts upon.

The problem is that frequently these steps are *not* given the focus or priority they need which deprives the members of enough reason to act *consistently*. Volunteer organizations are notorious for fudging on these steps, giving them tacit attention or ignoring them altogether. One hobby club that I belonged to was in complete disarray and as I asked many of the members what the club was supposed to be all about, hoping to hear a consistent vision or mission, I heard a wide variety of things. I got an earful of grousing. No vision, no mission, no goals – just grousing. In a business scenario you pitch the vision, get the ball rolling, get some buy-in and act. But in volunteer organizations, it takes more to get the vision to stick, get the momentum going, and build the synergy to *keep* the momentum going.

More often, however, the problem is one of *default*. The organization starts on the right foot and for the right reasons, but the group dynamics or the personalities don't mix well. When volunteers get frustrated or angry with each other, they pick-up their bat and ball and go play somewhere else. It usually is not a *lack* of synergy that chokes an organization, but a form of *anti-synergy* that leaves a handful of people doing most or all of the work and the rest acting like an unwilling, demotivated, and grumbling mass. At this point the leadership of the group defaults to someone who probably isn't the best prepared to lead and is doing so because the vacuum of commitment has allowed them to become the de facto leader. This starts the organization down a path of dysfunction that is tough to unwind, starting with leaders who have taken the job for all the wrong reasons. Sometimes this happens with the best of intentions, but I have seen enough of this that about two-thirds of the time it is a strong but ill-equipped personality who ends up in charge and then won't let go.

The Solution to Both Problems

Both problems have the same root – volunteer organizations have to be run *better* than most businesses. It has *everything* to do with why people are willing to give freely of their personal time, money, and devotion. If you have not done the legwork necessary to justify all that as a leader, do not expect anyone to follow you.

Now, there will be some who will say, "Bongard, you're all wet. You just have to run your volunteer organization like it's a business."

Who is a Volunteer?

While this may seem like a fairly basic and obvious question, one look at academic sources will already demonstrate that, for the sake of clarity, it would be wise for me to define in this book, who we are talking about when I refer to who volunteers are and how I define them. It should be obvious by now, that the way I approach volunteering and writing about leading volunteers, is from the viewpoint that the individual who is volunteering is generally doing so for good and laudable reasons *and* because the ORG gives something back that is personally important to them. That could be as simple as finding good fellowship, gaining information or skills, sharing assets they might otherwise not have access to, or could not do alone. Likewise, the individual who is leading volunteers – even if he or she is being paid to do it – usually gets involved in the organization because there is some connection to the principles or ideals of the organization. There are plenty of volunteer leaders who are essentially mercenaries, but at some point there has to be some sort of *genuine* connection to what the organization is about. If there isn't, there is usually an immediate disconnect between the uncommitted leader and the cache of volunteers he or she is trying to lead. While the leader may see the activity as a *job*, the volunteers opted in because the volunteer believed in what the group is about (vision and mission). This is a subtle but important difference. It's like a pastor of a church who doesn't believe in God but continues to do the work because it's his or her *job*. The rest of his or her members are probably in the pews because they *do* believe in God. As crazy as this sounds, this kind of mismatch happens *all the time* – leaders who end up in charge of groups they have no business leading.

It's one thing to be a hired hand leading other hired hands to do a job. You can work at a company leading a crew of autoworkers who assemble parts for Chryslers and in your private life be an avid Ford nut. The pay you gain to do your job allows you a certain amount of disconnect with your private life. Many of us don't like working that way, but the reality of things are that we make choices all the time based on our needs, and sometimes these are awkward compromises. But when it comes to our *convictions*, our *preferences*, and the *way we spend our free time*, a Yankee fan will not join a Mets or Red Sox fan club. What you do for pay and what you do as a volunteer often times come from two different places in your head or heart.

Getting Connected

When I was a lot younger, I owned a home in Ogdensburg, New Jersey. It had a *long* driveway lined with hedges that had been planted by the original owner and were about seven feet tall and almost three feet thick at the top when trimmed. That's a *lot* of trimming to do, but I was young and overly optimistic when I looked at the house. I didn't think twice about it – at least not until it came time to *trim* them.

I had an electric hedge trimmer that I had gotten from my father. It was an old but very durable Black & Decker that I had grown up with as a child. We had the thing forever, but it was built like a tank – no cheap plastic tool here – and, in true handyman form, it was well worth keeping. It weighed a ton, and the switch would get balky every so often, but it was tough, and tough is what I needed to get the job done.

The first time I tried to do the job, I grabbed the trimmer and uncoiled my extension cord only to discover it wasn't long enough. A quick trip to the local lumber yard solved that and soon I had just over a hundred feet of extension cord laying down the drive to the end of the hedges. It just made it, *kinda*. The outlet was just inside the double-wide garage and I was able to just reach to the end and fire the trimmer up and start cutting.

In less than a minute, the trimmer quit. Thinking it was the trimmer's notoriously balky switch, I unplugged it and walked back up to the garage (it was uphill of course), took it to my workbench and plugged it in. Nothing. Grrrr. So I took the handle apart to fix the switch, but nothing appeared to be wrong with it. I finally tried a different outlet and the trimmer sprang to life. I then hoofed back down to the end of the driveway, plugged in the trimmer and...nothing. Dead. This time I decided to follow the extension cord back up to the garage only to find that the cord had unplugged itself from the socket. It *should* have been the first thing I checked, but I went through all that other stuff first and wasted a lot of time and effort.

As dumb as this made me feel, I know I'm in good company because I see leaders and leadership teams make the same silly mistake *all* the time. The very *first* thing you need to do is check to make sure you are connected – positively connected – before trying anything else with your organization. Being *absolutely, completely, and redundantly connected* is not optional, a peripheral, or something that should be assumed in any way. Without real and genuine connection to your members, everything else you do is wasted effort. It's like waving a hedge trimmer at the hedges with the power off. You accomplish nothing.

You may be wondering why I'm being so emphatic about this, but the answer is simple. Most leaders or leadership teams either misunderstand what constitutes *enough* in the way of connectivity with their members or, underestimate what really has to be done. They either think their members don't care, that the ways they communicate with their members are sufficient, or they don't understand how volunteer members are so very different from the employees they are used to working with and leading. These issues are what this first section is all about – getting you plugged in so you can get to work!

KEY TWEAKS TO GO

1)

2)

3)

4)

Chapter 7

Hard and Fearless Questions

"The answers you get depend on the questions you ask."

Thomas Kuhn

"Successful people ask better questions, and as a result, they get better answers."

Anthony Robbins

Wood Badge and Courageous Questions

Have you ever had the experience of working in a job or being in some kind of program or game where you have a set of performance measures or criteria to judge how well you do? If you have – be honest now – have you ever done it or played at it long enough to figure out how to do it in a way that gets you the maximum number of points needed to get a great score? I think we all have at one point or another. It's human nature to figure out "the system" or find the "cheat code" to insure the best possible scores. There is a well-known personality test called the Predictive Index® used by many organizations. This behavioral test is designed to provide a personality profile based on an individual's self-evaluation, so there is really no way to "score higher" on the test. You are, after all, what you are. Nevertheless, there are several websites that will tell readers how to get "better" scores. As tempting as that may be for some, it really amounts to falsifying your personality profile in order to appear as something you are not. Manipulated numbers, twisted facts, skewed metrics, biased perspectives – these are all part of what happens all too frequently in our world. It's nothing new, but occasionally when the stakes are really high, the results can have disastrous consequences. I am old enough to remember hearing the body counts every night on the news during the Vietnam War and to understand how quickly these eroded General Westmoreland's credibility when we were told we were winning the war.

The awful thing about the kind of mindset that spawns "playing the game" is how it creeps into what you do. Almost no one who ever gets caught in this trap ever thinks of this kind of thing as "cheating," but cheating is what it really is. Yet, when it comes to asking hard questions about how we are performing as individuals or as organizations, we can easily get caught up in the need to appear to be right rather than the real need to find out what is really going on. Let me explain by relating a personal story that illustrates my point.

The Boy Scouts of America have an adult training program and award called Wood Badge which is the highest and most historic adult award you can earn in the entire Scouting program. The *Wood Badge of the 21st Century* (as it is officially known) takes over 18 months to complete, involves a full week of class and lab instruction (the lab being an array of outdoor camping experiences), development of a personal vision and mission statement, and execution of a set of five personally planned projects that align with the vision and mission statement. "Your Ticket," as this plan is known, is complicated and is like completing five Eagle Award projects and are true tests of leadership and management. The program teaches some of the best leadership trends and practices currently used in corporate settings and is a highly regarded program. Simply put, it's a big deal to earn your Wood Badge. It is one of the few awards given *worldwide*, so that recipients anywhere in the world will automatically recognize someone else who has earned the award.

The last requirement in the program is to conduct a 360° survey wherein the Wood Badge trainee goes back to

110

those who were impacted by his projects to get evaluations of his leadership, project execution, and other aspects of what he did. Each trainee has to write his own survey, with the intention of teaching the trainee the value of doing an honest postmortem or after action analysis. *That*, as I said, is the *intention* and it has tremendous value if done well.

Each trainee has an advisor, so when it came time for me to do my 360°, I took the intention to heart and wrote up what I thought were some really deep, honest, and analytical questions so that I could get a real grasp on how well I had done. I showed it to my advisor and he read it, put it down and told me I was crazy. I was really taken aback and asked him to explain. To my utter shock he simply stated that no one asks questions like that, and that, if I wanted to pass the program, I needed to ask questions that guaranteed a positive response and good feedback. I was simply stunned! He then proceeded to suggest a set of questions that were so "safe" that there would have been no chance of me getting a bad score. I remember driving away from that meeting feeling about as low as I ever have as a member of Scouting. I was disgusted at the idea that what I was really going to learn by doing it his way was how inquiries and surveys can be rigged to always show success, and I was supposed to *willingly* participate in this. It made me sick.

The next morning, I got up and looked again at his suggestions written across the draft of my survey, red ink and all. As I shook my head I thought to myself, "What part of 'On my honor...' is this?" "What part of the Scout Law starting with 'Trustworthy' was at work here?" For the life of me, I could not imagine where this could fit. As disgusted as it made me feel, I realized that my advisor's "advice" was not only counter to the intention of Wood Badge, but to the very core of Scouting itself. I popped the top of the kitchen trash can open and dumped his notes and suggestions into the can.

Later that day I sent out the original version of my questions to an array of people I had served and worked with over the past eighteen months. I figured I either was going to go down in flames and know *exactly* why, or feel pretty good about what I did in the projects, and there too, I would know *exactly* why. In either case, it was going to be real and not contrived. I could live with that.

A few weeks later, all of the surveys had been returned and two things were abundantly clear: the surveys were overwhelmingly positive and my advisor was profoundly miffed that I had ignored his "advice." To this day, I still have all the survey responses and remember the experience of reading each one and the feeling at getting honest feedback as one of the most rewarding leadership experiences I have ever had. Not just because of the positive response, though that certainly makes it feel all the better, but because it took guts to ask the hard questions and I have never quit asking them ever since.

Lots of leaders nowadays are afraid of what might happen if they don't pose the questions in a way that guarantees success or great marks and that is really sad because it is just a high end way of deluding yourself. Groupthink – the kind of blind, automatic agreement to things and ideas that is based more on going along with the crowd or being afraid to disagree – is born out of this kind of mindset, as are all kinds of other lies we love to tell ourselves about our organizations and how well we are doing. But the fact of the matter is that unless we are willing to drill down into the reality of what is happening in our organizations, unless we are willing to ask those hard and courageous questions about how good or bad a job we might be doing, then our organizations are doomed to mediocrity or worse.

So, what if?

If nothing else, this book is designed to ask some really hard questions about how we lead volunteers, what we assume in leadership, what we assume about our organizations, and proposing ways to think differently to get better results out of running our volunteer organizations. Who knows? Together, we may find that our world really *is* upside down, but if we can find ways to better lead volunteer groups, we may find some solutions for our businesses and NPOs as well.

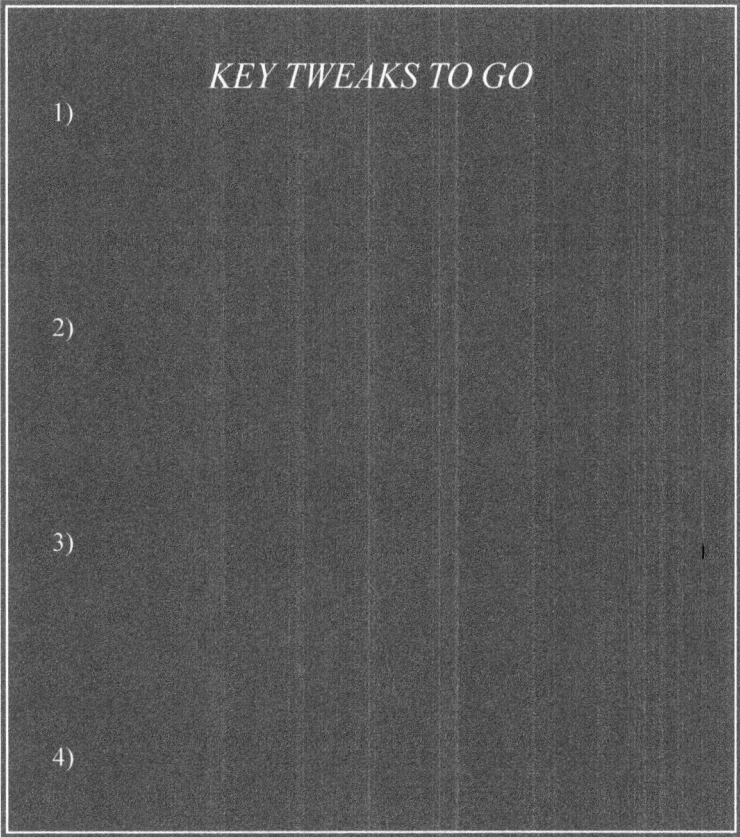

KEY TWEAKS TO GO

1)

2)

3)

4)

Chapter 8

The Sovereignty of Communication

"You can have brilliant ideas, but if you can't get them across, your ideas won't get you anywhere."
Lee Iacocca

Mass Communications that Work

No one argues over how important or critical communications are in the life of any organization, but there is a lively debate on how communications can be done effectively, especially when it comes to dealing with organizations that have members with commitments scattered hither and yon.

Smaller volunteer organizations tend to put their communication eggs all in one or two baskets – a website or an e-mail mailing list or perhaps an old-fashioned newsletter – but the reality of the communication world in the 21st century is that people now have more communication choices than ever before. The profound irony of modern communications is that instead of making communications more uniform, the variety of choices has made communications instantaneous *only if you are on the right channel*. You can get news instantly – but only if you are there to get it. For all the benefits of modern technology, you still have to reach 'em where they is, not where they ain't.

The Conversation

When I was growing up, my dad opened a small hardware store in our neighborhood that serviced the west side of our town. Dad was very handy, knew how to fix a lot of things, was dedicated, and hardworking. He did whatever he could for the neighborhood and when someone brought him something that was broken, he tried to find ways to fix it. As the family business grew, we ended up sharpening tools, doing bicycle repairs, lawn mower repairs, and at one point my grandfather even fixed cuckoo clocks. Dad poured endless hours into that store to make a living for us, but what made him and the store so special wasn't everything he did, but how *engaged* Dad was. Gunther Hardware was a

Solid communication at the level of conversation *is the doorway to the house, the ticket to the show, the way in, the grease on the gears, the tires on the car, and the premium gas in the tank.* Period.

gathering place. Dad made friends with everyone, or at least he tried to, and his secret to success was simply this: conversation. Dad talked to everyone and he sought to have meaningful conversations at every opportunity. What kept our little neighborhood hardware store alive for so long was not how well-stocked or how pretty it was. It was the guarantee of good conversation, solid information, and the friendships Dad made happen by engaging his customers.

As I moved into my professional career, I became part of a number of companies and operations, but the ones that were the most satisfying, rewarding, and meaningful were the ones that had leaders at the helm who understood the value of *great communication* and practiced that craft as if it were the same kind of conversation that went on at Dad's store. Every one of the wonderful mentors I've been blessed with has stressed in one way or another, the imperative of communicating well, and that by doing so in the most personal of ways, is *the* way to get the most traction with people.

Solid communication at the *level* of conversation is the doorway to the house, the ticket to the show, the way in, the grease on the gears, the tires on the car, and the premium gas in the tank. Period. Without it, everything else in an organization just *grinds.*

This may not be anything new. Any leader worth his or her salt understands this on some level, whether they practice it well or not. What almost everyone misses is that meaningful communication *inside* an organization or volunteer group happens differently than in any other kind of organization. It has to do with a principle I call *the sovereignty of communication.*

The Sovereignty of Communication

When it comes to volunteer members, the bottom line is simply this: Ya gotta reach 'em where they is, not where they ain't.

If you work for someone other than yourself, the company you work for has probably set up a number of things for you to help keep you in the loop with the rest of the company. You probably have a desk, cubicle, or office assigned to you. Along with that, you probably have a phone extension perhaps with a unique number where you can be reached. You may have some kind of instant messaging system and may even have a video conferencing address or log-in that you are a part of. You may have been assigned a fax number, an e-mail address, or perhaps an in-house mailing address. The company and, maybe even your division or team, probably has an established routine set up for meetings and, whether it is formally established or just a matter of protocol, there is usually some form of internal memo patterns or reports that follow along established guidelines. These are all ways that you communicate with the rest of the company and the company communicates with you.

All of these things have been *assigned to you* by the company. The company has control over all of these. If you leave the company or, God forbid, you are fired, all of these connections go away. The company is in control of all the communication channels – *it* determines how you will communicate regardless of whether *you* like using a particular system or not. *It* – the organization, or more specifically, *the leadership* of the organization – has the *sovereignty* of communications.

However, if you take a look at the local mutual interest or skills organization you belong to, whether it is a hobby club, church, Scout troop, etc., in the vast majority of cases, your group does not dictate much of anything in the way of communication channels *to* you – certainly not in the way your company does. Some communication protocols may exist, and most of the time those will be pretty informal, but your church is not going to issue you an e-mail address, give you a phone number, tell you what pew to sit in, and give you a Twitter account. *You* pick all of that. *You* choose your personal e-mail account and give it to folks you *want* to communicate with. *You* contract for a phone number, pay the bill, and choose who you will take calls from and who you won't, who you will text, or who will have to wait for a response. *You* choose which e-mails to respond to and which to ignore (or delete) and when you might visit the group's website and for what reasons. *You* ultimately are in control of how you send and receive information to and from the groups you belong to. *You*, the *individual member*, have the ultimate control over what you are willing to pay attention to and *how* you *prefer* to get your information. *You* – the member – possess the *sovereignty* of communication, NOT the leadership.

Let that sink in for a minute.

At the very least, this puts most volunteer organizations and the leadership of those ORGs at a distinct *dis*advantage. Not only does the leadership have to figure out *how* to reach you, it also has to reach you in a way that you will pay attention.

Here is the *real* kicker – while many ORGs will ask for your address, phone number, and e-mail address as a matter of course when you apply to join – *rarely* do they ever ask you something like, "What are your three preferred ways of receiving communication?"

What this really means is that most ORGs desperately need to reach their members to keep them motivated and focused on what is going on in the group, and yet haven't the foggiest idea how to reach each member in a way that will command their attention because the leadership does not possess the sovereignty of communication – the member does. Blissfully ignorant of this *vital dynamic*, most volunteer ORGs struggle to communicate with their members in ways that leverage responses and then blame the lack of involvement on members that don't care.

This is called *attribution error*.

The *real* problem is that members probably don't know what is going on because they have never gotten the message in a way that they will pay attention to and in a timely enough manner to make sure that they *want* to participate, or at least understand the need and obligation to.

You see, it really goes back to what I was saying in the beginning about Dad's store and what made it so successful. It is all about *conversation* and in order to have a genuine and meaningful conversation, you first have to be able to communicate using preferred channels. In a volunteer organization, that means reaching out to them *their* way.

When it comes to volunteer members, the bottom line is simply this: Ya *gotta reach 'em where they is, not where they ain't.*

The Power of Sovereignty

All the other things hinge on who ultimately has the sovereignty of communications.

I suspect that many with management, leadership, or human resource experience will say something to the effect of, "Well, this is simple, Tim. You just tell them how they will get their information. Just establish the channels for them." It seems to make sense, but if you truly feel that way, you have misunderstood the power of the independent mind and nature of volunteer members. The wildcard in this is *commitment.* Dictating works on employees in a company because even if they don't like it, they may still be motivated enough by their paycheck and benefits to do what they otherwise would never get around to. But most volunteer organizations don't have those pressure points or that kind of leverage that can be used on their volunteer members. For that matter, turning someone into an employee is an automatic means of raising the level of expectation with regard to their commitment. A level a volunteer may not be thrilled about.

You see, a key fact often overlooked or obscured when dealing with volunteers, and a key point leaders of small groups need to really understand, is that first and foremost, volunteers *volunteer* their time. They give their time when they want to, and not a moment before. If they hear about an event that isn't all that attractive to them, the vast majority will find something else to do. If you treat them poorly, ignore them, make them do things they don't like or endure things they wouldn't normally put up with, don't expect them to hang in there and hang around. They will, as my dad used to say, "Take their bat and ball and go find somewhere else to play."

Get this dynamic straight: What they endure at work, especially if they don't care much for it, will NOT be endured when they are on their own in your organization. Expect them *not* to put up with it, and to probably tell you about it in no uncertain terms. If they don't tell you, rest assured, they will tell their neighbors – something no small neighborhood or community organization can afford. So the stakes are higher when trying to get it right with volunteers, much higher.

"But they have an obligation to the organization!" I hear you say. To which I ask, "Obligation?"

Which comes first? The cart or the horse?

In volunteer settings, *obligation* is something the leadership *has to earn* – over and over and over again. It doesn't stop. You gain a sense of obligation from members once you have convinced them that the vision, mission, and goals of your organization are worthwhile and worth their time. You *earn* obligation when you have communicated frequently enough and well enough and effectively enough to earn their commitment. A sense of obligation is a direct result of their sense of commitment.

Little or no communication equals little or no commitment.

No commitment equals no obligation.

Do you see how this works? You simply cannot expect members to do anything just because they signed up. The initial enthusiasm that caused them to join will only go so far – and, on average, that it is a *shockingly short* distance. As a leader you have to make volunteers want to participate because you don't really have the leverage to compel participation the way you might at work. If you do succeed, it will probably be short-lived since most people belong to these kinds of groups because of the joy it brings them on some level. And when you quit making it fun or something deeply and personally rewarding and turn it into work, then your volunteers will simply go away.

So again, you have to *reach them where they is, not where they ain't*. It applies to the channels of communication you use and it applies to the way, and the what, you communicate as well.

The sovereignty of communication truly belongs to the members in all-volunteer organizations – *they* are leading the dance steps. Leaders need to understand that and adjust to the dance accordingly, or they won't have dance partners for very long.

Their Way

So what would the results be if we, as leaders, actually did it their way? What would that *really* mean?

To grasp the difference in the dance, you have to change the way you think about or conceive of your volunteer members. Instead of thinking about them as being like unpaid employees (something most of us default to without even thinking about it), volunteer members need to be thought of as something much closer to *customers*. Volunteers choose to participate, choose to belong, and choose to get news about your group more like they are consumers and *not hired help*. This really is the transformational key. As a leader, if you want one constant guiding premise on to how to handle anything with your volunteer members, always think of them as your *customers*, and you can't go wrong.

If you approach them as customers, then the issue of internal communications with them becomes much more an exercise of seeking dialog than making statements or announcements. Instead of putting up a website as one of only a few ways of communicating with your group, and then expecting them to eagerly come to visit, you need to think in terms of going out and finding your lost sheep and making sure they get the message, regardless of which way the message needs to go out or what the message might be. By doing this, you will begin to approach communications as an act of winning them over, convincing them again and again of the worthiness of your product, and getting them to invest in it. What they will give in return is their time and money.

From a leadership standpoint, this brings the constant pitching of the group's vision, mission, and goals into sharp focus, as does the need to continually mention them at every opportunity. From a personal standpoint, it will force you as a leader to be far more personable with your members, respecting them and treating them more like family, than expecting things from them that you may not have earned yet. In doing so you will make the first steps towards building rapport, which is so vital to the survival of any volunteer organization, but also make transmission of any message far easier. Once you have earned their respect and given them the understanding that they matter as individual members – each and every one – getting them to pay attention and give their commitment will be far easier.

This cascade effect of benefits generated by thinking of your members as being much more like customers continues with you as a leader getting to know them better, understanding what makes them tick, and anticipating what they will want and what they might be willing to do. Again, I saw this over and over again in my Dad's store. He got to know many of his customers as personal friends and, in doing so, knew the kinds of thing they might be interested in. He would then act as a connector between his customers and the product and services he could offer them. In exchange, he earned a level of loyalty that helped our little store live long past when the doors and windows should otherwise have been shuttered. It works the same way in any volunteer organization. If you, as a leader and your leadership team, act in a way that conveys that you are the lookouts for opportunities to do what your members really want to do, and then double down by acting as the facilitators to get those activities rolling, they will participate and respect your leadership, because that's what leadership really is!

Semaphore Syndrome – A Failure to Communicate

The biggest mistake most ORGs make is not *fully* understanding the significance of *quality* member communications.

Simply put, communication efforts with your membership *is not* just an event. It *is not* just an activity. It *is not* something you just do once you decide to let your people know what you have planned or is important news to the group. Communications is all of that, but attitudes and mindsets similar to this dilute the importance and power of internal ORG communications.

Get this straight from the start: *Quality internal communications to your members is your ORG's life blood. It is the lynchpin that holds the vision, mission, and operation together. It is the keystone holding up the rest of the organization's operations. It is the conduit that brings the power of solid leadership to your people.* Face it, if you are unwilling to put forth the effort to get this part of the organizational management and leadership done fully, pack up and go home now. Save yourself and all those around you all the wasted time, effort, and agony that will surely follow from a failed attempt at trying to get your ORG healthy and working at maximum efficiency. Because, *without quality communications, you are dead in the water.*

The biggest failing of modern ORGs, and perhaps even in business itself, is understanding that quality communication begins *with the consistency of doing it.* Tech, webs, cells, tweets, PR experts, English majors, and all the rest, are all useless window dressing unless you are *really* out there communicating. We take all that other stuff and put it ahead of *the act*, and as a result, ORGs are notoriously *bad* at communicating.

Want proof? Marinate on this for a moment: Many ORGs now have webmasters. How many still have a position called "Communications Secretary" and of those that do, what does the Communications Secretary actually do or manage?

Every time I have dealt with, seen, or heard about an ORG that was in trouble, close examination revealed that poor internal communications were *always* part of the mix, if not at the heart of the matter.

Leaders do not seem to understand that poor communications is not just overlooking follow through on a pre-event action item. Poor ORG communications is not an organizational thing we didn't have time for. Poor internal communications with your members is not just an annoying thing that we all tend to push to the back as an act of collective procrastination.

Let's call a spade a spade here: Poor internal communications is a *failure* to communicate internally with your members – a *critical failure*. It is as bad a failure *of organizational stewardship* as the treasurer having no clue what the balance in the checkbook is or the leadership blowing the treasury on a personal junket to Bermuda. It's a cancer. It's the termites that will eat away at your ORG from the inside out. But here's the worst news of all: The effects of poor internal ORG communications are hardly ever static. Poor internal communication is destructive. It is literally a *silent* killer. If you are not doing a top notch job of communicating to your members, whether you realize it or not, your ORG is suffering. You just haven't gotten the message yet.

You reap what you sow, and as true as that statement is for the quality of the lives we lead, it is a pivotal statement for our organizations.

It is as fundamental an understanding of organizational health as fully comprehending that organizational health depends upon good management that, at its core, is all about leading well, which is *dependent* on the quality of communications.

A leader needs to do a number of things well, but if the leader is a lousy communicator it won't be long before *any* leadership initiative grinds to a halt – essentially stillborn for lack of the critical messages that need to be conveyed.

What it does take, and what most ORGs fail to do well is *make the effort*. For most, the effort is lackluster, partial, and incomplete – and the ORG reaps what it sows, or, more accurately, what it *fails* to sow.

Quality communications is *so* simple. It does not take any special tools or skills. It doesn't need anything high tech. Those things can help, but before you use them, you have to do one thing and do it well, over and over again – ***you have to reach your audience where they is, not where they ain't.***

Again, to be clear on this, in corporate settings, lines of internal communication are usually mandated by the company and the systems the company uses. Employees are issued a telephone extension or cell, given a company e-mail address, assigned a place to sit or an office or station where they can be found. Every company has established ways of getting information out to their employees and this is so automatic and assumed that most of us don't even give that a second thought. It's just the way things are done.

But when you get to church or your bowling league, your hobby or hunting club, or the non-profit you volunteer at, the assumed lines of communication usually aren't *actually* there, and most of us are not aware of that either. The ORG assumes automatically that you use your phone, e-mail, and snail mail as your primary ways of communicating. You, on the other hand, default to your own ways of communicating – the ones that you – the receiver – establish and prefer. And here is the first major communication problem experienced by most ORGs: *how does the ORG know where you are?*

This is exactly what I ran into when I assumed the Ranger's position at Camp Acahela in the Poconos of Pennsylvania. When I got there in early 2004, Acahela was a neglected mess. I needed to get some help quickly and put the word out to our volunteers that I needed help. But little in the way of help came. For the first year I had only a handful of helpers and it took almost a year before I realized that my pleas and calls for help were not getting through.

This was a mystery. The professionals at the office had advised that I announce work weekends on our website and to send out bulk e-mails to the list of volunteers they had, but, generally no one ever showed up. Sometimes, several old-timers would come, and I assumed that they had gotten the messages – that is until Charlie Jackson clarified the whole situation for me. The conversation went something along the lines of me thanking Charlie for showing up for a planned work weekend, to which he replied, "What work weekend?" I was confused. "Aren't you here to help out today?" I asked. He replied that he was, but he didn't know about any work weekend. I was even more confused. "It was on the website and e-mails were sent out,"

I said. He scoffed and told me he didn't know anything about that and that he didn't even own a computer. Even more confused, I said something like, "Well how the heck am I supposed to get in touch with you?" That's when he started poking his finger in my chest and growled something akin to, "Send me a postcard. Call me on my house phone. But don't bother with that computer stuff – I haven't got one, and neither do any of the other guys coming up here to help you." He quit poking my chest and just stared at me like I had rocks in my head – which, at that point, was exactly how I felt.

It never occurred to me that none of the regulars who were showing up didn't have a computer. I had just been following Council instructions to send out e-mails and post notices on the website to get help because I assumed they knew what they were doing. When I finally sat down and thought about it, I realized that almost none of the volunteers were coming to me from those notices, and if that wasn't working, then how was I supposed to get in touch with any volunteer? Out of stunned curiosity, I started asking any volunteer helper or potential helper I ran into what their favorite ways of getting messages were and I was shocked. As crazy as it sounds, it quickly became apparent that the council and I were really clueless when it came to communicating with my volunteers at the camp. You see, the basic problem that Charlie helped drive home so clearly is that, in most volunteer scenarios, the communication channels *are really based on the preferences of the volunteers or members*. In other words, **you have to reach 'me where they is, not where they ain't.**

Semaphore Syndrome

The old communication signaling technique called Semaphore is a perfect example of this phenomenon. Semaphore is essentially signaling with flags. If you want to send a message, you spell the message out using a code where each letter of the alphabet and numerals is represented by the way the sender holds the flags as shown in the illustration below.

The military and groups like the Boy Scouts and US Forest Service used to use this technique for line of sight communications between locations or ships for decades. The Navy still uses the code to communicate between ships in close proximity, such as during refueling procedures at sea. It is a handy way of being able to communicate, but it also has a few drawbacks based upon what it was designed to do.

As simple and easy as semaphore may be to use, one thing absolutely *must* happen, or the entire system falls apart: The message receiver has to be paying attention and watching for an incoming message. Semaphore, as it was taught in Scouts, even has an "acknowledged" signal to confirm the receiver got the message – but they have to *see* the message first.

Obvious, right?

Your ORG may have Semaphore Syndrome if:

- You have not accounted for the fact that *receiver established channels are based on personal preference.*
- Sender is usually ignorant of the receiver's preferences or capabilities.
- Sender defaults to several streamlined ways of communicating in the name of efficiency or ease of use for those doing the work, without considering receiver preferences.
- ORGs generally fail to differentiate between passive and active communication techniques.
- Many of the common default communication techniques used are passive.
- Worst offense of all in this generation: "Timely" communications usually are not.

First of all, both the sender and receiver have to be proficient enough to send the signals and decode them clearly (this includes knowing how to spell of course). The sender and receiver both have to be in clear sight of each other and able to clearly see the position of the flags. Most of all, the sender and receiver need to know where the other is. Semaphore is an interactive form of communication – both parties actively have to participate. So if the sender is up there on a hill wagging his flags for all he's worth, the receiver needs to be paying attention. This means the receiver *has to be watching for and properly interpreting the message.* In a best case scenario, and working the way the creators of the system intended, both parties send signals to indicate a readiness to receive the message, receive the message itself, and acknowledge receipt of the message. This may sound cumbersome, but until the last decade or so, and before the introduction of cell phones and inexpensive handheld radios, semaphore was pretty efficient.

Back in the early seventies when I was trying to pass my First Class rank tests in Boy Scouts, learning semaphore or Morse code was still part of the Scouting requirements. It seemed like a pretty good idea at the time, but let me take a moment to frame this in the technology of the time to give you some perspective. Wrist radios existed only in the minds of the author and fans of Dick Tracey, the closest thing to a cell phone was Captain Kirk's communicator from *Star Trek*, and the CB craze was just getting started. Getting a message from one side of the lake at an encampment to the other meant you either walked around the lake or sent a signal.

Semaphore has some drawbacks too. It is imperative that the signaler and receiver *pay attention to each other* and *know where the other is* at the appointed times to insure the message gets through. It is also entirely dependent on the sender and receiver being proficient at the code and spelling. If the system was used as intended, and the sender *and* receiver could spell, then things usually went pretty smoothly. But when proficiency wasn't what it should be, or if the sender *or* receiver wasn't very good with the code, interpreting the code or spelling, mayhem would quickly follow.

The absolute worst scenario was when one or the other party simply wasn't where they should be or paying attention. Young teenage boys are not the most patient or attentive things in the world, so getting distracted, missing an appointed time, getting lost on the way to where you were supposed to be, or any number of other possibilities could effectively kill *any* communication efforts. And in the field on a camping trip, you usually had one of two choices in communicating: Using a code like semaphore or Morse code, or walking over to someone to pass the message along. This makes the potential for communication failures imminent and pretty commonplace. Thankfully, a solution is easy, as long as you ae willing to reach your members *where they is, and not where they ain't!*

Chapter 9

The Flexible Matrix Solution

"The most important trip you may take in life is meeting people halfway."

Henry Boye

Flexible Matrix Communications – How to Solve Semaphore Syndrome

The solution to Semaphore Syndrome is a classic illustration of why this handbook is called *Tweaks*. There is not one, huge, earth-shattering idea that changes the internal communications paradigm in ORGs. It is understanding and using an array of simple, small changes to get your communications efforts into alignment with what your members want and need. More than anything else, this collection of ideas is designed to break the stranglehold that current thought and practice has on ORGs when it comes to the issue of internal communications.

Start with the Failures

It should be clear from the previous chapter if your ORG has a case of Semaphore Syndrome and, if so, how bad it is. Before you can fix what is wrong with your ORG's internal communications, you have to understand where things are not working. In general terms, especially in volunteer organizations, the failures can be any one or a combination of the items in this list:

- Not understanding you are competing for your members' attention and time.
- Not knowing what communication channels your members prefer.

- Assuming the channels (methods) you are using are sufficient.
- Relying upon one or two channels to handle all internal communications.
- Relying on one person to handle all the internal and external communications.
- Messages to members are too infrequent.
- Messages to members are sent out much too late.
- Messages are far too routine.
- There is no understanding on the part of the leadership about active and passive communication techniques.
- Unrealistic expectations about member participation.
- Defaulting to a "corporate" communication mindset.

Each one of these on their own can spell trouble for an ORG, but when you start combining them together, the effect quickly multiplies. They also tend to reinforce each other, so that one bad approach supports another and so on. It's like bad, home-brewed chemistry. For example, ammonia has fallen out of favor as a household cleaning agent because it makes most people gag. Chlorine isn't much better. Both compounds are still included in many cleaners even though breathing either of them is not very healthy. However, things get really bad when you combine something like Mr. Clean (lots of ammonia) with Comet (a chlorine cleanser). The result is a chemical reaction between the two that can create ammonium chloride which is seriously toxic. This same kind of wicked additive chemistry is what you get when you combine some of these seemingly inoffensive communication problems and not fully comprehend how destructive or incapacitating they can be. Ammonium chloride won't simply make you gag more than ammonia or chlorine; it will make you pass out first before it kills you – much the same way combined internal communications problems will cause an ORG to pass out long before it finally squeezes the life out of the ORG entirely.

Competing for Their Attention

You may be thinking that this whole communications problem is easy to fix by simply mandating where your members need to go in order to get information. However, that ignores some very important paradigms that go right to the heart of how volunteer organizations differ from corporate organizations. Unless you have ever had the experience of actually leading volunteers, you are very likely not to going to believe this. There is a prevailing belief in leadership circles that the hardest and most difficult form of leading occurs in corporate settings. After all, it takes a *professional* to get it right – at least that's what most people think. But corporate leadership benefits from the leverage that is part of the employment agreement. That is, if you do your job well enough, you get to keep it. In fact, most employers will be kind enough to make it worth your while by paying you and giving you benefits. That *does* have the effect most of the time of keeping an employee at work when they would rather be home taking a nap or playing golf, and it *does* provide leaders and managers with at least some modicum of leverage when dealing with their employees.

As I've said before, volunteers and ORG members do what they do because *they want to*, not because they *have to*. They pick and choose their participation and, with the jam-packed lives we all lead nowadays, you often have to compete for their attention. If they don't like what they are told or don't agree with what they are instructed to do, they are very likely to take their coffee and go home to find something more entertaining to do. This is not an exaggeration, it is a fact. The leverage point a leader has with volunteers is not the employment agreement, but the vision and purpose of the organization and if it happens to be something the volunteer wants to support. It's all about what they are willing to do. So, knowing that, it is simply wiser and more efficient to reach your membership by *their* preferences, not *yours*, especially on the front end of getting an ORG back into healthy shape.

Mandating any line of communication can come much later in the process after the culture and consistent operations of the group are firmly in place. Even so, you always have to remember the difference between what drives a volunteer (desire and passion) and what drives an employee (leverage) and never, ever forget it.

Where are They? - Begin with What You Know

As I have said before, the principle you are trying to engage is simply this: *Ya gotta reach 'em where they is, not where they ain't.* The most obvious way to start that process is to use what you *do* know. This may sound ridiculously simple, but it is amazing how often this is overlooked in ORGs.

Please understand, I'm saying this from practical experience. I've made this same mistake several times over. After a good six months or more of working with the few volunteers I had in the very beginning of working as a Ranger at Camp Acahela, it *still* hadn't registered with me that none of these old guys probably had a computer or Internet access. I simply *assumed* they did. Then again, I never took the time to ask. I never got personal enough with each of them to find out. *That* changed immediately after the chest poking I got from Charlie Jackson.

I had one rudimentary list of volunteers left for me from the previous Ranger and another from my boss. Neither had a lot of information, and most of it was really old, but at least it was a start. I called everyone on the list, let them know I was the new Ranger and that I was updating my list of volunteers – could I update their information and count on their help in the future? When I started, I thought I was doing some fact finding, but I soon discovered that this was even more of an exercise in relationship building and I switched gears. Here was a chance to share a little of the vision I had for the camps and instill some sense that I was trying to get things moving again.

It also gave the folks I was talking to a chance to vent some of their frustrations and concerns over things that had occurred in the past. I didn't want to get tangled up in a lot of that, but it was long overdue and was something I needed to listen to in order to get a better sense of what had happened. In the long run I ended up with a better understanding of how my grand old High Adventure Base had devolved into a barely functional Cub Camp. Giving the volunteers a chance to vent was like draining an infected wound. Some were so frustrated that they vented and said they had had enough and their time of service was done. Those received my sincere thanks and I told them I would keep them posted on progress in the future and that the door was always open in case they changed their minds. Others had their interest piqued enough to want to know more, while more than half were eager to help. All of this came with a willingness to want to know more of what was going on and what opportunities there would be to help. In the end, working the old list gave me far more than I bargained for or could have ever imagined, even as I reestablished the best ways to communicate with my volunteers!

On the opposite end of the spectrum, I had a recent experience with a local hobby club that underscores how damaging it can be to ignore the principle outlined above.

A national chapter of a large model building organization had a list provided to them by their national headquarters that had over 150 names, addresses, phone numbers, and e-mail addresses on it. Most clubs would *kill* for a list like that. In addition to what their national office provided, they also had several club lists accumulated over the course of several years that had another 50 or so members or past members with the same kind of information on it. So far, so good.

They had a major annual event coming up and spent several months ironing out a new website, complete with a new domain name. They sent out a few tacit announcements and passed around some fliers announcing the annual event. In years past, about 200 people would show for the event. This time, about a dozen people showed. Not so good. What happened?

Well, a bunch of little things all added up to hobble what had been a big success in the past. A change of location and a change of domain name certainly didn't help. But the biggest failing was that the Board really didn't have a solid handle on where their 200 potential members were – and they steadfastly ignored working this major asset. Instead of actively chasing down their members to let them know what was happening, much in the same way I did at Acahela, they relied on a number of rather passive attempts to communicate and they paid the price for it.

However, that isn't the worst failing, believe it or not.

At the Board meeting immediately after the lackluster showing, the Board discussed what happened and concluded, much to my dismay that, "members nowadays simply don't care."

Really? Seriously?

This obviously wasn't the first time I've ever heard a leadership group conclude this. The leadership team at the Scout council said the same thing about the Acahela volunteers. I've heard this over and over again from a number of leaders and leadership groups, but it rarely has anything to do with the potential drive of their members. It has far more to do with the lousy, poor, and uninformed way ORGs try to communicate with their members. They violate the idea of: *Ya gotta reach 'em where they is, not where they ain't,* and then blame the members for the results.

This principle, or more precisely, the violation of it, is rampant in our organizations – professional or volunteer –

and it has to do with the level of effort and commitment of the leadership to do a craftsman-like job in communicating, and that often comes because assumptions are made about what needs to happen and how it should be done.

Find Out What Communication Channels Your Members Prefer

As I mentioned earlier, the primary reason for chasing down what members you do know about is not only to find out if they are still willing to help, but what is the best way to get news to them of events and work sessions. At Acahela, I asked each one, "What are the three best ways for me to reach you? What ways am I guaranteed to be able to get news to you about what we are doing, and know that you will pay attention to it?" Two things immediately happened. First, the reaction I got most of the time was a chuckle and something like, "Well, gee, I never thought about that. Let's see. Uhmm," and then eventually we zeroed in on the three best ways *for each member.* That provided the second thing which, still to this day, always fascinates me – and that *is the wide variety of communication preferences people have.*

Again, think about this for a minute. Modern communications are *supposed* to streamline the way we communicate - to make communication more efficient and to basically standardize how we pass information back and forth between one another. But instead, all we have really done is multiply *the number of ways* to communicate, or what I refer to as "channels." That is what makes it so hard to know what your members are paying attention to. Nowadays there are a bewildering number of choices:

- Landline telephone
- Cell phone
- Work number
- Fax
- Video face-to-face

- Video messaging
- Standard e-mail
- Facebook messages
- Facebook posts
- Twitter tweets
- Internet messaging
- Text messaging
- Calendar invites
- Paging
- Radio or Plectron
- Postcards
- Newsletters by post
- Special letters or appeals by post
- Newsletters by e-mail
- Special letters or appeals by e-mail
- Face-to-face verbal communications
- Hand-outs at meetings
- Websites
- Internet forums
- Bulletin boards
- Advertising or newsprint articles

That's just for starters!

Picking three channels that each member prefers *is not* a democratic exercise in finding out what three channels or methods are *most* popular so you can focus on those. It is truly a matter of discovering how each *individual* member *prefers* to be communicated with. If you take the time to do that, and then actually communicate with them in those preferred ways, the results are far more productive than any other technique you can use.

In this process of discovery I can guarantee that you will eventually stumble across something else that is not on the list above. In the development where I live for example, the community communicates with its residents by leaving newsletters and bulletins under a rock each of us has at the end of our carports. I'm not kidding! The community leadership cannot legally leave unposted material in the mailboxes, so the driveway rocks serve as the mailboxes for "official" or important community news. Since I live in Arizona, we don't worry too much about inclement weather, so the "Mailrocks" are actually a lot more efficient and are far more functional than it may sound. When residents see something under their carport rock, they know it's important. It works because *it reaches them where they is, not where they ain't.*

Don't Assume You Know

Use the Matrix strategy even if you already have a list that contains a couple of methods of reaching your members. Why? You need to *confirm* their preferences. Don't assume. In the hobby club I mentioned earlier, when I poled the Board members what their preferences were, two significant things became clear: 1) the Board wasn't paying any attention to the channels they created for the other members and, 2) texting was the most preferred method of effectively reaching Board members. Ironically, texting was not anywhere in that ORG's communications scheme. Unfortunately, it never occurred to anyone on the Board that if they weren't following their own scheme, there was little chance their members were either. This ORG simply had no clue how to effectively and efficiently communicate with its members and this, in turn, compounded other problems as they tried to move their ORG forward.

The lesson here is to do the legwork you need to in order to reconnect with your membership on a *personal* level and find out what *exactly* what they prefer. Then once you have done that, begin to do the same with every new member and possible contact you can find. After attempting to track down all of the old volunteers at my camp, I then started showing up at events where I knew I could get in touch with other possible volunteers, both in Scouting and around the community. *Everyone* got the same questions when it came to staying in touch: *What are the three best ways for me to reach you? What ways am I guaranteed to be able to get news about what we are doing to you, or know that you will pay attention to it?* In doing so, you are letting them know you are serious about communicating, and the response will tend to be more reciprocal than if you make the communication question a secondary piece of information gathering or an afterthought. You are, in essence, cueing up your audience by asking for their preferences.

Use a Matrix to Communicate

Once you have gathered all the communication preferences, the best way to manage it is to create a Matrix using a database, spreadsheet, or some other kind of list. You will probably discover a fascinating array of member preferences – it will be a real mix – but the Matrix will help you keep things straight. Each time you have a key or major event, be sure to let your membership and interested parties know by using the matrix to get the word out. The same goes for the usual monthly announcements and newsletters – use the matrix as the basis for sending out the information.

So how does this actually work? Say, for example, you have 33 members. Each member has three preferences, so the total possible preferred ways of communicating will be 99 (3 times 33). When you look at the 99 possibilities, 20 may be e-mails, 25 may be text messages, 12 may be postcards, 15 may be cell calls, and so on. Therefore, you create a message that can go to each of these preferred channels, then send the tailored message to each, by sending out the e-mails, the text messages, the postcards, etc. This is, without a doubt, more complex and time consuming then sending one blanket e-mail or posting it to your website, but there are multiple trade-offs. The biggest trade-off of all is insuring that *all* of your membership and interested parties have received a message via channels *they prefer*. There will be a much higher percentage of folks actually seeing the news and paying attention to it. By reaching them on *multiple* preferred channels, you are not only letting them know the message is important, but one channel acts to reinforce the other – remember that you are competing for their attention as much as you are competing for their participation. Again, aside from reaching your people where they are most likely paying attention, the extra effort also communicates a willingness and concern on the part of the leadership to pay attention to the member's specific wants and needs.

The Generational Phenomenon

One of the stranger things I ran into as I continued to use the Matrix was that, in some ORGs, the span of technologies preferred by members and interested parties can be pretty impressive. By the time I left the Boy Scouts as a Ranger, I was reaching my maintenance volunteers with a wild array of preferences that spanned postcards for the old-timers and text messages and tweets for the teens – and just about everything in between. While this sounds like an operational nightmare, it actually wasn't that bad and if I had to look at it in a negative light, I preferred to see it as a "*success problem.*" It truly indicated that the programs we were running and the interest we were generating were cutting across a bunch of boundaries and genuinely reaching a wide cross section of our total volunteer population.

Don't Assume the Channels you are Using Are Sufficient

The other near fatal assumption leaders tend to make about their ORG's internal communications is that the communications regimen they have in place is *sufficient* or *adequate*. If you stop and think about it, the question should *not* be, "Is our communications regimen *adequate* or *sufficient?*" However, it seems that most ORGs think in terms like that. The question *should be,* "Did we get the message to *everyone?*" If you are honest and use a critical eye, using anything less than the Matrix to communicate to

ORG members and interested parties will likely yield an automatic, "No."

In addition to the story I related earlier about the hobby club, I can cite more examples of where the leadership of an ORG assumed that the communications situation was covered when it really wasn't. Often, those leadership decisions in the name of expediency or convenience lead to self-destructive communication strategies. For example, one state conference in a church congregation on the east coast decided that it would be a great idea to create an electronic (e-version) of their newsletter that would go out to all their lay volunteers. Initially, members received both the printed version by post and the e-version by e-mail, with the promise that members would continue to receive both. (Mind you, the denomination didn't ask which they preferred.) At some point, someone in the congregation decided that this was redundant, so the snail mail version was halted – but many of the members were older without any capacity or desire to receive the electronic version. Participation dropped as a result, but no one at the denomination seemed to connect the dots that the reason might have something to do with communicating to fewer members. It took time for members to realize that they were not getting the newsletter. The problem did not surface at the leadership level until they started getting calls asking if the newsletters had been discontinued. Aside from sending the unintended message that the administration didn't care about older, non-computer savvy members, it illustrates how assumptions like these can kill active participation and frustrate volunteers into quitting or giving up.

ORG leadership must apply careful thought to the entire process to insure that everyone is covered and taken care of. Even then, the best well-intended effort can fall short. A major university, for example, installed a program where students and staff could be notified immediately of any threat, danger, or crisis and provided instructions or direction to make sure everyone remained safe. The system sends text messages to cell phones to make the notifications, but a big problem that seemed to escape everyone at first was that most staff members are not allowed to have their cell phones on or out on their desks – a rule designed to insure the integrity of student record confidentiality. This would not be so bad if it accounted for only a handful of staff members, but the number of individuals affected are in the hundreds. The lack of global awareness of this confidentiality rule coupled with the assumption that *everyone* carries a cell phone meant that the administration confidently believed everyone was now safe, and as a result, no other form of immediate notification was worked out to provide any form of communication back-up. This is not only a breach in smooth and complete communications, but creates a potentially dangerous situation where a large number of staff members could miss important communiques. The lesson here is not to assume your communication regimen has it all covered. You need to walk through the *entire* process to insure everyone can get the message in more than one way and then go out and check!

Routinely Use More than One Channel

Compounding a lack of clarity or understanding where members are, when ORGS try communicating with them, is that ORGs frequently default to using only one or two channels or methods to do it. Again, call it expediency, call it convenience, or call it a lack of understanding, but using only one or two ways to communicate with your members is a sure-fire way to hobble far more than just your communication efforts. We have already seen that ORG members, especially volunteers, communicate by a different set of rules than employees. You will always have to give some level of consideration to the independent nature of your members – how they think, how they act, and what they might be willing to do. You can't take these points for granted the same way you would if you were dealing with employees.

You cannot simply dictate how they will receive their information either as you reduce your effectiveness by doing so because they say, "Well, OK, I won't participate if that's what it takes," or, "It's too inconvenient," or, "Too much trouble." If you are a fisherman, you know you need to cast the net to catch the fish. The fish usually don't seek out the net and simply jump in. Why we think members are more likely to find the net and jump in is a testament to our overconfidence in what our ORGs are offering our members. In fact, if we are making our members take the initiative on this level of communications, then the program side of things must not be functioning at a high level of efficiency either – meaning a member has to work at finding out little to nothing is actually going on. That spells automatic *disillusionment.*

If you know the channels your members prefer, use them. If you don't, use an array of them and find out for sure.

Use more than One Person to get the Job Done

We will explore the idea of being sure folks are in the right jobs for the best possible reasons a bit later, but for now, let's take a look at the old-fashioned idea of a Communications Secretary and how to get this communications job done.

Years ago it was pretty common for organizations to have two secretaries on their Executive Boards, not just one. The Recording Secretary took care of keeping the records and minutes of the group, while the Communications Secretary took care of all the correspondence and might double as the newsletter editor. That was 50 years ago, and since then I've seen that most ORGs of less than 250 members have dispensed with having two secretaries and combined the responsibilities. This, in most cases, has yielded the result that the communications side of the job falls by the wayside. The level of effort applied to the position just isn't there the way our grandparents used to do it, and the associated tasks are quickly becoming a lost art.

Let's be honest here too. Many ORGs suffer from too

few volunteers willing to step up and help run the ORG. When it comes time to fill the elected officer positions, there is a split between folks wanting a position for the prestige of it and finding a body to fill a spot where the member won't have to spend that much time. Yes, there are plenty of volunteers out there that understand the joke of, "The job only takes an hour or so a week," when they are spending far more time on it than that, but the norm is more likely to be the job needs about 3 hours a week and the member tasked with it is spending 15 minutes before the meeting banging out the report so they don't show up empty handed. That isn't getting the job done, and one area where this happens with chronic regularity is *communications*.

Instead of approaching the Secretary's position as we commonly do nowadays, I would suggest that we go back to having two different positions and resurrect the title and job description of Communications Secretary. This person would be tasked with any correspondence needed by the ORG, but would also head up the entire suite of communications efforts in the ORG. Can this be done all by one person? Probably not once things are really rolling, so whoever lands in this spot *must* be a capable leader – someone who can delegate effectively and create a team that can handle the website, the communications matrix, and the creative writing of blurbs, announcements, and other public relations tasks. In other words, as I see it, the Communications Secretary in a fully functional and healthy ORG, is the leader of a very active *team* of folks who specialize in presenting the ORG to the community and the world.

The building of this team begins with the Matrix and getting the word out to members about events and important news. It is easy to look at the Matrix of preferences and gather a few people willing to help with getting the word out: one handles e-mails and text messages, another handles a phone chain, a third takes care of sending out snail mail, and someone else takes care of the website. This coordinated effort grows over time, and with it, the ability to insure that messages are going out on a timely basis and are varied enough to spark and capture the attention of members and other interested parties. At the start, the effort begins on a smaller scale and is set up in a way where it can easily grow – the coordination and execution of the special team vision is the *primary* responsibility of this resurrected Communications Secretary position.

Aside from the results it will yield, there is another monstrously important reason to try to do this. This approach does not create a single position, but creates an opportunity to form the first of, what should be, numerous special teams within the ORG. The big difference is that this one reports *directly to, and is managed by,* the Executive Board, and does so in a way that shows the rest of the ORG how special teams should work. Therefore when, at a later date, the ORG needs to explore securing a new piece of property or designing a new facility or program, the ORG will already have a working template on hand that says, "Here, do the job the way the Communications Special Team (or committee) does it." *This* is how to divide up the work, make the work efficient and effective, and set a standard of performance that will drive the ORG towards being a highly effective group with substantive organizational health.

Make the Messages Frequent Enough

These next couple of points all work hand in hand to get and rivet the attention of your members and other interested parties. These are simple, but critical points. The first is to make sure your messages happen frequently enough.

Sending out ORG announcements too infrequently communicates that not much is really going on or that the leadership is not on top of their game on either the communications or program fronts. Sending out announcements or reminders too frequently is almost as bad. It can make the ORG sound or appear desperate and turn off recipients. There has to be a balance and each organizational situation will have to find what is too much, what is too little, and what is just right. In most cases, it will probably be a timely, long range "plan for" announcement, followed up by a specific reminder, and then a final "48-hour before" reminder. Using the array of communication preferences, this will probably do the trick and gain the maximum possible participation level.

Be Sure Messages Are Timely

Timeliness of the messages is imperative. If we routinely mess up on the timeliness of messages, it can do irreparable harm to an ORG and get your members to view ORG activities with a critical eye. If your ORG membership is suffering from a case of the bad attitudes, this may be one of the reasons why.

Once, a club I belong to, sent a notice that a membership meeting was being called to hold the club's elections. However, there were a few problems with the execution of this:

- The *first* message about this went out 2 ½ hours before the meeting.
- It announced a *new* meeting location.
- The message went to less than half of the total membership because the e-mail was only sent to those registered to the club's news group (about one-third of the total group).

No surprise here, but no one showed up except the current officers, who then explained away the lack of participation as evidence that the membership simply wasn't interested enough to be involved. This was hardly the case, but it is shocking how often I have seen this same thing play out over and over again in ORG after ORG. Management does a poor job of executing their duties and the blame is laid at the feet of the members when they don't participate.

148

With the busy schedules we all have and how ORGs have to compete for the attention of their members and potential members, getting the word out about events needs to happen *early enough* and *frequently enough* to insure the time will be set aside and the members can and will attend.

Another unanticipated consequence of using the Matrix at Camp Acahela was the discovery of how many members actually preferred postcards as a way of receiving communications. That forced me to announce things much earlier than I had been, which moved the preparation planning for the event to a spot a couple of weeks earlier on my calendar. The earlier preparation eventually morphed into *better and more complete preparation.* This translated into better execution of the events, as well as pre-event communications. This little tweak forced the entire chain of activities associated with each event to be done in a way that was better for my ORG, and the results showed. When I first started, I had as few as a half dozen, unorganized volunteers I could count on. Six years later, I had a list of over a hundred volunteers I could tap into and get regular participation out of. Here, as elsewhere, the little tweaks add up.

Beware of Routine Messages

One danger in all this is to make the messaging strategy you use *too* routine. If the same kind of templated message comes out too routinely, the lack of variety will quickly cause the messages to lose their intended effectiveness. Like a Major League Baseball pitcher, you have to mix up the pitches in order to keep the batter engaged. A certain amount of routine is good, but you also have to modulate the message to keep the recipients curious enough to want to read or see what the messages say.

Making every message a priority has the same negative effect as well. NASA has learned this lesson several times in the history of their operations when every activity ended up being labeled "Mission Critical." It became clear during the investigation into the 1986 *Challenger* disaster that the classification was used so often that *everything* became "Mission Critical," which not only diluted the label, but had a seriously negative impact on how operations were handled. Critical items were missed as a result, and the same kind of thing can easily happen in your ORG to diminish the impact of your communication efforts. So modulate your messages.

Let me put this in clear, unmistakable, operative terms: When both sides of the communications equation – sender and receiver – are taking a passive approach to communications, active engagement **is highly unlikely.**

Understand the difference between Active Outbound and a Passive Resource

The worst and most common mistake most ORGs make is using only *passive* communication channels in order to get their messages out to volunteers. Volunteer leaders sending members to only their website demonstrates that leaders have little to no appreciation for how to *really* get a message out in a way that encourages and motivates members to participate. Unfortunately, by misusing this asset, our websites have become as much of a curse as they are a blessing. It's the communications equivalent of owning a beautiful Steinway grand piano and only ever learning how to play *"Chopsticks"* on it.

There seems to be this nearly automatic default in most ORGs to, *"send the members to___."* The blank is usually filled in with something like, "the website," as if the web is the magic bullet solving all communication problems. Yet, it is not. Websites are passive forms of communication where information is posted and the member has to go looking for it. That's easy on the staff, but lousy at *engaging* the members. Again, keep in mind that as an ORG you are probably competing for your members' attention, so how intelligent is it to depend on *them* to go get the latest news?

The forms of communication discussed above break down into passive and active. Think about your situation at work. *Active* is stuff that comes roaring across your desk in the form of urgent e-mails, incoming phone calls, the IMs that pop up on your computer, or the memos dropped on your desk – *the message comes to you,* the receiver. The *passive* stuff is like the Help library in your computer program, or the company employee network that holds all the forms and policies – *you have to go find it,* whatever "it" happens to be. Which of these gets your attention more quickly and more often? If you are anything like me, it's the *active* stuff. If we do this automatically at work, why then, when we get to our churches, bowling leagues, clubs, or any ORG we belong to, do we think our members – with everything else going on in their lives – will be rushing with joyous anticipation to the group website to get the latest and most important news?

Let me put this in clear, unmistakable, operative terms: When both sides of the communications equation – sender and receiver – are taking a passive approach to communications, *active engagement* **is highly unlikely.**

Again, let me be clear. I am not saying that websites or other forms of passive communication are not important or should be abandoned. Hardly! But they *are not* and *should not* be relied upon as *the only* mode of communications to your members. If that is the one dance step you are using, close up shop and go home. Your ORG is already well on the way to dying, you just haven't realized it yet. Sorry to be so blunt, but this is an ORG *killer*. Communications that really work and help ORGs grow and get healthy are ones that involve *active* engagement – and that means *you* going after *them,* not them coming looking for you.

Use *active* channels augmented by all the passive resources you can offer – this is the best combination of communications tools you can use.

KEY TWEAKS TO GO

1)

2)

3)

4)

Chapter 10

Know How Committed They Are

"Commitment is what transforms a promise into reality."

Abraham Lincoln

How Committed are They?

Try thinking of your membership as *customers.*

In the business world, no customers equals a dead business. You can't run a business without customers. Neither can you run a volunteer organization without volunteers. It's as simple as that.

When you start thinking of your members as your customers, a side benefit will be that you will start to realize that you have all kinds of different customers, with different levels of interest. This is perhaps the most misunderstood aspect of volunteer membership. The vast majority of volunteer organizations *never ask,* "How committed to our program are you?" No one ever asks how much of a fan or how serious you are about whatever it is that the organization does. It is simply assumed that you are devoted because you plunked down the dues or filled out the application. But in reality, there can be a very wide range of reasons for someone to join a group and an equally wide assortment of motivations and levels of commitment that come with it. Being an employee has a way of leveling out this commitment and interest issue. If you don't care much about your job you end up opting yourself out. However, in a volunteer organization, you can have members who are enthusiastic obsessives, passive financial supporters, and then everything in between those two points.

You have to find out. You have to *ask*. If you don't know, it will be like charging into battle without knowing how many troops you have or how well-trained they are. Your program is dependent on a certain level of enthusiastic participation in order to make it work. If you have a bunch of the enthusiastic obsessives and only a few passive supporters, it's probably going to be a pretty lively group. On the other hand, if you have only a few enthusiasts but a whole pile of passive supporters, getting enough critical mass to do much of anything is going to be laborious. So, find out. *Ask*. It may be one of the most revealing leadership exercises you will ever participate in, and one of the most useful.

Remember, the bottom line when it comes to volunteer members is this: Ya gotta reach 'em where they is, not where they ain't.

Just as an experiment, if nothing else, try asking your members where they fall in the list that follows. The first few times I tried something like this I was stunned by the responses. In each case I had overconfidently assumed that all of our members were either fully on board or just too busy to participate – basically a chocolate or vanilla approach. What I discovered was a much broader and wider set of flavors with a lot of nuances added in for good measure. In several ORGs I've helped lead, the opinions shared on why members felt the way they did was incredibly valuable intelligence and then helped guide and shape the steps we took thereafter. Instead of shooting in the dark and thinking we were providing what our members were interested in, we got the specifics and knew. No more guesswork, *we knew*. Use the list to get a handle on where your group stands, but then I would encourage you to dig deeper. ***Get personal.*** Find out the reasons why. If nothing else it will be one more thing to build rapport by showing you genuinely care, but it will go well beyond that. The consequences of knowing where your group stands, individually and as a whole, will make a huge difference on all the things that will follow. Try the following list. Suggested descriptors could be:

- Obsessive fanatic
- Dedicated member
- Enthusiastic member with plenty of available time
- Enthusiastic member with limited time
- Ordinary member with plenty of time
- Ordinary member with limited time
- Casual member – neutral feelings
- Fan of the organization, but not active
- Barely active members – other commitment issues
- Barely active member – not happy
- Inactive member – no real issues with the organization
- Inactive member – not happy with the current administration
- Inactive member – financial issues
- Inactive member – distance or health issues

You can find out any number of different ways but the *most* effective is a personal approach. Go around to your members and simply ask. Meet them at meetings and ask. Call them on the phone and ask. This may take a little time and may not seem terribly efficient – an almost counter-intuitive way to find out, but in many cases the reasons members fall away have something to do with a lack of *connectedness*, so using a personal approach may have more benefits that you may initially realize.

If you have a fairly large group, doing this as either an ongoing project or as a group project conducted by the leadership team as a whole is a good idea. But be careful about handing it off to a committee or "survey takers" – *that* will signal an impersonal approach that could do more harm than good.

You might also think about incorporating it as part of a new member on-boarding process or some kind of member "health check" or "idea sweep." In the former, you ask these questions several times throughout the member's life span with the group, gauging if his or her interest is rising, falling, or stable, and why. In the latter, if the leadership team decides to interview members for new ideas and initiatives, these questions can be part of the overall suite of questions asked. Regardless of which way you do it, make sure you convey genuine interest in the well-being of the member – it's all about *the members*, not what you can get out of them.

KEY TWEAKS TO GO

1)

2)

PART III

Triage for Ailing ORGs

"It is not the strongest of the species that survive, nor the most intelligent that survives. It is the one that is most adaptable to change."
Charles Darwin

This is where we get into the nuts and bolts of how to fix and fine tune volunteer organizations. Perhaps things are bad enough in your ORG that you flipped here for immediate help and solutions – that's OK – this book is designed so that it can be used that way. But you may be reading along following the progression of thought that will give you the "big picture" needed to better understand these unique organizations. That's good too and eventually I hope you do both.

Every ORG can be improved. *Every* ORG from time to time shows some form of distress. The trick is to know what to do. This section will give some very practical advice on what can be done immediately while also looking ahead to what *should* be done as your organization grows towards maturity.

Chapter 11

Symptoms of an ORG in Distress and 14 Things You can do Now

"In any moment of decision, the best thing you can do is the right thing, the next best thing is the wrong thing, and the worst thing you can do is nothing."

Theodore Roosevelt

Triage and Zombies

One of the things that amazes me about leading volunteer organizations is the sheer number that function at levels that in the corporate world would simply be unacceptable or get hidden as the business' deep dark secret. While there are plenty of examples of well-run volunteer organizations, many are in need of serious first aid or are walking around like they are the undead, zombies that need to seriously meet their end before they do any more damage.

Part of the problem is that usually in a volunteer organization, the infrastructure is not there to step in and fix a group that is in deep trouble. In organizations where local groups act as chapters of a larger regional or national organization, the national group normally won't step in to fix broken groups preferring to follow a "survival of the fittest" strategy where sick clubs need to heal themselves or simply dissolve. This puts many clubs at a real disadvantage since the leadership is usually ill-equipped to solve the myriad of problems a group can face. Add in what we have just learned about the dynamics and mindset of most volunteers and fixing broken groups becomes a daunting challenge under the best of circumstances.

Making the problem even worse (see, the zombie analogy may be pretty accurate.) is that most volunteer leaders who inherit disasters like this default to blaming the symptoms as causes of all the group's troubles. The rant usually starts with, "What's wrong with these people?" and ends with, "There is such a rotten atmosphere and attitude around here." Occasionally, the rant gets aimed squarely at a membership group that is looking for, or desperately hoping for, *something* to get better. Instead, they get blamed for the zombie-like nightmare they have become a part of.

Seeing *symptoms* as *causes* gets plenty of doctors and healthcare experts into hot water, so as volunteer leaders, we need to make sure that we aren't guilty of the same crime and look deeper to gain a handle on what needs to be done.

Make no mistake: Lack of participation, apparent lack of resources, having no organized program, suffering a lack of direction, lack of cooperation, and a discouraging atmosphere are all signs of an organization in distress and in need of help. These are *symptoms* of more significant operational problems – that's the bad news. The good news is that these operational problems are typically easy to correct.

14 Things you can do Right Now

I'm willing to bet that a fair number of readers are skipping ahead to this chapter with the hope of finding some *immediate* help and ideas so that they can do something, *anything*, to help their ailing ORG. That's fine – there are a few things that you should do immediately regardless of how good or bad the situation is. In light of that fact, the way I'm going to approach this chapter is to give you what you need to do *now* with the understanding that you will go back and read about the connected issues as soon as possible. If you have been reading progressively through the book you know by now that many of the things that help make an ORG successful are all interrelated, so in doing one thing you are very likely effecting something else or several other things. So it is vitally important to get as much of the whole story and background as you can. So, with that out of the way, expect that as we move through each of these 14 things you can do immediately, I'll be directing you back to other parts of the book so you can dig in deeper.

#1 – Do no harm

Never forget this first rule of ORG first-aid: *To the best of your ability, do no harm.*

This sounds like a pretty obvious statement on the surface, but trust me, there is a natural inclination in humankind to step into a flawed situation and immediately reduce everything to rubble and start all over again. This sounds crazy, but I've seen it. While I am now ashamed to admit it, I've actually done it. The dynamic is like a homeowner who buys a home that needs some tender loving but gets carried away in the demolition phase. Before you know it, the house is a complete wreck and a simple renovation project has gone from restoration, to remodeling, to remuddling overnight.

The greatest way to do harm is to *assume*. Even if you have been watching a disaster befall your organization and unfold before you, there are probably a few things – details and nuances – that you may not either know in full or even know at all and these little things often have outsized consequences. So before trying to take any action or even making any plans, it is prudent to check yourself by doing a bit of fact finding and reconnaissance. The more information you have, the better and it will keep you from doing something that you may have to retract later. When things are not going well in an organization, it's a steady hand at the helm that does the trick. Again, don't assume anything. The best way to *do no harm* is to make sure you understand what is going on and what has happened.

#2 – Understand how things got the way they are

The second task you need to face when walking into an ORG that has problems is to not only figure out *what* has happened, but *how* things got to be the way they are. Having a good, accurate picture of *what* is going on and *how bad* the damage is takes time, maturity, and objectivity. It takes a bit of skill to sort out what *has* happened, what *is* happening, and where all of it is headed. All of that information can be overwhelming. However, gathering good intelligence is vitally important if you are going to properly diagnose what needs to be addressed and in what order.

When you stop and think about it, evaluating the status and health of an organization is not all that different from any emergency situation that firefighters, police officers, or paramedics respond to. In each case, emergency management personnel of all kinds are taught to look around and take everything in as they arrive on the scene. Information gathering is critical because it does absolutely no good to begin treating an accident victim in the front seat of their car if the car is sitting in a pool of gasoline and smoldering. Likewise, a downed powerline in the immediate area or even touching the car is a critical bit of information responders need to be aware of. In both cases, these situations will alter the approach the responders take and rearrange priorities. Every emergency situation is different and has its own unique set of problems. Therefore, critical evaluation is imperative.

On the other hand, time is not exactly your friend in situations that are beginning to slide out of control. I've seen several seemingly stable organizations turn into a train wreck with shocking speed. When the seeds of destruction finally begin to bloom, the rapid compounding of problems can escalate so quickly it can take your breath away! Just like in emergency management, you have to work quickly and yet be as thorough as possible. And just like in emergency management, having a good idea of *what* happened will go a very long way towards knowing what steps to take to fix the problem. Most solutions are not like resetting a circuit breaker or plugging an extension cord back into the wall. Occasionally, the problem may be as simple as that, but usually it takes a series of steps to set things right again. That may mean taking things back to a place where they were working before everything came unglued. That may mean going back to a state of Poor (on our scale of Ugly, Poor, Good, Better, Best) and then figuring out how to move towards Best while avoiding the pitfalls. Regardless, knowing *what* happened is a critical step in the process.

#3 – Get a good handle on how bad things really are

The third task you need to face when walking into an ORG that has problems is to figure out just how bad things really are. The first couple of times I found myself involved with organizations that needed help, every situation seemed so different. It was bewildering! But then after a while, the more situations I saw the more I realized that they actually fall into several categories. Over time, I came up with an easy way to identify where an ORG was in the process. This helped me create a framework of steps to follow in order to correct the situation at hand. Simply put, all organizations have a life cycle and the patterns they experience fall into groupings or phases. In the next chapter I go into this in greater detail and have made each phase easy to understand, but the thing you need to know here is this: where your ORG is in regard to these stages will dictate the assets you will have to work with and the kind of work you, as a leader, will have to do.

Understand that knowing *what happened* is very different from knowing *how bad things really are.* The two are like the heads of Hydra, the terrifying multi-headed monster that Hercules battled in Greek mythology. Either one can kill you. Evaluating how bad things are will uncover if things are still unraveling. Let me explain this with two illustrations.

One organization I stepped into was my son's Cub Scout Pack. When we returned for his second year as a Cub Scout, the leadership team had decided they had had enough and were going off to do something else. The Pack had dwindled to about a dozen parents and kids and the leaders had simply lost interest over the previous year. Their solution was to announce that the Pack was closing and they promptly vanished. It was a lot like a hit and run accident – the damage was done, but the perpetrators were gone. That is about as simple as it gets when you need to hit the reset button, so it made stepping in and getting things going again fairly simple. Overcoming any objectors wasn't an issue and those left behind were at least willing to give fixing things a decent try. Knowing what happened made it clear that a lot of what worked before could probably be recovered, and taking the steps to get things going again was pretty clear cut.

On the other hand, I was also part of a hobby club that can best be described as the worst cauldron of simmering discontent and bone-headed leadership I've ever encountered. Once a championship organization that had won National Chapter of the Year several years in a row, it was a shadow of itself when I joined just a few years later – just the news that it was hobbling hadn't caught up with its reputation yet. From an ORG-watchers perspective, this really had me puzzled for a while. Regular member business meetings were so poorly attended that sometimes only three or four people showed up. The monthly activities were far better attended, but it seemed like an entirely different group. As it turned out, the members of the Executive Board felt that spending one night a month running the board meetings and then another weekend a month engaged in the club's primary activity was enough. That should have been a clue that worse things were yet to come.

When I joined, the existing Board had been in place for a couple of years – long enough to establish a few routines and settle into an established way of doing things (for better or for worse). To their credit, they tried to create a handbook of how things should be done based on what they and the previous Board had done. However, they were blind to some of the bad habits they had sown or things they had neglected. When the torch passed to a third set of Board members, no one realized that there was a time bomb ticking that was about to go off. A few months into the new administration, the website went down, the club lost its domain name, and the prized flying field was suddenly no longer available for the club's use. Compounding matters, no complete membership list containing names, addresses, phone numbers, and e-mail addresses had been compiled. It seems that early on, an earlier Board had reacted to a fear of the wrong kind of people (read government) knowing who our members were, so no information was kept on file. Making matters worse, it became apparent the old Yahoo! Group that had been used as the club's primary communication tool was out of date and had not been maintained. In no time, what had seemed to be a solid, well-designed and organized group collapsed like a house of cards. As the Board scrambled to fix things, a lack of clear information or understanding of what was going on inhibited all efforts to get the ship righted. The club gravitated towards a split that it, in hindsight, should have seen coming. Older, senior members wanted to simply go their way and fly. Younger members wanted an opportunity to learn the craft and skills needed, as well as have some fellowship. Just as it seemed like things were going to come back together again, this underlying fault line gave way and the club split. It was ugly and it crippled the group that remained for months.

The Board that remained was faced with the tremendous challenge of getting things back in working order, but instead of following the steps outlined here, they never fully grasped what makes volunteer members tick and tried repeatedly to get what few members were left to do things in a way that volunteer members simply don't respond to. Eventually, the new Board settled into running things in a way that satisfied their own interests and how they wanted things done. If anyone else wants to join in, swell, and perhaps, over time, they may be able to regrow the group.

Consider the *organizational culture* that this mindset fosters. It's a sad epitaph. Fully comprehending what happened and then understanding how bad things are should help inform what needs to be done, but it also takes a willingness to listen and learn from the mistakes of the past. If you don't you are doomed to repeat them. Instead, work the rest of this list, understand how volunteer members think, and strive to make things better.

#4 – Take a tour – MBWA

In his book *Lincoln on Leadership,* Don Phillips makes the point that Lincoln spent less time *in* the White House and more time out in the field than any other president in the century before. When he wanted to know how things were going, he made a point of going to see for himself and made the most of what he saw. It wasn't that he didn't trust the people working for him or could not delegate – he probably did more of that than any other president as well, but he understood the value and spin-off benefits of seeing things first hand and making his presence felt. Likewise, both Nimitz and Halsey did the same thing in the South Pacific during World War Two, making their presence known at the front lines and seeing how things were with their men. More recently, and in a different kind of environment, business leaders like Bill Mulally of Ford and Carlos Ghosn of Nissan stunned their own corporate cultures by actually going to their plants and mingling with the plant workers to get a true handle on the problems both car companies were experiencing. Visiting the troops won't tell

166

you everything, but it will tell you a lot more than what you can learn cloistered in your office. You *need* to go and *talk* to your members.

The very idea of MWBA, or *Managing By Walking Around,* may seem either inconvenient or smack of trying to be some kind of social butterfly, but in reality the things you will see and hear and the subtleties you will observe can, *and will,* have a profound effect on the rest of the process. It may even change the perception of how *you* are seen as a leader. In volunteer organizations populated by members who can come and go as they please, *you* taking the time to find out what *they* feel and think is like adding a binder to paint, accelerant to cement, or fertilizer to a plant. You will be demonstrating that you really care and that is the currency traded by volunteer members.

So, how do you find out what your members really think?

Go find them and *find out.*

One simple and practical observation about this idea before we move on: You can't lead from the front by sitting behind a desk or safely ensconced behind the podium at the front of the room. You need to get out there and be with your members.

#5 – Take an inventory

One of the very practical things that will happen by getting out of the office or out from behind the podium is you will be able to see just what kind of assets you have to work with. It is vitally important that you not only have a good idea about *what is going on* with your people, but *what you have to work with* as well. I'm not talking about doing a physical or staffing inventory. I am referring to a strategic inventory where you look at *everything* to see what you might have to work with.

I have to admit that I first learned this as an object lesson with the first home I purchased on my own. It was a small Cape Cod that had been cobbled together and when I got it, it needed a lot of tender loving care. Actually, it needed a complete rebuild and I quickly got in over my head. I was on my own and money was tight. I remember one weekend having no cash for materials and feeling so frustrated, overwhelmed, and absolutely stuck. I wanted to sit down and cry. Not knowing what to do, I said a prayer asking for some help or direction and the thought came to me to *do an inventory*. It was an idea that the other half of me quickly dismissed, but it came to me again that I needed to take a good look around and see what I actually had. Pad in hand, I went room by room and wrote down what I had in the way of materials. I wrote down what projects I was working on, what was working, and noted what had been completed. The inventory kept expanding in scope. When I got to the kitchen, I wrote down what I had in the way of food. In the basement I noted what I had in the way of fuel oil and then what firewood I had out back.

In a few hours I had a fairly complete idea of where things stood and I discovered, much to my amazement, that I had *plenty* to keep me busy for, not only the current weekend, but several of the weekends ahead. I also had a much better idea of what needed to be done and I was able to clearly see a few strategies that I had previously missed that I could get to work on right away – I already had what I needed from assets I had previously overlooked. When I finally stopped for the night, I sat back down on the edge of my bed and said a word of thanks. Despair had been replaced with hope and boy, was I grateful!

Now I don't mean to make more of that than it really is. No miracle like the multiplying of fishes and loaves occurred, but I *did* become aware that the Good Lord always provides and we simply are too dense to see it. I have never forgotten that lesson and whenever I step into someplace either familiar or not and start thinking to myself, "Oh boy," in that kind of tone that is bracing for the next bit of bad news, I know it's time to start by taking an inventory.

Keep an open mind. Ask yourself, *"OK, what have I got to work with, and what has potential?"* It doesn't matter if it is stuff or people or processes or programs, but take a look at what you have available and chances are you'll find you have far more than you think you do and some solutions will be immediately at hand.

Stuff

Again, when I took over as the Ranger at Camp Acahela in northeastern Pennsylvania, I walked into an organizational nightmare. The camp itself was in a state of serious decline and had experienced several years of neglect, not because the previous Ranger didn't care, but due to budget constraints. Virtually all the funding available for operations was being funneled into our other camp, Goose Pond Scout Reservation (GPSR). GPSR was the gem of the Council and it showed. Unfortunately Acahela, where I lived full-time, was on the short end of the funding stick. To compound matters, the corps of volunteers that was supposed to help with the camps was barely functional – I had no idea who could help me. In addition, my timing for arriving on the scene could not have been worse. There was over a foot and a half of snow on the ground and, without a garage or maintenance building, I had no idea where the bulk of my equipment was.

It's one thing to step into a new job and try to learn the ropes, but stepping in and having to sort out everything was quite a challenge. It occurred to me that approaching this new position in a traditional corporate fashion would not work half as well as approaching it like I was leading one of the clubs I belonged to. Therefore, I adapted the strategies that are outlined here. I not only needed to figure out what happened, why things were the way they were, but also what I had to work with, whether it was equipment, buildings, spare parts, or people. I needed to figure out what was working, what was barely working, and what had quit working and needed attention. So the kind of inventory that you have to do in situations like this is more along the lines of accounting for what is present and what state it is in, versus counting widgets or noses.

This process yielded some immediate results, but it was an ongoing process. It took several hunting expeditions and treasure hunts in order to figure out what I had. I kept the inventory going as an open-ended project as I moved through the days and tasks needed to get things back in order.

At first, I couldn't find more than half of my equipment or tools such as a generator, two lawn mowers, and a garden tractor. They finally appeared one day in early April when the snowbank on the side of the house melted enough to reveal where they were. This was obviously both good and bad – at least now I knew where the missing items were, but sitting all winter in a snowbank is never good for machinery. It took a fair amount of work and time to get all that stuff out of the snow and in working order again.

People

My team of volunteers was another matter entirely. The list I had was out of date and the volunteers I could find had this way of looking around and letting out low whistles or would silently shake their heads as they wished me luck. *That* didn't bode well.

One day, after a light snow the night before, I found a set of tire tracks that came into the camp and went right down to the cabin furthest from the Ranger Station. Then there was a set of footprints leading from the vehicle up to the cabin. When I took a closer look, I noticed that the size of the footprints were *immense.* I stand six foot and have a size 12 boot. This guy had a boot size close to a 15 and my first thought was, *"Oh nuts!"* as I took a good look around to see if King Kong was anywhere nearby. It wasn't until he returned later that day when I finally met the guy. He was a bear of a man, yet one of the nicest guys I ever met. We talked for a long while and over the years that followed he became one of my most valued volunteers and the one that also caused me the most frustration at times. Suffice it to say that the people inventory you do will be the most complex of all and the one that, above all others, will be ongoing. Learn to be a people watcher and evaluate those whom you work with and work for with a healthy amount of open mindedness and grace. Snap judgements about people have no place in a community where one of the ongoing dynamics is that people are *growing* as individuals. Keep your eyes open, but your heart open as well, so you end up leading like a good parent.

Processes

Two of the bigger challenges I had at both camps were the water systems. The instruction sheets left by the previous Ranger had only the barest explanation of what to do. As grateful as I was for that, it didn't explain how either system worked, and as it turned out, there was a huge set of differences between the two. I felt very uncomfortable with the, "Hook system up, connect lines, turn on," approach and had a terrible feeling that if I flew into summer armed only with that, it was going to be a disaster. I started asking around and, to my dismay, no one had a clear picture of how Acahela's system worked. We knew a bit more about Goose Pond's, but the documentation wasn't there and neither was any comprehensive understanding of either system. Even the map of the system that existed at the time was in a scale that did not provide much in the way of detail.

Camp Acahela's water supply system was fortunately an above ground system of heavy polyethylene pipes and tubes. The whole thing laid on top of the ground feeding all the various sites, cabins, and buildings. After trying to bring the winterized system back to life, and running into a host of problems, my German temper got the best of me and I began walking. With a notepad in hand and a 100' tape measure in the other, I progressively walked every foot of the system 100 feet at a time annotating exactly what I had. I noted every joint, valve, fitting, and patch, and even noted the diameter of the fittings and pipes plus the materials they were made of. Anything I thought might be important or informative got written down on the pad as I filled page after page with details. I then went back to the Ranger station and put all the mains and various legs of the system into a database and created a more detailed map for each section. As I did so, it was as if the system itself was explaining to me how it worked or why it worked the way it did. The process eventually revealed all the system's secrets and helped explain its quirks. It even showed – in shocking clarity – where the system had simply been patched over and over again instead of addressing recurring problems. That was one I never expected, but was very happy for. In fact, once it was done and I was able to show it to others, a lot of, "Well, why the heck," questions evaporated. It was like turning on a light.

It worked so well, I replicated the process with GPSR's system as best I could (half of the GPSR system is underground and remains a foggy mystery) and then tackled every other system that had left everyone else scratching their heads. When I left Acahela after over eight years of service, I was still taking process inventories and still learning.

The fact is, a process is a recipe. If you put it down on paper and then *look* at it – I mean really study it – solutions should jump off the pages at you. You will wonder why no one saw it before but, regardless of the complexity of it, mapping the process and doing an inventory of it yields *tremendous* results.

The point of all this is that when you step into an ORG as a new leader or into an ORG that is having some problems, regardless of their severity, doing an inventory of how things are and what assets you have should not be an exercise in seeing how much junk you have, but in seeing how much *potential exists*. This is, as I've explained before, the time you figure out where you are on the scale of Ugly, Poor, Good, Better, Best, and that can rescue you from certain despair.

#6 – Lead from the front

In the opening days of World War II, Vice Admiral Robert L. Ghormley was the Commander of the Southern Pacific Theater of Operations and was in charge of the campaign for Guadalcanal. Never heard of him? Not surprising. While more and more of the heroes and personalities of WWII fade from our collective memory, Ghormley has long been forgotten as the leader whom Admiral William "Bull" Halsey replaced. The fight for Guadalcanal was America's first concerted effort to stop Japan as its forces advanced all across the Pacific. It was a grueling, difficult battle that was fought with few resources and has gone down in Marine Corps history as one of the Corps finer moments. But in the opening days of what became a six-month battle, things were not going well under Ghormley's command.

It wasn't that Ghormley was a lousy commander, though there can be no arguing that Ghormley was rushed into a command that he may have been ill-suited for, as the record clearly shows that he was a fine administrator. But scholars and historians also agree that Ghormley was guilty of two critical leadership failures that resulted in his lackluster performance as the area commander and caused his eventual removal. First, he allowed himself to be inundated with the administrative details of his command. Second, and this is the one that really did him in, was that he was absent from the front.

If you are going to lead, you need to be in the thick of things and be willing to be out in front. The days of sitting on your horse overlooking the battlefield and sending instructions by messenger to those in the thick of the fight are long gone. Yet, I still see leaders in volunteer groups who think standing behind the podium or sitting at the head of the table are enough. Worse yet is the volunteer who collects jobs and responsibilities like they are collectible patches and revels in the status of the job while doing little to get the job done. In either case, those kinds of leaders are more interested in the status of it all than in really knowing what to do, and when the slogging suddenly gets tough, they either vanish or send someone else. In reality, a volunteer leader has to lead from the front and set an example for others to follow because volunteer members react very quickly and powerfully to leaders who expect *them* to do the things that the leaders themselves are unwilling to do. Even if you are not in charge of a particular event or activity, but are the ultimate person in charge, you still need to be there to show support and help set the tone. Do not fool yourself into thinking that your absence does not matter or won't be noticed. When you are not actually doing the role of Commander-in-Chief, you still need to participate as *Member*-in-Chief.

One reason for this is simply a matter of scale. In small, mutual interest and skills organizations, anything with a group membership of 150 or less, you are *always* visible. Whereas, in a big corporation, the public participation still needs to be regular and meaningful, but there are often several layers a leader has to think about at once. For example, if you are the head of a large department, you have to be there in a meaningful way for your staff; but at the team level, occasional visits are more appropriate. The key in *all* cases is *regular and meaningful* visits and to make sure that what good you do is consistent with your conduct the rest of the time. Professionals and volunteers alike will catch on very quickly when visits or walk-throughs are just for show or just to crack the whip. In volunteer ORGs, that *cannot* be the only time they interact with their leader – it has to be more personal than that. The acid test is this: for every member you meet, can you identify something about them

174

on a personal level or something beyond the organization that you know about them? If you do, you are on the right track. If you don't, you haven't dug deep enough yet.

Whatever you do, especially at any time when things are critical, as the leader, you have one place to be both figuratively and literally, and that is at the front, in the thick of what is going on. Take a look at any endeavor in history, big or small, military or business, professional or volunteer. If there is any kind of crisis and the group has successfully navigated through the crisis, the leader is going to be leading from the front.

#7 – Brainstorm some solutions and a plan of action

Brainstorm Good Ideas

Horatio Hornblower, C.S. Forester's fictional naval captain, was described by Forester as having a particular routine he would engage in while working out problems or ideas. While pacing his quarterdeck, he gradually moved through a series of possibilities in solving a problem by first creating as many possible solutions as he could and then testing each in turn by playing the scenarios of how each would actually work. Gradually, he would eliminate one after another until finally finding the best solution. This process of working through all possible scenarios and outcomes, enabled him to solve the problem, and to have several contingency plans if things went amiss.

This is almost identical to the processes described in *Creative and Critical Thinking* (Moore, McCann, & McCann, 1985) and also at the heart of what Burger and Starbird describe in *The 5 Elements of Effective Thinking* (Burger & Starbird, 2012). I read the first book in a Logics course while at Northeastern Bible College back in the mid-70's when I was working on my Bachelor's Degree. It radically changed my approach to school and to doing things. In very practical terms, the concept plays out like this:

- Necessity is the real mother of all invention. Cool fads die quickly or get shelved if there is no real need for them.

- The problem delimits or describes the parameters of the needs or what needs to be solved.

- Begin by creating as many solutions to the problem as possible regardless of how daffy, crazy, or implausible they first appear.

- Once this list is exhausted, begin to cull the ideas by eliminating the worst based on solid and logical objections – not personal dislike. Is the option technically possible? Is it impractical? Too costly? Already being done?

- When *eliminating*, you are really only *setting aside*, since you may have to come back to it when it turns out to be the best option anyway. But when eliminating don't just find one objection and set it aside. Work all the way through using that possibility to find as many faults as possible. This may in turn reveal other options or alternatives.

- Eventually you whittle the list down to one or two *best* choices – in this case meaning "better than all the others." Then you test the possibility by playing each out completely in your mind. Build it, do it, walk it, assemble it, do the transactions in your head. Like the process Marsh Williams used when designing the self-loading mechanism that is at the heart of the M-1 Carbine rifle and almost every other semi-automatic rifle built since. Williams designed, built, and tested the mechanism in his mind while doing a stint in solitary confinement in prison to keep from going crazy. (Accurately portrayed by Jimmy Stewart in the 1952 movie *Carbine Williams*). This refines and tests the idea even further.

- At that point, the idea can be reviewed by others, gathering input for further testing and refinement, but also to gather synergy in making the idea go. This may reveal sources of materials and other necessities that can make the idea flourish or function even better than originally conceived.

- During this time, the plan is committed to paper, operational items or a "punch list" and/or schedule of execution is put together, and one final review is given while team members are brought up to speed on the details of the plan. This may include training in more complex operations.

- Dress rehearsals or flaws revealed during training are addressed.

- The idea is finally launched with an eye towards ongoing corrections, improvements, or engaging alternatives or contingencies as things move forward.

The heart and soul of the process, the real key, is the working through of the idea, the testing of it to check its validity, and if the solution can be destroyed or undone. Lockheed's SR-71 Blackbird was categorically the fastest airplane ever mass-produced and in military service. It flew faster and higher than anything else (including Russian missiles) for decades and was a technological marvel. The design itself solved many engineering problems using essentially the same process just described. What finally sidelined the Blackbird were technological advances that finally put it at risk *and* did the job it was doing cheaper, faster, and safer. The constant checking and testing of a concept is an absolute. Then again, any good engineer will tell you the same thing.

#8 – Tackle the life threatening "criticals" first

A Boy Scout Troop that cannot go camping. A church that has lost it's building to fire. A barbershop harmony chorus that has lost its meeting hall, or a rocketry club that has lost access to its flying field. Each of these scenarios are life threatening situations that an ORG can face. It can be a disaster brought on by poor management, leadership, or some failure of organizational stewardship, or it can be a situation that the ORG had little or no control over, such as a freak act of nature. Unfortunately, there will be things that will happen to your ORG that can challenge its very existence.

By far, the best approach is to split your efforts into two distinct thrusts. The first is to craft a plan to fix or restore whatever happened and get things back on track with a new suite of assets to replace the old. The second thrust, is often the most overlooked, and may take even more creative effort than the first. There is a real need to keep your members moving forward and keeping the ORG functioning in a very real and productive way.

Say for example that a barbershop harmony chorus

Keeping the membership involved is critical.

has been meeting at the local VFW Hall for years and has a fairly healthy group. One night the VFW Hall has a fire that guts the place, leaving the chorus without a place to meet. What do you do?

The typical response is to halt operations while a new location is found. Some ORGs may respond quickly and locate a new hall, but it may cost more money, be in a less desirable location, be smaller, or have other issues. Regardless, some part of the Board needs to find a new, temporary location while continuing to scout for new permanent locations. However, either process may take a while. So what else should be done? Depending on the complexity of finding a new meeting place, the group can exercise some contingency plans that could end up turning a negative into a positive.

First, make sure everyone knows what has happened and what steps are being taken to rectify the "big issue." Next, be sure to calm the troops by letting them know that as the "big issue" is addressed, the ORG will focus on keeping the group *productively active*, though it will take some flexibility on everyone's part. The chorus, for example, could meet at several members' homes. Using a quick survey of the group, several members have garages big enough to hold the whole chorus, while several others could host one of the four-part sections. After discussing it with the Board, a plan is created where the chorus would obtain a hall once a month for a full chorus meeting and rehearsal, then the following week the sections divide up and meet at several of the members' homes to practice their parts. The week after, the whole group would meet at one of the big homes, followed by more section practices the following week or a group field trip to check out a new temporary or permanent location. Any way this goes, the idea is to keep the bulk of the members doing what they are supposed to be doing, or at least something akin to it in a way that helps to continue to move the membership forward.

If a Scout Troop suddenly can't go camping for a few months while some issue gets straightened out, then they should switch gears and apply their efforts to other activities or find a different way to camp (a member's backyard, a relative's farm or property) or try a different outdoor activity that hasn't been done before. If a flying club loses its plane, perhaps they can contract with the local flying school to use one of their planes. It all depends on what the group is about and what creative options can be tried – and it may be trial and error to find things that work – *but keeping the membership engaged is critical.*

This is why it actually takes *two* leadership teams to deal with a crisis like this – one to handle the "big issue" and the other to handle ongoing operations until some form of "normal" can be restored. There is enough creative thinking and work to keep two leadership groups going at once and this is why: When a group is run by one or two leaders and then stumbles into a crisis like this, the wheels can come off and things grind to a halt. It is simply too overwhelming for one or two people to handle under most circumstances.

Proper handling of an ORG-threatening crisis should go something like this:

- The Board meets to evaluate the situation and assigns two work groups: one to handle correcting the problem and another to help continue day-to-day operations in some modified fashion.

- The first group should look for *both* temporary *and* permanent fixes and pursue those options until suitable permanent options are found.

- The second group should work to calm the troops, keep everyone together, and coordinate *productive and useful* activities that can ultimately contribute to the group in the long run.

- Once solutions are found, the membership should be consulted in order to gain buy-in from the members. Ideally, all steps should be approved by the membership and the members should be kept apprised of the steps being taken.

One final note of warning on this topic. These events can be *seismic* and there may be members who will use circumstances like this to their own ends. (Yes, there *are* people who are wired like this.) Some folks simply are not very patient or just have an agenda all their own. Don't be surprised at the appearance of a counter-leader who may convince several mates to jump ship and start their own thing because of the troubles being experienced by the home ORG. Keep calm and cool. Try to reason them back into the fold, but don't waste too much energy on it. Instead, focus on short-term and long-term solutions and work doubly hard at working together as a team or a family.

#9 – Then work some "visibles"

As important as it is to handle the life threatening issues of an ORG, you cannot neglect those day-to-day tangibles. I have seen a number of Boards desperately handling some huge problems with such devoted focus and mostly unseen by the members, that they neglect or put on hold regular operations for long periods of time, ignoring the concept above about thinking with two heads. The result is they lose their members while fixing the main problem. There has to be some balance between the criticals and the daily workings that keep the members engaged.

Sometimes it's the little things or the meaningful gestures with your members that matter the most and will act as something tangible they can point to as progress being made. I've seen this play out both ways in ORGs that were in trouble, but these little things can often time have outsized results and benefits.

That first year I was at Acahela I had very little in the way of a budget to work with. There were so many things that needed attention. I distinctly remember my first walking tour of both Goose Pond and Camp Acahela. The Pond was in great shape. Things looked pretty good. When I got to Acahela I was dismayed at how run down and forlorn the place looked. There was a lot of cleaning up to do – that was an ongoing project in and of itself – but the general condition of things needed to be brightened up.

One of the first things I did was to rehabilitate the signs throughout the camp. Using a cache of stain, varnish, and paint that was sitting around, I created a colorful variation of the original signs. At first, staining the signs was an act of poverty – I didn't have enough nice exterior grade paint to paint the signs, but had plenty of stain and varnish. It ended up looking a lot better.

So instead of just doing white or yellow lettering on brown signs, as is the norm in of many of our state and federal parks, I upped the game by staining the background wood and then added a colored border with fresh white lettering. I also standardized the hodgepodge of signs by replacing some of them and replaced missing signs in the upgraded style I had created. I was able to do all this with the materials on hand and in a matter of weeks. I was reinstalling refurbished and newly crafted signs on a regular basis. Much to my surprise, the effort had an outsized result. Folks coming to visit the camp consistently commented that they liked what they saw in the effort to refurbish *the entire* camp, and a comic irony was I heard over and over again was, "Oh, it's great to see that the Council is finally sinking some money back into the place!" All I had been able to do at that point was whack weeds, mow lawns, and put up some new signs, but the results looked like a lot more. I never had the heart to tell any of them in that first year or two that no real money had been rerouted or channeled into the camp and I was only using surplus stuff and junk I had unearthed and repurposed.

Changing a logo, coming out with new branding, or putting a new face on things is an old marketing trick and if all you do is a logo, stationary, or retreading an old program with a new name, you are very likely going to run into trouble. But if you do something genuine that indicates a *real* trend and *intent,* then you will be onto something. The trick is to first find all the assets you have available to you and then find something visible that will help folks know you are serious about getting things fixed and headed in the right direction. If you do that, the result will be folks stepping up and asking how they can help, and *that* is *priceless.*

#10 – Fix / Improve communications

I have written an entire section on internal communications and there are several things you have to grasp right from the start with volunteer/member ORGs. The problem is that most folks *think* they understand how to communicate well when in reality they only have only a vague understanding of the nuances of the art of communication. Make no mistake, communicating effectively to a group is a *nuanced* art form – it takes a practiced hand to do it well and one that really understands the details of what works and what doesn't. An old Scouting story illustrates this perfectly.

Outdoorsman have this unwritten rule that if you are lost or in trouble in the woods, the universal signal for help is to fire three shots in the air. Well, a search was started one time for a couple of inexperienced hunters at the start of archery season. They hadn't shown up at home after their first day out and two more days passed before the pair were found. They were hungry, thirsty, and freezing from exposure. When the Ranger who found them asked what had happened, they explained that their GPS receiver had died, there was no cell service. They had gotten themselves lost and simply didn't know what to do. Finally, the older of the two remembered hearing about the universal rescue signal so they tried that. "What happened?" asked the Ranger. "Well," said the lost archer, we kept firing three arrows into the air until we lost them all, but that stupid signal didn't work at all."

Nuances.

OK, for those of you who may not be outdoorsman or didn't get the joke, arrows make little or no sound at all. The signal is supposed to be three *gunshots* – *bang, bang, bang!* But the point remains, you have to use the best tools available in the best possible way in order to get the best possible results and *all* of it has to be deliberate. It's not a matter of passive activity.

First, *ya gotta reach 'em where they is, not where they ain't.* If you don't know the channels your group is paying attention to, then you can't insure they are getting the message. Second, you can't expect them to come and find you, you have to go to them. Posting something to your website and then expecting your members to flock to you like a hoard of invading Visigoths or Vikings only demonstrates that you are an archer in the woods shooting arrows into the sky as a signal for help. Third, make sure that all your communication is *timely*, as in *plenty of advanced notice,* with a reminder. Modern communications can get messages out right away, but you still have to give your people enough time to put it on their calendars. Leaders that consistently advise their members of upcoming events only a few days from the event can hardly blame their members if they don't show up. Yet, time and again I've heard these same leaders gripe that their members simply don't care (yet *another* glaring example of *attribution error*). It is not that they do not care. Our lives are busy. Any organization interested in getting me to attend anything has some serious competition to contend with in booking my time and the wise leader would make sure I get their event message far enough in advance that I can plan to be there.

Good communication is pivotal and there are a lot of things to consider. Make it timely, focused, and deliberate.

Then go read the rest of Chapter 8 on the Sovereignty of Communications and the section on Semaphore Syndrome.

#11 – Find your crew chiefs

Early on you need to get a handle on who can help you, but also on how they can help you lead others. The modes of organizational growth in Chapter 13 will spell out the transition from you working alone to working with a team of leaders that you can confidently delegate responsibility to. This doesn't mean a team of fully trained individuals who can step into your shoes right now. Dr. David Jeremiah, a well-known pastor and host of the radio and television ministry called *Turning Point*, has said that the best advice he was ever given on the topic of delegation was that if someone knows 75% of what you do in a particular job, to give it to them.

The trick in volunteer/member ORGs is finding competent and willing individuals to help. Even harder is finding someone who catches on to what you are trying to achieve and can lead others. With all the projects we had going on at Camp Acahela when we got things running, it became a matter of necessity to find folks who could act as team leaders to keep various projects moving forward. This helped me multiply my efforts, but also helped us get several things done at once without me having to split my focus among all of them. So cultivating a competent team of "Crew Chiefs" is one of the things you can and should start as you begin to set things right.

#12 – Get rid of boat anchors

At the same time, don't hesitate to *fire* a volunteer if you have to.

Yes, you heard that right and yes, you *can* fire a

volunteer. If in the process of culling through your members you find someone in a position of authority who isn't getting the job done, then coach them up and encourage them in every manner you can think of. Bring them up to speed. Get them on board. Mentor them into becoming the kind of person you need them to be. But if they refuse or resist your every effort, after a reasonable amount of trying, *jettison them*. You can retire them, you can give their responsibility to someone else, or you can simply make staffing changes, but get them out of the place where they are gumming up the works.

Boat anchors come in several forms. There is the "Promiser" who makes all kinds of promises but never follows through. There is the "Collector" who collects tasks, jobs, and responsibilities and then is too busy to handle them all. There is the "Centralizer" who is similar to the Collector, but he or she actually does the work but then does it in a way that they make themselves indispensable, and when they disagree with something, the trouble soon begins. There is the "Naysayer" who is skeptical about everything and every effort. Then there is the "Bureaucrat" who pledges support from his or her area and then deliberately withholds the promised support as they try to starve your effort or stonewall it until it goes away. In every one of these instances, my advice is this: Try to get them on board with what you are doing. Give that a worthwhile effort. Failing that, cut the chain and sail on.

Occasionally good people will turn into boat anchors for various reasons. Never burn a bridge, but don't tie your boat to a burning pier either. There have been a number of people I have cut loose for one reason or another. I've been saddened each time I've had to do it, but every one of them earned it when they did something so egregious or so out of line that parting company was hardly a surprise and certainly not without clear cause. After a time, a few – a *rare* few – were welcomed back into the fold, but also under agreed conditions. The bottom line is always this: *I* am not the organization and *they* are not the organization. *We* are the organization. If things are not being done with the collective *we* at the heart of it, then an adjustment needs to take place. Get your people into the places they belong and where they can do the best good. If all they are willing to do is damage or fight every step along the way, get rid of them, either out of the position or out of the group.

#13 – Does everyone know their neighbor?

The idea of "team building" has become so watered down and so overused that it can elicit a collective groan if you even suggest doing any kind of team building activity. However, the fact of the matter is that building your group into a *family* is a healthy and very productive thing to do. I think part of the problem is that nowadays we go about it in ways that do not work well and may even drive people apart. Not everyone is the same. Some folks are very sociable and others are not. One group that is part way between are the folks that *yearn* for belonging but aren't much good at it – I've seen this more often that those who are semi-sociable. So the challenge is finding ways in your group to prevent your program from cultivating wallflowers.

I first got a handle on this when trying to run my son's Bear Den in Cub Scouts. Joe surprised me one time by complaining near the beginning of the year that he didn't know anyone in the den. I was shocked. These guys had been together in other dens for over a year or two prior to that, but when he told me that he didn't even know half of the names of the other boys I was floored. We talked about it for a while and I was surprised to realize that he had been attending meetings with these guys for months and had no idea who they really were. He didn't know their names, where they went to school, or what they liked. We did all kinds of projects the year before, been to all kinds of activities and all he could do is recognize guys he had in his den and say, "Hey you." *This* was not good.

If you think ice breakers and get-to-know-you sessions are tough for adults and that you loath them like I do, wait until you consider doing it for a bunch of little boys and their dads! For the life of me, I could not figure out a way to tackle the problem successfully head on. Then I had a brainstorm. We were coming up on Thanksgiving and Neckerchief slides have always been a tradition in Scouting. I dreamed up a cute slide that looks like a funny, goofy turkey that had our pack number on its chest. It was made of bits and pieces of stuff: a PVC pipe coupler, some colored Popsicle sticks, two giggly eyes, a small nail, some black pipe cleaners, and some glue dribbles – lots of *guy* stuff. Putting the thing together required a *bunch* of simple steps and typically on projects like this all the kids would assemble their own little projects on their own.

Not this time.

I pointed out that I thought the individual approach was OK, but we could all do better if we worked together, so instead of each Scout working on their own, we would make a whole batch of these things *together.* It would be a collective effort. I still remember the panicked look on everyone's faces, parents and kids alike – it was priceless. I then explained, showing a finished prototype, how the whole thing went together, from raw parts to finished piece. Everyone was hooked and the excitement was growing.

Each member of the den was assigned a task. We started by doing the feathers together. One boy cut the ends of a Popsicle stick off producing two round ended "feathers." He then passed them to the boy next to him who used a brown colored Sharpie to "paint" the base of the feather. He then handed it to the next boy who added a curved blue stripe. That boy handed it to the next who added a curved green stripe above the blue one. He passed it to the next boy and so on until orange and yellow stripes were added. Then one lad added fine black lines in between each color while one the last boy added a dash of white paint to the top of the feather. Each slide required eight feathers and there were 10 boys in the den, but the project quickly escalated. They were having such a good time, that they quickly churned out more than twice the number needed – so many in fact that when I suggested we use the extras to make slides for the Den

Leaders and Pack Leaders it just bumped the level of pride and enthusiasm up a notch. While all of this was happening, the boys were *interacting*. Names were suddenly exchanged and they began to not only work *together*, but *to get to know each other*. It worked for the parents too who were just as enthusiastic as the kids. The activity *forced* close interaction, which is the real, genuine goal of *real* team building, not *faux* team building.

Making feathers occupied the first week. When we

came back for the second week of the project, everyone was excited and enthusiastic. We were also able to kick up the complexity a notch. Now that the boys had experienced working together, we could try doing tasks in smaller groupings, which, unknown to them, was helping them to break down barriers between them and help them get even a little more personal. Some boys worked on coloring the body, some worked on coloring and building the face. Others worked on making the legs or helped put all the pieces together, but in each case it always took more than one boy to do a certain task. By now, the enthusiasm was building to a near frenzy as we chatted up the idea of presenting the slides to leaders at the whole Pack meeting in another week or so.

At the end of that meeting we had a group huddle where I explained what had happened – not just in building a great set of slides now spread out on the table – but that every time one of the boys would wear the slide or see it, they could say to themselves, "My Den and I made them, and it was fun!" Even more than that, I told them, "You proved to yourselves that you are a family and that from here on out you are going to stick together and do things *together*." The details of getting to know each other flowed from there – as leaders we didn't have to tell them that. All we had to do was keep reminding them that they were now a *family*. Years later, that group of boys had the highest level of cohesion and collective rank advancement in the history of our Pack and Troop.

As crazy an idea as that was, I think that stands as one of the best team builders I have ever been a part of. The point is that knowing your neighbor is a vital part of small organizations. In fact, in the class of group that I refer to as Mutual Interest and Skills Organizations or MISOs – those groups that are centered around working together to improve or share skills or interests, getting to know each other in a safe and friendly fashion is paramount to the success and continued health and growth of the organization. There are

190

lots of creative ways to do this – from team builders or group projects to doing clinics to creating a member yearbook with interesting and fun facts folks might be willing to share. Yes, finding the thing that helps folks get to know each other can be awkward, but if you think of it in terms of how to make your group more like a *family*, you are on the right track.

#14 – Rediscover your mission, vision, and purpose

At some point in your recovery process a funny thing should happen. Either you or one of your fellow leaders or a devoted member is very likely to find some old document or photo or something that jars loose a memory of what the group is really all about. Do not miss or dismiss this golden opportunity because it means you are on the cusp of renewal or revival.

Churches often go through periods of renewal and revival where they rediscover their mission, purpose, or vision. It may be a brand new approach or way of doing things, but eventually it ties back to the founding reasons for the ORG's very existence. All kinds of organizations can experience this. At some point in time, you will *rediscover* why you exist, what you want to accomplish, and how you want to impact the world around you. When you do, don't miss the opportunity to plug back into your organization's founding concepts and ideas. If you want to find a productive use for traditions and ceremonies and anchor points to the past, this is it. But again, it has to be productive. Like team building, vision, mission, and purpose statements have been used and abused to the point where they have lost their impact and meaning. Such as the Scout that can rattle off the Scout Law and Scout Oath like it's a legal disclaimer at the end of a radio ad for a car dealership, or the church member who can name all the books of the bible at lightning speed. You have to wonder how much of it has really sunk in.

Often times when an ORG is in trouble, a good part

of the problem is that they have drifted away from or forgotten what these statements actually mean. Few ever really go completely out of date to the point where they have no relevance at all. At the very least the *intent* should be there, and usually that is all you need. Establish the link back to your legacy, and then built on it from there.

Every one of these steps is a miniature of the practices and skills you need to put in place to keep your ORG healthy. Once you have gotten the ship righted, the work has really only begun, and that's where the rest of this book comes into play.

KEY TWEAKS TO GO

1)

2)

3)

4)

Chapter 12

The General Theory of Pets and Understanding the Kind of ORG you are

*"Don't be what you ain't, jess yo' be what yo' is.
If you am not what you are, den you is not what
you is..."*

*Lyrics from "Don't Be What You Ain't"
by Edwin Milton Royle and George V. Hobart*

Anyone with a lick of common sense will tell you that a turtle isn't a cat, a cat isn't a dog, and a dog is neither a parakeet nor a hamster. All are pets, dearly loved and appreciated by their owners, but no one would tell you that they are all essentially the same and should be cared for in the same way. The care, feeding, breeding, and maintenance of pets varies from species to species and no one in their right mind would try to care for a guppy the same way they care for their dachshund. Each general class of pet has a different set of rules that have to be followed if the pet is going to live a happy, healthy, and long life. These sets of rules are essentially paradigms, just like the paradigms that rule scholarly studies or any other complex operation. But we don't even think about raising pets in terms like that. We just accept that there are commonly understood rules of care – *depending on the kind of animal of course* – and then do our best to take good care of them.

Let me repeat that: *take good care of them.*

Marinate on that phrase for a moment.

Taking good care of them is the cornerstone responsibility of any leader worth his or her salt as we have already discussed. It is the true essence of quality organizational stewardship, at the heart of servant leadership, and the vital attitude needed to keep organizations healthy and growing. In order to do that and do it at the best possible level, we have to engage our people *where they are* and meet their needs with the best possible set of operational paradigms. Again, this is common sense.

Every organization has its own vision, mission, and purpose along with its own way of achieving them. These things shape the kind of organization you are.

There seems to be no problem in corporations with defining and applying various definitions and categorizations to all kinds of corporate entities: Partnerships, sole-proprietorships, LLCs, S-Corps, and so on.

There is a problem however when it comes to studies and literature on leading *volunteers,* especially *volunteer* organizations. A survey of Google Scholar or any major book store or online outlet will quickly tell you that there is a plethora of books and works on volunteer studies that assumes that there is only one kind of volunteer organization and one way to run it. Some studies have been specifically devoted to discovering a unified understanding of what volunteerism is, what kind of organizations they are, and how they should be run. Dig a little deeper and you will find that scholarly works and government studies alike generally hold to the idea – the singular idea – that volunteers are those who give their time to a cause for the purpose of achieving some specific work, and that all this free work has a value at the human resource level that needs to be managed properly to the point that volunteer management is becoming a big business. Continue down the path and you will discover that the overwhelming number of studies, opinions, and advice being offered has far more to do with the business end of volunteerism and running NPOs than it does with running the local sewing circle.

The problem stems from studies done in concert with the Department of Labor and with business scholars who have tried to apply business rules and logic to running *all* kinds of organizations, including volunteer organizations. There is some understandable logic in this – the belief that the business way of doing things trumps all other ways of doing things – but that does not mean that this *assumption* is correct or even applicable in some cases. The problem also stems from a blindness to the wide variety of organizations that actually exist apart from corporations or larger NPOs (which have become more and more a variation of corporations). At the very least you are left with the impression that *most* volunteer organizations are NPOs that exist to provide volunteer assistance to one cause or another, and most of the books and academic work is this field is geared to that end. But is this really the case?

One study that seemed to point to a potential flaw in our generalized understanding of who volunteers are and what kind of organizations they belong to was uncovered in the Pew Research Center's 2010 *Internet and American Life Project*. While the results focused on the impact of religiosity and how the Internet is used, the results included a fascinating look at volunteers and volunteer organizations in general. Overall, the data gathered indicates that there is a substantial need to look more deeply into this cross-section of our culture, but it also indicates that the focus we currently have on volunteerism and volunteer organizations may be akin to studying an elephant and ignoring everything but the trunk. The trunk may be fascinating and do most of the work, but we are missing a lot of elephant if we ignore the rest of the animal. Here are some highlights that are worth considering:

- The Pew study discovered *28* different kinds of groups, most of which are *volunteer* groups that are *not* the focus of most labor or academic studies on volunteerism.
- The Pew study found that while there is a significant difference in how much participation there may be between those considered religious and those who do not consider themselves religious, participation overall is far from dead.
- Most individuals belong to more than one organization, and significant percentages of Americans belong to and participate in multiple organizations.
- Most of the organizations cited, and the responses from those surveyed, indicate that a significant number participate in an effort to *find* community or as a form of *fellowship* with those who have similar interests.
- The ways that members communicate go well beyond the old standards of postal address, home or personal phone number and e-mail address. Individual members – *volunteers* – in many cases are using different channels to communicate.
- The list of organizations cited included: Charitable Assistance Organizations, Mutual Interest and Skills Associations, Community Enrichment Organizations, Social Enterprises, and Community Initiatives, in addition to, traditional NPOs.

Volunteer organizations vary as widely as corporations can. Here are just a few of the types of ORGs out there in our communities:

Type of Organization	Purpose	Generally Staffed by	Examples	Notes
Corporations	Business entities created to provide products or services and earn profits for their owners or investors.	Professionals, employees. May seek volunteers for specific tasks.	Home Depot, Lowes, IBM, Apple, SpaceX, GM, Ford, Dell, Hospitals	For Profit Entities. The focus is on business and there are a wide variety of ways that corporations can be organized and officially chartered, creating a unique set of dynamics for each.
Charitable Assistance Organizations	Provide some form of assistance to other individuals or groups	Professionals and Volunteers	St. Vincent DePaul, Red Cross, Habitat for Humanity, Salvation Army	Organizations focused on doing things for others as opposed to doing things for self
Social Enterprises	Organizations who not only generate income, with the specific goal of improving life or situations in one form or another. They tend to be a hybrid of what we think of as For Profit or Not for Profit here in the US.	Mostly professionals, employees	Goodwill, GCU as a For Profit University	This is a class more commonly discussed and practiced in Europe, though it is making inroads here in the US.
Community Enrichment Organizations	Organizations specifically designed to provide or sponsor services or assets to the greater community with the intention of improving or enriching individual and community life	Professional Management Staff and Volunteers	Libraries, universities, Arts Centers, Museums, "Living Museums" (such as Mystic Seaport Museum), Shriners	These can begin as or be maintained as government entities for the common good. Libraries are a good example of this.
Mutual Interest and Skills Organizations	Generally groups that share a similar interest or hobby with the goal of sharing information, fellowship, or growing in a particular skill or practice.	Generally Volunteers with some professional staffing at higher levels that answer to the volunteers	Churches and religious groups (congregations), Hobby clubs (IPMS, NAR, NMRA), Boy and Girl Scout Units, Hunting or Rod & Gun Clubs, Car and Motorcycle clubs, Choruses, Toast Masters	In some cases the group exists to share assets that a single individual would be unlikely to obtain on their own, such as a lease on property or ownership of specific equipment.
Sports Leagues	A sub-group of MISOs, focusing on a specific sport. Softball Leagues, Bowling Leagues, Little League, Pop Warner Football, any organization where a sport is actually practiced.	Volunteers	ABC Bowling Leagues, Little League, Pop Warner Football	Competition as well as skill development are a large part of individual participation in these

199

Type of Organization	Purpose	Generally Staffed by	Examples	Notes
Societies	These are groups that band together because of a common profession, skill, or experience. Belonging here usually requires having been a part of something else currently or at an earlier time thereby providing a shared experience and culture among the members.	Volunteers with some professional staffing at higher levels that answer to the volunteers	Alumni Associations, Professional Groups, Veteran Groups, Masonic Lodges, Elks, Moose, etc., Rotary Clubs	These groups often adopt activities where they then act as sponsors to a specific cause or some other group.
Fan Groups	A sub-group of Societies because there is often a culture attached to the group	Volunteers	Celebrity Fan Clubs, Sports Fan Clubs	Fantasy Leagues tend to straddle several classes at once.
Community Alliances	Groups that band together to specifically assist professional organizations. Similar to government services, but working side-by-side with established professional groups such as Police or Teachers.	Volunteers	PTA/PTOs, Neighborhood Watches	These groups assist established professional groups in one form or another, functioning as auxiliaries or as liaison organizations between professionals and the greater community.
Government Services	Groups created to provide necessary community services that often require specialized skills, perhaps even certifications. They are generally created to augment what the government may not be in a position to offer the community through its budget alone.	Professionals augmented by Qualified Volunteers	Fire Departments, First Aid Squads, FEMA volunteers, Health Department Volunteers, volunteer police or deputized law enforcement.	These groups take the community alliance idea a step further by actually becoming or existing as the government or existing professional agency chartered or authorized by the government to act as a government agency. It also includes corps of volunteers who augment government staff as needed.
Community Initiatives	Temporary ORGs that are designed to meet specific problems, issues, or needs. Usually disbanded once the issue or need has been met or addressed.	Volunteers	Political action groups, benefit or fund-raising initiatives for the sick, injured, displaced, etc.	These have a very short lifespan, making the study and tracking of them extremely difficult.

200

At the very least, these charts should make it clear that more specific research and focus are needed on these various kinds of organizations if we are going to understand what makes them tick, how to get the most out of them, and how to manage and lead them in the best possible fashion.

Now, I want to be explicitly clear on what follows. This is not intended to be a criticism of any scholars or academia in general.

I grew up in the shadow of New York City and, as a young man, I have experienced gridlock in lower Manhattan first hand. Back then, in the early '70s, the city was far more "rough and tumble" than it is now, the traffic situation was far worse than what it is today, and gridlock was not just a momentary thing but something that could cascade into a blocks long nightmare lasting for minutes on end. You simply sat where you were with little or no forward motion for, what felt like, forever.

When I look at the current state of academic inquiry into the field of organizational studies of volunteer organizations, I'm reminded of those Manhattan gridlocks and it breaks my heart. I have spent most of my adult life leading in both corporate and volunteer organizational settings and I can tell you from the street level view, that as researchers and academics, we need to find a way to end the gridlock and get out of the rut that volunteer studies have been mired in for the last two decades.

Why should we care? Thousands of small volunteer organizations are saddled with the challenges they face in leadership, organization, and operations. Just imagine what could happen, how much more we could accomplish, how much wider and broader the impact could be if we broke the gridlock and *really* understood the dynamics and inner workings of the wide *variety* of volunteer organizations around us in far more detail. We could begin to differentiate *and care for* our volunteer organizations in ways that are specific to *their* needs, just like differentiating among goldfish, hamsters and dachshunds.

We have a tremendous opportunity here to reset the trajectory of not just one but several streams of leadership research that, in every case, could have a profound effect on how organizations are led and how to craft organizations that can deliver on the wide variety of reasons people volunteer in their communities in the first place. Studying NPOs is only the tip of the iceberg.

Scholars, please *hear* this: We *need* studies and quality academic work focused on Charitable Assistance Organizations, Mutual Interest and Skills Associations, Community Enrichment Organizations, Social Enterprises, and Community Initiatives, in addition to, traditional NPOs and For-Profit Corporations. Each have their own unique organizational structures, demographics, make-up, and *needs* and right at this moment, those needs remain largely unexplored and unanswered. My challenge to academia and the business world is to take a serious look at the field of leadership in this wide and wonderful variety of organizations that exist in our communities apart from the traditional For-Profit/NPO classifications. Every church and organization in our neighborhoods, cities, and states could use the results of these studies.

Not surprisingly, academics have moaned, for years, over a lack of progress in the field of volunteer leadership and many volunteer leaders have been left feeling like they cannot find the help that really applies to their particular organizations.

In a nutshell, the problem is that academia and the business world look at volunteer organizations like they are one kind of animal, and never really see or understand the variety of ORGS that are out there. The current dominant approach to volunteer studies is akin to having a PetSmart store with one line of food, toys, and care products for all animals. There are an awful lot of unhappy pets out there to prove the point.

Understanding what *kind* of organization you have is very important but also understanding what *shape* your organization is in is even more critical. Having a good, solid handle on both enables leaders and managers to make intelligent and insightful decisions so that they can lead their ORGs away from a hobbled existence to robust health. Just as it is important to differentiate if you are caring for a goldfish, hamster, or dachshund, you also need to know how healthy your pet or ORG actually is. In this next chapter I've outlined an easy to remember way to determine how healthy your Org may be and where it is in its life cycle.

KEY TWEAKS TO GO

1)

2)

3)

Chapter 13

Stages of ORG Health (Modes)

"The secret of success is consistency of purpose."
Benjamin Disraeli

Some ORGs are like beautiful old homes or like well cared for classic cars. They are in great shape, have owners that lavish just the right amount of care and maintenance on them, and are poised to continue on for years to come. I think we all wish that most things in our lives were like that. Then again, some ORGS are more like a beautiful old project car or home that just needs work and some tender loving care to restore it to its previous glory or even better. Vestiges of the former vision are still there. The potential can still be seen. Being able to imagine what it could do, how wonderful it would be to see it cleaned up and in good order are easy to conceive. The excitement of imagining those things gets you going, and like any restoration effort, the trick is to see things realistically and understand that it takes a lot of effort, requires many steps between the start and finish, and it will not happen overnight.

Evaluating where you stand is not easy. There can be an awful lot of emotional connections involved in preserving old homes, old cars, and ORGs you care about. It's not easy to be realistic. Personally, I tend to be overly optimistic in such things, thinking that as long as you don't have a tree growing up through the middle of the thing, there is hope. That is probably not the best approach, but it is better than looking at something that could survive and caring so little that you figure it just isn't worth the effort. The trick is, as *objectively* as possible, to figure out *where* the ORG stands and where to go from that point. Sometimes a tune-up, some adjustments, or quick makeover is all you need.

So what are the first steps you take to *actually* save the ship, fix up the old mansion, restore the dusty car? What do you do first to fix a broken and ailing ORG?

In most cases, it's a lot like any emergency response situation, home restoration, or auto restoration project, and it frequently requires some kind of rapid response to stop any downward spiral that can eventually kill the ORG. In emergency management situations, when you arrive on a scene, you have to:

- Evaluate the situation,
- Improvise a plan of action,
- Stabilize the victims,
- Restore basic function,
- Medicate and heal,
- Then rehabilitate.

Likewise, in rehabilitation projects, the steps you take run something like this:

- Evaluate what damage there is,
- Figure out what works and what doesn't,
- Do a thorough inventory of what needs to be done and what assets are on hand,
- Organize the work and set up a plan with workers and subcontractors,
- Stabilize the foundation, then the structure,
- Solve any leaks above and below,
- Replace rotten materials,
- Reinforce where needed,
- Undo bad renovations or remuddling,
- Work from the bottom up and the inside out.

When it comes to saving your ailing ORG, tear pages

from the handbooks of Emergency Management, Emergency Medicine, Damage Control, and Building and Auto Rehab projects. The basic steps are very similar and keeping these handy as useful analogies can provide you with insights when you get stuck or the slogging gets pretty heavy.

- Do Triage – Determine where the most critical and urgent needs are first. Follow the same kind of protocols emergency responders do.
- Figure out where you are - where are you in the modes.
- Dust off the forgotten reasons why you exist.
- Take an inventory of what you have, what you need, and what you can get.
- Save what you can, create the rest, and set aside some things for repair later.
- Time – You can't make sauerbraten, the famous German marinated pot roast, in an afternoon. On the other hand, you can't afford to waste time either.
- Rehab and renovation are a progression just like UPGGB.
- Semaphore Syndrome & communications (life blood and blood pressure).
- Forget titles and focus on needs first. Then get the right people into the right places as it shakes out.
- Immediate tactical needs to long-view strategic concerns.
- Work the modes.

Work the Modes

Any approach you take to trying to solve your ORG's problems begins with asking hard, honest questions. This may seem pretty obvious, but as we've explored already it is actually a bit more difficult to put into play than you might think, and with good reason. There is a very natural tendency to want to overlook the bad news and seek out only the good. Over time, as adults, some of us actually become very good at asking questions just the right way to insure the news is overwhelmingly good. We do this in our personal lives, at school, at work, in our relationships, and in our spiritual lives. The experience that I had in Wood Badge training in Boy Scouts that I mentioned earlier, really drove home how deliberate and counter-productive this kind of self-induced blindness can be.

And that is my point. Any good effort to help your ailing ORG *must* begin with a hard, brutally honest evaluation of where things are, what assets you have left, if your ORG's vision and mission have any spark of relevance and life left in them, and if there is a good chance of viable life after crisis. Without this *honest* assessment, you can't possibly begin to solve the problems in an orderly and rapid fashion.

The first thing you need to determine in helping your ailing ORG is to understand where your ORG is on the scale of *functionality* – what's working and what isn't – because this will give you, almost instantly, a handle on diagnosing what needs to be done and what direction to head in. The problem is that most organizational development models don't lend themselves well to this. The idea of "life cycles" or similar ideas are good in their own way, but they don't help much in situations where everything seems to be falling apart. Many of them tend to focus on aspects of leadership, or human resource development, or vision and mission creation. Unfortunately, that doesn't really help when the problem is that your ORG *has* a vision but the ORG leadership is acting like they can't remember what it was or where they put it. Besides, the steps in most of these models are hard to remember and don't adapt well to the organizational first aid that needs to happen to get things pointed in the right direction again.

So where does your ORG stand? The best way to find out is to read over the list of Modes that follow and take an inventory. Where are you on this continuum of organizational life? You may discover you have elements in several of these Modes at one time. That's good! It means that there is some life, but also shows where some deficiencies need to be addressed. The great part about the Modes is that they provide an almost instant road map on what needs to happen, who needs to do it, and how to get to the next level, all eventually leading your ORG back to full and robust organizational health. So let's move on to understanding what the Modes are and how they can help. Remember, honest knowing begets realistic action and the best results.

The first couple of times I found myself involved with organizations that needed help, every situation seemed so different. It was bewildering! Then, after a while, the more situations I saw the more I realized that they actually fall into several categories. Over time I came up with an easy way to identify where an ORG was in the process. This helped me to create a framework of steps to follow to help correct the situation at hand.

Summary of Modes

When your ORG is sick and needs help to get on the right footing, it's better to imagine the process more like a continuum, as opposed to a cycle. Think of it like a ladder where each successive step up is an improvement. Every ORG is somewhere on this scale regardless of its situation, how old it is, how healthy, or how sick it might be. The titles and analogies associated with these steps make each mode or stage easy to remember and will give you a handle on where your ORG is on the scale. From worst to best, the stages run like this:

- **Damage Control Mode**: The place is a wreck, nothing is working right and a lot of things need to get fixed quickly. The ORG is in danger of sinking and failing to exist.
- **Dutch Boy Mode**: You or a handful of people have plugged the holes, but help is needed to really correct the problems and get things moving again.
- **Tom Sawyer Mode**: Volunteers and other help are starting to show up and share in the work of getting things reorganized and moving again.
- **Follow Me, Boys! Mode**: Leadership is starting to kick in and others are starting to assume some of the responsibilities of getting things going again. *Model* or *Template* program is likely to be used here.
- **76 Trombones Mode**: People want to get involved and are willing to join up. The band hasn't learned to play well together yet, but a *Personal* or *Individual* program has begun to come together.
- **Mozart Mode**: The group has learned to play well and play well together. Efforts of individual sub-groups complement one another.
- **Pangs of Birth Mode**: The group is either ready to think and act globally, taking on a larger outreach, or is ready to spin off new groups, to expand upon the original mission.

One other mode, **Rio Lobo Mode**, is not listed with the others because it is a dead end or a rest area. I'll get into describing it later in detail, but this Mode is when an ORG has settled into a comfortable place and has quit moving forward and is simply treading water.

Your ORG *is* somewhere in this list. Now, I'm a very

visual kind of guy and each of these stages or Modes relate to some old movie, show, or story that is easy for me to relate to, but because some of these are now considered "classics" or are obscure oldies, it would probably be useful to explain each in a little more detail. I'll sketch out each of these stages or modes below, and then we'll follow up each with more detailed discussions on confirming the diagnosis and some practical ideas on how to get things better.

Deeper Discussion and Prescriptions

Before we do that though, it's important to understand that while an ORG may be in one mode, it may have some characteristics of some of the others. Like a teenager growing into adulthood, ORGs can waffle back and forth between maturity and immaturity, trouble and success, good conduct and bad. So in this continuum, it's not as if you complete a grade and move into the next, but more like moving into maturity – there is that time when waffling between phases is painfully normal.

As much as these things drove me nuts in school, a Venn diagram is a pretty good tool to help describe this effect. The Modes tend to overlap, so they look a little like this as they are unfolding. Assuming the ORG is in Damage Control Party Mode and in need of a complete overhaul, the progression to complete health should look a bit like this:

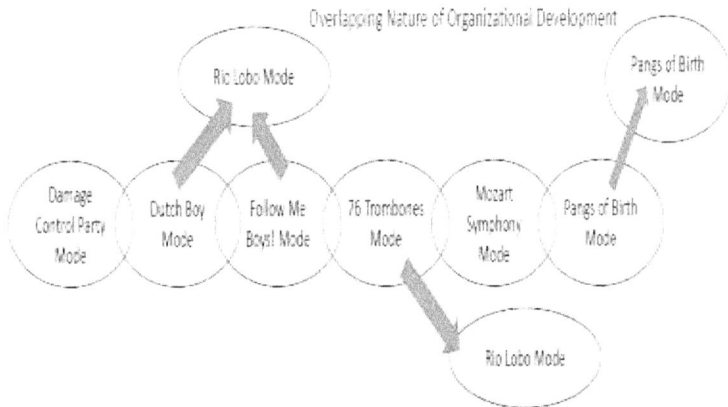
Overlapping Nature of Organizational Development

As you can see, there is this transition between each Mode where characteristics can overlap and, as I said, this is normal. In fact, don't be too surprised if you find that while you are in the midst of Dutch Boy Mode you see some attributes of 76 Trombones Mode beginning to show themselves. That's great! It's an indication that there is life in the ORG and hope for the future. These signs may come and go – just like the signs of maturity in a teenager – so don't give up hope or despair if they are there one day and gone the next. Remember that this is a progression – *Ugly, Poor, Good, Better, Best* – and continue to work up the scale. The other two things the diagram shows are 1) how Rio Lobo Mode can happen at any time, and 2) the dynamic of Pangs of Birth Mode. In either case, these two Modes will take the ORG in new directions and may cause either a part of the ORG or the entire ORG to have to re-evaluate where they are in the continuum and reformulate a strategy for moving forward.

The guidelines and prescriptions of what to do that follow are deliberately generalized since every situation and the condition of each ORG is going to be different. I also want to guard against the concept turning into a one-size-fits-all approach to remedy situations. Templating or the practice of applying a technique again and again once it's been learned is a good and natural thing to do, but it can also be overdone and this is one of the banes of modern business practice. When a leader or manager gets into the habit – the ugly habit – of constantly using the same template of action over and over again, there is a real danger of the leader *and* the ORG becoming a "one trick pony" where it only knows how to do one thing and do it one way regardless of how good or bad that one way may be. This eventually leads to forms of legalism and squelches creativity, and this is one of the main reasons I dislike one-size-fits-all approaches. It's another fantastic way to *kill* synergy, so don't fall into that trap.

So remember that the Modes are *wide open frameworks where you can improvise and adapt within them* and this should maximize the potential impact of your own customized plan of action for your ORG. Understanding all that, let's get into some prescriptive specifics.

A WORD ABOUT DESCRIPTIVES AND PRESCRIPTIONS

- EACH IS DIVIDED INTO 3 SECTIONS.
- *PLANNING STYLE* IS WHAT *YOU* NEED TO DO, HOW YOU NEED TO PLAN.
- *YOUR MAIN WORK* DESCRIBES WHAT *YOU* NEED TO BE DOING AS AN INVOLVED AND ENGAGED LEADER AND MANAGER.
- *TEAM COMMUNICATION* IS HOW WELL THE GROUP IS COMMUNICATING WITH EACH OTHER.
- *BOSS COMMUNICATION* IS HOW OR WHAT YOU NEED TO COMMUNICATE WITH OR TO THE GROUP.
- *YOUR NCOS* DESCRIBES YOUR ABILITY TO DELEGATE AND THE LEVEL OF TRUST YOU HAVE FOR THOSE YOU CAN DELEGATE TO.
- *YOUR FACILITATION ACTIVITIES* DESCRIBES WHAT YOU ARE DOING TO SUPPORT THE ACTIVITIES OF THOSE WORKING FOR THE ORG. ORGANIZATION.
- *VISION CASTING* DESCRIBES

Damage Control Mode

When I was a kid, *Voyage to the Bottom of the Sea* was a big hit on TV and every week, Admiral Nelson, Captain Crane, and the stalwart crew of the submarine *Seaview* roamed the oceans of our world saving us from all kinds of dangers. There were the usual sci-fi themes, but one of the things I remember was it seemed like the Damage Control Party was the busiest group in the whole crew. They were constantly keeping the *Seaview* from sinking, and getting her back into tip-top shape. They would go in, see how bad things were, and then improvise some quick fixes that eventually matured into things being completely repaired.

When things are at their worst, or when a crisis hits and your ORG has taken a real beating, or your ORG has been neglected for a long time, this may be exactly where you are – and it's a dangerous place to be. Left alone, the problems can quickly escalate and the damage begins to compound on itself like interest on a high rate credit card. One problem leads to another and causes things in one place to get worse elsewhere. If things aren't brought under control quickly and the flooding stopped, the ship is going to sink – period!

The most important things you can do in this Mode are to figure out just how bad the damage is and if the ship can be saved. As noble as going down with the ship may be, it may simply makes more sense to salvage what you can and start over again. But in many cases rediscovering what you actually have may be enough to bring new life back to your ailing ORG. You may find that a few simple steps can stabilize the situation enough to get folks back on board and moving in the right direction again. Getting a handle on what assets you have on hand to work with is also key at this stage.

Organizational Characteristics
- Baby, you are on your own! Little or no help.
- Not much is working.

- Not much is in place to help make things work.
- General disarray.
- Lots of unanswered questions.
- Either no vision or no charted course to reach it.
- Little or no help.
- Few viable assets *apparent.*

Your Leadership Situation

Planning Style:	Urgent issues & on-the-run needs
Your Main Work:	Hands on; Investigative
Level of Team Communication:	Very low
Level of Boss Communication:	OMG! High
Help:	Very low; little organized
Your NCOs:	Few if any. Not really an asset
Your Facilitation Activities:	Not much – no help
Vision Casting:	Creation high, embryonic effort

Your Immediate Leadership Prescription and Goals

- Keep the ship from sinking.
- Evaluate the needs.
- Construct a basic needs plan and steps to take.
- Begin to do the work.
- Place a call for help!
- Promote the need for immediate help.

Dutch Boy Mode

Dutch legend has it that a little Dutch boy saw a leak in one of the dykes that kept the sea out from the lowlands and plugged the hole by sticking his finger in the hole until help could arrive. Two things have to happen here in this ·Mode – the holes in the operation need to be plugged and the

Dutch Boy needs to scream for help! You can't take a "build-it-and-they-will-come" approach at this stage. Just fixing the major damage in an ORG is not going to get people to automatically flock to your efforts. You need to be out there *screaming* for help until help arrives and people begin pitching in.

In this Mode you not only have to have a handle on what needs to be fixed, but why it should be fixed. Dusting off that lost or misplaced vision and mission of the group may just be the reason needed to inspire others to help, but it will also provide you with the message you need to energize your evangelism efforts. Someone needs to see what has to happen and start to take action. They also need to get the message out to start rounding up the help needed to make the repairs. Remember, you *can't do this on your own*, nor should you *want* to.

Organizational Characteristics
- You, Baby, are still pretty much on your own!
- Some stuff is working, patched together.
- Some things in place to help make things work.
- Some disarray. Little in way of materials.
- Needs are much more apparent.
- Developing vision and *provisional* course to reach it.
- Awareness of the need for help is growing.
- Inventory of what is available is coming to light.

Your Leadership Situation

Planning Style:	Still urgent issues & on-the-run needs
Your Main Work:	Still hands on; Directive
Level of Team Communication:	Low, starting
Level of Boss Communication:	High, urgent items
Help:	Low; individualized

	help beginning
Your NCOs:	Few. More soldiers than leaders
Your Facilitation Activities:	Starts. Provide direction to help you.
Vision Casting:	*Creation high, long range and immediate plans can take shape*

Your Immediate Leadership Prescription and Goals
- Plug the holes! Keep the leaks to a minimum.
- Evaluate what you can do, what others need to do, and what pros should do.
- Begin the job basics.
- Be sure to do something people can see.
- Promote your efforts loud and clear!
- Recruit for regular, deeper help.

Tom Sawyer Mode

In a scene from Mark Twain's classic tale *Tom Sawyer*, Tom is assigned the task of whitewashing a picket fence. Fence painting is a pain, but painting a picket fence is especially a bother and very time consuming because of all the various parts and angles that need to be painted in order to get a great looking fence. If you do it poorly, a badly painted picket fence looks especially bad. Tom really isn't thrilled about this task and, quite accidentally at first, begins to get his friends to help him paint the fence. More activity gains more attention and pretty soon kids start to come and pay him for helping paint the fence. Eventually, he isn't painting and everyone else is – and he's making money while he's doing it! That comical outcome is essentially the lesson of this mode – getting folks excited enough about what you are doing that they come and freely give their time and assets to the tasks at hand.

At the heart of this Mode is *promoting and planning*.

You have to promote what you have in mind to do, but you also have to have it planned out well enough that when someone shows up to help you don't have them standing around waiting for instructions while you figure out what to do. Nothing ruins potential volunteers or enthusiasm faster than not being prepared for the help when it finally arrives.

Organizational Characteristics
- Help is starting to arrive.
- Work is beginning to gain momentum.
- Awareness is on the upswing.
- Enthusiasm is beginning to grow.
- Needs are beginning to be met.
- Casting the vision and *provisional* course to reach it is beginning to go public.
- Positive feeling is growing.
- Inventory is clear.

Your Leadership Situation
Planning Style: Moves to gangs and solos.
Your Main Work: Some hands on, moving to directing others in tasks. More supervision.

Level of Team Communication: Moderate
Level of Boss Communication: Strategies
Help: Moderate; crews help.
Your NCOs: A few. Start finding winners.
Your Facilitation Activities: Moderate. Provide materials and guidance to the helpers.
Vision Casting: *Promote like a fiend. Evangelize!*

Your Immediate Leadership Prescription and Goals
- Get the tasks moving.
- Get some crews excited and moving.

- Begin routines, document.
- Be sure to do something people can see, promote your crews.
- Promote your vision loud and clear!
- Keep recruiting for regular, deeper help, specialized help.

Follow Me, Boys! Mode

A great Disney Movie from 1966, *Follow Me, Boys!*, tells the tale of a man, Fred McMurray, who finds his own calling and purpose by starting a Boy Scout Troop in the small town where he settles. It's a great movie that teaches some great lessons, but one of the subtler lessons is what happens when you take a template, or what we might think of as a ready-made program, and put it into action. Over time, Fred McMurray's little troop develops a personality of its own and begins to do some things that give their troop a unique identity, but it takes time. The other lesson that goes hand in hand with this is that if you remove the hands-on leadership at this juncture, the program is likely to fall apart.

This may sound like a contradiction, but it goes back to what I said earlier about how the leadership of the group has to change and morph as the organization develops. A one-size-fits-all approach misses this nuance. As I said before, *nuance and subtlety are the secret ingredients to successful leadership*. At this stage, hands-on, almost fatherly or motherly, guidance is what is needed to help the ORG gain a steady footing. Later on, training the ORG to develop some kind of leadership legacy that preserves the developing culture of the group yet brings in fresh and new leadership is essential. This Mode also demonstrates the kind of mentoring leadership that is ideal for the transition that has to occur at this point in an ORG's recovery.

There is a difference between the activities that an ORG will concentrate on as a start-up, or when it is in the throes of re-starting after some serious ORG trauma, or the activities that take place when the ORG is under a healthy full head of steam. Seeing the difference, and especially the subtle steps between those points, take a special kind of mentor-like or parental leadership. The gap between emergency activities and full-on program is significant and most leaders fail to realize this and push themselves or their ORGs to try and make this jump too early, often with disastrous results. It takes an alert and patient leader to envision the steps in between and move the ORG successfully through this Mode. This is not a long or complex mode, just one that is marked by patient preparation. As a leader, you are setting the table for the things to come, staging for future events.

This is why one of the best tools to use at this point is "canned" or "template" style basic programs. It may not be the level of experience your ORG had before any crash, but it *is* essential to getting the wheels back on and training new people in what needs to be done.

Organizational Characteristics
- Help is active and begging to mature.
- Work is active and regular.
- Awareness is maturing, synergy beginning.
- Enthusiasm is present and strengthening.
- Needs are being met.
- Casting the vision and *promoting the mission* are now public.
- Positive feeling is growing further.
- Inventory and assets are growing.

Your Leadership Situation

Planning Style:	Focused on specific teams, solos, activities
Your Main Work:	Some hands on, moving to directing others in tasks. More supervision.
Level of Team Communication:	Moving higher

Level of Boss Communication:	Strategies, eye on future and long term
Help:	Solid; crews helping regularly
Your NCOs:	Fair number, expanding, solid work
Your Facilitation Activities:	Now routine. Provide materials and guidance to the helpers.
Vision Casting:	*Promote like a fiend. Continue to evangelize!*

Your Immediate Leadership Prescription and Goals

- Look to solidly establish and anchor routines.
- Set crew protocols, establish esprit de corps.
- Document how to do things.
- Keep doing something people can see, promote your crews.
- Continue to promote your vision loud and clear!
- Keep recruiting for regular, deeper help, specialized help.

76 Trombones Mode

Another great tale is *The Music Man*, a pretty famous musical in its time. The story is about a traveling salesman, Harold Hill, who is more con artist than salesman and he convinces an entire town to buy a slew of musical instruments to create a municipal band to eradicate the threat of delinquency in the town. The only problem is that Professor Harold Hill is perhaps the biggest delinquent of all – the musical band organizer and salesman can't even play an instrument and plans on skipping town before even teaching a single lesson. There are some great lessons in enthusiasm and promises you make and then may not be able to keep – cautionary points for our purposes here – but the reason for my selecting *76 Trombones* as the theme for this Mode is that it reflects the primary need in this part of an ORG's recovery or growth, and that is the need for cooperation and teamwork.

As an ORG gets the things that can make it run in proper working order and gets a program of activity going again, the next step is to develop the teamwork needed to move on to the next step. The goal in this mode is to establish the roles for each section of your operation, get everyone moving in the same direction at the same time, and get them all playing off of the same sheet of music. Easy, right? Just like a marching band, imagine what it's like if each section and member is playing whatever he or she wants, in their own time, moving in their own direction, with their own plan. It would be a calamity!

The leadership homework done during *Follow Me, Boys!* is what helps to set the stage for *76 Trombones*, and it puts into practice the cooperative atmosphere and teamwork necessary to restore full health to the ORG. This is where the family mentality of the group comes into full blossom and members realize that they are no longer in it just for what *they* can get out of it, but that they are part of something bigger and have figured out how to put that into action with the members around them. BUT, if you try to institute full-on teamwork too soon, or do team-buildering or similar activities without the rest of the scaffolding in place from the previous modes, the efforts often don't get the traction you expect. It's a lot like going on a first date and talking marriage before you are really even sure you like each other. Team-building is part of a logical progression, but it has to come at the right time and be introduced in the most productive way possible. You also have to realize that this is not the end, but continues to build towards the next steps.

Organizational Characteristics
- Help is now segmenting into groups.
- Work is fully engaged, following plans.

- Awareness is full-on. Promotion by action.
- Enthusiasm is high.
- Needs are being met.
- Emphasis on teamwork, team building.
- Positive feeling continues to grow.
- Inventory is clear, cycling.

Your Leadership Situation

Planning Style:	Looks bigger, longer. Focus on groups and projects
Your Main Work:	Fully into directing others in tasks. More supervision than hands on.
Level of Team Communication:	High
Level of Boss Communication:	Strategies & Long Range Needs
Help:	Lots of it. Needs attention to stay organized
Your NCOs:	NCOs develop into crew bosses, crew chiefs.
Your Facilitation Activities:	Moving to high. Provide materials and guidance to the helpers. MBWA.
Vision Casting:	*Promote like a fiend. Evangelize and update!*

Your Immediate Leadership Prescription and Goals
- Routines established.
- Crews, help, organized and established.
- Assignments become routine.
- Work organized into programs with own recruiting.
- Vision clearly established and articulated.
- Recruiting continues.

<u>Mozart Symphony Mode</u>

Mozart is regarded as one of the greatest if not *the* greatest classical composers of all time. When you listen to his music there is a beauty that simply blossoms out of the complexity and intricacy of it. In the highly fictionalized play and movie about Mozart, *Amadeus*, the chief protagonist and a contemporary of Mozart, Salieri, does a splendid job of explaining those intricacies and the complexities of Mozart's work, which is also reflected in how complex it is for a full orchestra to play seemingly flawless compositions. I tried to master the clarinet as a kid and learned a little guitar, but I completely lack any sense of rhythm and just don't have the wiring to be a good musician. Still, I can easily see that the larger the musical group, the more complex the problems of playing well together and having the music come out as intended by the composer. The point is that as hard as it may be to get folks to play well together in *76 Trombones* Mode, getting them to a point where they are high performing and able to improvise new things is another matter entirely. Mozart Mode is all about high performance and developing that capacity to break new ground – how to get there, how to cultivate it, and how to maintain it.

Organizational Characteristics

- Help is now segmenting into groups.
- Work is fully engaged, following plans.
- Awareness is full-on. Promotion by action.
- Enthusiasm is high.
- Needs are being met.
- Emphasis on teamwork and team building.
- Positive feeling continues to grow.
- Inventory is clear, cycling.

Your Leadership Situation

Planning Style:	Looks bigger, longer. Focus on multiple operations
Your Main Work:	Fully into directing others in

225

	tasks. More supervision still. Little hands on. More training.
Level of Team Communication:	High
Level of Boss Communication:	Still High, Strategies & Long Range Needs, focus on coordination at top
Help:	Lots of it. Needs attention to stay organized with help
Your NCOs:	NCOs develop into crew bosses, crew chiefs, helping lead sections, projects, operations
Your Facilitation Activities:	VERY high. Provide materials and guidance to the helpers. MBWA. Focus on direction
Vision Casting:	*Promote like a fiend. Evangelize and update! Look for new birth opportunities.*

Your Immediate Leadership Prescription and Goals

- Make sure routines are trained, taught, and refined.
- Crews and help are organized and established – each recruiting. Have their own identities established.
- Look for new opportunities and options.
- Work organized into programs with own recruiting.
- Vision clearly established and articulated for multiple operations.
- Recruiting continues at higher levels.

Pangs of Birth Mode

So is there anything beyond being a high performance team? If this book is all about restoring health to an ailing ORG, isn't reaching high performance and full health the end of the story? From my experience with ORGs of all kinds, I have observed that one of the biggest traps an ORG can fall into is not realizing that it's pregnant. As silly as this may sound, I think most organizations reach a point where a split, splinter, or spin off is a *natural* outgrowth of the ORG's development. However, we often treat such things as subversive or the work of destroyers or malcontents in the organization. While that may be a possible explanation, treating every situation like this is, I believe, a mistake.

This Mode is all about *thinking through options*. Seeing an organization expand its scope to a much bigger arena is the natural outgrowth curve of a successful ORG. Giving birth to franchises or chapters can be a good thing. Sometimes I think we do a disservice to our ORGs when we try to hold something together that really needs either a splitting off or, better still, a divorce. The trick is to realize when an ORG needs to subdivide and then give some serious thought to the idea of how your ORG can deliberately prepare for giving birth or evaluate the wisdom of allowing prodigal groups to go their own way.

Organizational Characteristics

- Some uneasiness and internal conflicts; vision & mission struggles.
- Work is fully engaged but direction is in question.
- Awareness is full-on, searching for more.
- Enthusiasm is high with some conflict or questions.
- Needs are showing signs of not being fully met as before.
- Emphasis on teamwork, team building, but teams may be moving in different directions.

- Overall feeling that things are too big or that there is a need for change.
- Group has reached a segmenting threshold; 150 or higher.

Your Leadership Situation

Planning Style:	Parental; careful evaluation of future.
Your Main Work:	Leading discussions of group's collective future.
Level of Team Communication:	High
Level of Boss Communication:	Strategies & Long Range Needs
Help:	Lots of it. Needs attention to stay organized and focused without fracturing.
Your NCOs:	Maturing and now leading develop of others into new crew bosses, crew chiefs.
Your Facilitation Activities:	Highest level. Provide overall guidance to entire group. MBWA. Listen CAREFULLY!
Vision Casting:	*Remain open to creation or modification of vision for greater impact.*

Your Immediate Leadership Prescription and Goals

- Listen Carefully.
- Watch Carefully.
- Promote harmony and peaceful maturing.
- Act carefully and with Legacy in mind.
- Clarify Vision and Mission as well as goals.
- Recruiting continues.

Rio Lobo Mode

This final Mode is one that can happen at any time throughout the life of an ORG. It can be the result of having won a particularly hard-fought battle, and looks like a great place to be, but it can quickly turn into a trap. This Mode begs the simple question: When do the meadows and peaceful places become the valley of the shadow of death? When does success or prosperity turn into the quagmire of complacency? And how dangerous is that? Rio Lobo Mode is a constant, ever present temptation because it woos us to a place where the productive work stops, the party begins, and the vision gets lost like a set of car keys at a bar.

Rio Lobo Mode is dangerous because it is the complacency effect that can occur when ORGs get lazy. It is not the ORG as much as the leadership or perhaps the will of the majority, but in either case the situation is that instead of continuing down the path of maturity and on to full health, the ORG gets stuck in a siding – some nice, cozy place where it is content to just "hang out." It isn't going anywhere, growth has stalled, and in fact it may actually be sliding backwards, but the ORG is working harder at "station keeping" than at moving forward. Station keeping, or trying to stay in one spot, may actually be harder work and require more effort than simply trying to sail forward in an unrestricted fashion. Like trying to hover a helicopter by the pilot's skill and control inputs alone, staying in one spot is *very* hard work. Some leaders think that this is what they are supposed to do, but try standing still and balancing a bicycle – man, is that tough! It *can* be done, but you have to wonder why. Bicycles are designed to enhance forward motion, not stand still. The same applies to ORGs. *They aren't supposed to hover or stand still.* Rio Lobo Mode represents any time an ORG gets complacent and decides standing still is a good thing. Permanent station keeping for an ORG is death waiting to happen.

Understand that many ORGs suffer from some type

of debilitating dysfunction, or have somehow quit moving forward and are stuck in Rio Lobo, and this is one of the hardest places to get a group out of. If your church seems filled with "the dead in Christ" or your club with a bunch of mindless zombies, welcome to Rio Lobo! Figuring the way out isn't easy. It will take getting the majority of those with you to see that moving forward is ultimately better than camping out and just waiting to die. Go back and dust off your vision, re-evaluate and re-energize your mission, and set some new *active* goals that look beyond the ORG's comfy couch.

KEY TWEAKS TO GO

1)

2)

PART IV

Building for Legacy

"The best way to predict the future is to create it."
Abraham Lincoln

When you are building something with the intention of making it last, you *deliberately* do certain things that help it survive. Anchoring a part to another is what makes things stronger and better able to withstand the rigors of use and time. It's like the difference between building something out of plain building blocks or Legos – the Legos interlock, making the structure more durable. Likewise, contactors routinely use rebar, reinforcing rods that the builders bury deep in a concrete structure and often help connect one piece of the structure to another.

That same intentionality needs to go into our ORGs as we move from triage and first aid, to building for health, to building for legacy. Building for legacy is what you deliberately do so that the generations of leaders and members that follow will be able to build upon and continue the good work you have helped shepherd along, and how to keep the termites and vermin out!

While the exact number of experiments and attempts with various materials is not known, it is said that it took Thomas Edison thousands of tries before producing an inexpensive filament for use in an incandescent lightbulb that would be practical and inexpensive enough for everyday use. There were already a number of filaments available, but some were too expensive to be practical while other materials didn't last. The trick was to find something practical and affordable *that would last* and not go *pththt-zap!* after a few short moments of brilliant light.

That same rule applies to ORGs. It's one thing to *fix* an ORG, but another to get it so it *stays* healthy and has a brilliant future.

This section will provide some valuable insights into how to build an organization that is well-grounded and healthy and can *stay* healthy for years to come. This is the part of our discussion where we explore the things that help good ORGS run even better and to identify the things that can spoil that forward motion and really gum up the works. This will help you identify what is grease and what is gum – and provide the insights on what to do in either case.

Chapter 14

Mission and Program Aligned and Coupled

"There is a powerful driving force inside every human being that, once unleashed, can make any vision, dream, or desire a reality."

Anthony Robbins

Pathway to Member Maturity
This concept should be the ultimate driver or acid test to see if your vision, mission, and goals are designed as directive tools and not as some kind of literary or administrative exercise. If they are not connected to and helping drive your program, they are worthless. If your program is just a bunch of activities created to keep your members active and busy, but not connected in some tangible way to the ORG's mission, vision, and goals, then that too is probably missing the mark. The real question should be this: **What ultimately will every participant get out of being part of this group?**

From the earliest days of the Scouting program, preparing boys and girls to handle the situations life can throw at them has been the cornerstone of the organization. Most people would be very surprised to learn that the goal of the Boy Scout program is not to make Eagle Scouts of every young man that puts on the uniform. The real goal - as set by founder Lord Baden-Powell himself over a century ago - is to get every boy to First Class. For those of you who don't know the Scouting ranks, that means a lad earns Scout, Tenderfoot, Second Class, and then First Class. Following that are Star, Life, and *then* Eagle in the American program.

There are three distinct ranks *above* First Class.

So what is the purpose of this? In the early 1900s Baden-Powell designed the system so that a boy would learn everything he would need to save a life – either someone else's or his own – by the time he got to First Class. In the process he would learn to be fully responsible, self-sufficient, and able to lead others with confidence. Think First Class is a halfway goal? Think again! It is an obtainable standard of excellence upon which further achievement can be built. In other words, at the *bare minimum*, Baden-Powell wanted *all* Scouts to be *excellent* responsible citizens and leaders that were able to handle emergencies, and then set even higher goals for exceptional achievement above that.

> What many ORGs miss, is that every organization should have some kind of plan, concept, or established form of progression that helps members develop from new, novice members to experienced, well-trained and mature members.

It doesn't take much to see that this tiered approach is very different from what we typically do today. We tend to set end goals and often they are stated or considered in terms of "beginning with the end in mind" or what we want to accomplish. Baden-Powell's approach sets a solid, lofty, but attainable goal at the center of an ongoing continuum that can lead to great achievement. First Class is something to be proud of and exceptionally handy as any former Scout will tell you. That is why the military has often looked for former Scouts in their ranks as young men who were more likely to be prepared for any kind of contingency – the military didn't have to teach it, the former Scouts already knew it. How to think on the fly, how to save a life, how to act in an emergency, how to lead – that's at the heart of Scouting's motto *"Be Prepared."*

Now imagine what might happen in your church, club, group, or even your own Boy Scout Troop if you approached your vision, mission, and goals the same way. Imagine how this might change your programs, the impact this approach could have on how you plan your goals, and the development of your membership. The change could be both dramatic and profound – a high, proficiency-oriented but attainable goal in the center with a lofty, almost idealistic goal of excellence at the end. The result would be a membership standard that would surpass what we normally do today – and just imagine what a group like that could do!

What many ORGs miss, is that every organization should have some kind of plan, concept, or established form of progression that helps members develop from new, novice members to experienced, well-trained and mature members. What that might look like depends entirely on the organization, but it is something that every ORG needs to look at and address if developing the lasting power to be around a long time is part of what the ORG has in mind.

Setting Realistic Expectations

Passion is what really drives ORGs and it can be a wonderful motivator and driver as we will see in the chapters to come. But some ORG founders and leaders get so caught up in the program of their ORG that it soon displaces everything else. When programs become an obsession, it ceases to be a good thing and turns into something that can become a destroyer or silent ORG killer. It is therefore imperative that ORG leaders keep a realistic eye on the programs and the number of group activities they plan, realizing they are a means to an end – the things that *should* be extensions of the vision, mission, and goals of the ORG.

For example, the group that expects that their members will be participating in almost all of the ORG's planned activities and then sets up a calendar that would make a Little League baseball team cringe is bad enough, but when you combine that with a leadership attitude that doesn't understand or comprehend that you are competing for your member's free time, then you have real trouble brewing. A program hobbled by lack of participation is bad enough, but this attitude also tends to breed the idea that real members make the time to participate – and that is the kind of exclusionary divisiveness that ORGs need to banish if there is any hope of true organizational health. I've seen churches do this a lot, but I've also seen some other clubs create schedules that only a few of its members could keep up with. So having an activity calendar that is realistic and obtainable is not just a good idea, but critical.

I've mentioned this before: there is a real need for ORG leadership to understand and acknowledge that they are competing for their members' attention and time. And again, volunteers and ORG members participate on *their* terms, not yours. Simply stating that there is a meeting of the ORG like there is a meeting of your team at work *will not* produce the same results at the same level of compliance. Why? Participation in an ORG is *not* generally *compliance* driven. Sure, there may be some "mandatory" meetings for some reason or another, but if you make too many of your meetings mandatory, the activity quickly becomes another form of work and participation is very likely to drop. Yes, some ORGs by their very nature need to have calendar events like this. I was a member of a volunteer fire department and it was apparent that the departments that instilled a professional approach to their firefighting were the better departments. Sports teams tend to be the same way. But in both cases, there also has to be a balance of some kind that makes participation fun enough or attractive enough to give the time needed to reach maximum performance and maximum amount of participation. In ORGs, it's always a tricky balance.

Something old, something new, something borrowed, something worth going back to.

I was reading a biography about Teddy Roosevelt and the author made the observation that Roosevelt made it a habit to go back and find the traditional things that worked and had value. He would dust them off and breathe new life into them and add to them with new enthusiasms and new approaches. For years I had felt very self-conscious about being the same way. I have been criticized for being a bit of a sentimentalist at times, but here was one of our greatest leaders who routinely did the same thing! And as I thought about it, *many* of our finest examples of leadership would go back and mine the classical moves, concepts, ideas, and practices for ways of solving the problems of their day.

Israel's King Solomon observed in the book of Ecclesiastes that, "there is nothing new under the sun," and to a certain degree he is right. Especially when it comes to dealing with people or the issues of leadership. Technology screams forward with an ever-increasing velocity and with more and more new "stuff," but in the areas that really count like human interaction, leadership, and the art of following well, not much has really changed in several thousand years.

Just in case...

Writing vision statements, mission statements, and goal setting has received so much print over the last two decades that I almost hesitate to even mention what they are and how they should be created, yet I have repeatedly seen folks use these terms as if they were experts in their use and then discovered that they only *sorta kinda* know what they are really about, how to create them or, best of all, how to actually *use* them. One of the most tragic things in today's business practices is that we go through all the work of creating wonderful, lofty, impassioned vision statements, mission statements, and overarching goals and then relegate them to by-stander status or ignore them.

To address this and to make sure we all understand, here is a quick explanation of what they are, what they *should* mean, and how they *should* be used.

Vision, Mission, and Goal Statements

The *vision* of your group is essentially the answers to three questions. *"What are we all about?" "What are we all here for or concerned about?" "Why are we all banded together?"* When you collectively express the reasons why, the ideas or concepts should be broad enough to say, "We exist as a group because together we want to_____," and then fill in the blank. A *generalized* expression of what you do or why you exist is a solid place to start. *Vision* is the *"big picture." It is the why.* This should be a set of ideas that are long-lasting, something that 100 years from now could *still* be what the group is all about.

The *mission* of your group is a little more specific. It is essentially *how* you are going to pull off the *why.* If vision is the television series, then mission is the episodes. If vision is the book concept, then mission is the chapters. Mission explains the *"whats"* and *"hows"* of executing the vision. The expression of these ideas has a bit more detail than those expressed in the vision, but are still are more an overview of how things may be done than the specifics of how each thing will be done. Again, the expression of these ideas should be from the long view, ideas that 25 to 50 years from now would probably remain the same, even if techniques, technology, or society changes, or that they could be flexible enough to be updated as time goes on.

The day-to-day, what do we have to get done tomorrow, next month, next year, by the time we are five years from now, are what the *goals* are for. Goals are the expression of the collective will of the ORG and where the ORG wants to head and what it wants to do in the near and immediate future. This is something that the leadership should be working on all the time.

The goals should be constructed using the idea of SMART goals, an acronym that stands for *Specific, Measurable, Attainable, Relevant,* and *Time-bound.* Again, there are books and articles galore on this, so I won't go into it here, just make sure they remain flexible and that you always remember that these are guidelines and treat them that way.

Finally, your *program of activities* is the detailed expression of how the *goals* can and will be reached, provided of course that all four – *vision, mission, goals,* and *program* – actually connect. If they do not connect and have any real impact upon one another – meaning that one gives input and validity to another – then you will have meaningless smoke and no real fire when it comes to what your ORG is doing. This is a very real and very common problem that happens when ORGs have been on "auto-pilot" for any length of time. Folks are out there doing stuff and talking about stuff and yet there isn't anything really happening or the overall satisfaction level just isn't what it should be. If your people are just going through the motions, then you have a problem with your *vision, mission, goals,* and *program* being connected and aligned.

The best way to insure against that is to get into the routine of continually conducting, "stop, start, and continue," reviews of activities on a regular basis. Always go back and look at what you just did and ask, "What do we need to *stop* doing based on what just happened, what do we need to *start* doing based on what just happened, and what do we need to *continue* doing based on what just happened." Actually applying this practice on a regular basis demonstrates that your ORG is becoming a *learning* ORG, and is willing to learn and adjust by doing. Ask the hard questions and then take appropriate action.

KEY TWEAKS TO GO

1)

2)

3)

4)

Chapter 15

Synergy

"The whole is greater than the sum of its parts."
Aristotle

*"Synergy is better than my way or your way.
It's our way."*
Stephen Covey

I cannot remember exactly the first time I felt it, but I'm pretty sure the first time I encountered *fake* synergy - the kind manufactured by a leader telling a bunch of followers that they are all having a great and seriously productive time - was at a birthday party for one of my young neighborhood friends. Watching one of the local mothers flip-flop back and forth between sweet, encouraging words and searing growls at things not exactly going according to plan was scary and sad enough for a kid. Since then I have seen the same scenario play out when all the participants are adults, and every time I see it I'm transported back in time and my immediate thought is, "You've *got* to be kidding."

Over and over again, I have seen intelligent adults and reasonably good leaders act as if synergy were something that can be manufactured or ordered into existence. Some leaders and managers really do believe that if you cheerlead hard enough you can create synergy.

Synergy is not something you can drive or force into existence in any organization and certainly not into any volunteer organization.

Unfortunately, when it doesn't work as expected, these same leaders will very quickly revert to driving their people or demanding they have a great attitude, as if the attitude problem is the followers' problem and not the result of subpar leadership. This error in leadership and management judgment comes from the errant belief that if you do a few things to manufacture a feeling of synergy, that it will kick-start the process like squirting ether into the carburetor or an old lawn mower. While keeping a positive attitude plays a major role in getting synergy to occur, *faking it* does not make it real and when it is done badly enough it will actually kill synergy.

Let's clarify this again: Synergy is not something you can drive or force into existence in any organization and certainly not into any volunteer organization. It can't be manufactured like you are making widgets in a manufacturing plant. Synergy is the result of all the parts of your program, personnel, leadership, and organization melding together in a way that the sum of the parts ends up being greater than the whole, and your people *willingly* give extra to help build what is going on because they are fully on board, believe in what they are doing, and are having a very satisfying time participating. Do you see the subtle nuance here? Synergy is not so much what a leader or manager does, as much as it is a *reaction* by the followers to what is happening around them.

It is a by-product of when everything is working well and the organization is moving towards Best and moving away from Ugly. Yes, it is the result of good and positive attitudes, an expression of belief in what a group is doing, a willingness on the part of many of the members to not only participate, but to bring something extra to the table when doing so. However, it has far more to do with leadership character than manipulating feelings.

A leader who has an unquestionably upright character and understands servant leadership is far more likely to produce *genuine* synergy than the idiot leader who thinks driving and manipulating people works just fine.

You may think my use of the term "idiot leader" is harsh, but this really is a matter of common sense and wisdom. Perhaps I should use the term "fool" the way it is used in the Bible instead. Even the Old Testament scriptures repeatedly remind us that the character of a leader determines the *response of the followers* and make no mistake, *synergy* is a follower response. In the book of Proverbs there are numerous references to bad and abusive rulers and every time the response of the followers is to run and hide. Proverbs 28:28 says, "When the wicked rise to power, people go into hiding." We all know what it's like to work for someone that, every time you see them coming, you want grab your helmet and dive into the deepest foxhole you can find. This kind of response is not the kind of response that inspires synergy – quite the opposite. When a leader's conduct and character are so bad that it drives his people into hiding, the odds of him inspiring synergy by standing over his quivering, shell-shocked followers and yelling, "We are having a *great* time, aren't we?" are not very good.

If you casually read the book of Proverbs in the Old Testament or just blast through it once, you are left with the impression that it is a jumbled and random collection of sayings. However, if you study the book, reading it through several times and watching for themes, they start to bubble up to the surface and you see that they are ingeniously grouped together in almost a point/counterpoint fashion, like the comparing and contrasting of scholarly material. One of the themes that bubbles to the surface from Chapter 25 on, is the conduct of leaders and followers both good and bad, and the effect this has on everyone around them. Written by Solomon, who was the king of Israel, these observations about followers and leaders didn't make Solomon's original final cut. For some reason they were left out of the original collection. Verse 1 in Chapter 25 tells us that the scribes of King Hezekiah found and added these sayings at a later date and I think there is an interesting backstory to explain why.

Solomon was arguably one of Israel's greatest kings who reigned over the united kingdom of Israel from 970BC to 931BC, but he was not perfect. Also, the writer of Ecclesiastes and The Song of Solomon history, records that in his later years his quest to build Israel and demonstrate his own power and wealth may have gotten the better of him, and he, among other things, began to heavily tax the people of Israel. Solomon's omission may have had something to do with him seeing how conduct and character – things he observed all throughout his collection of proverbs – were present in him, both good *and* bad. His early years were marked by incredible synergy and Israel grew to its greatest heights under that kind of leadership. But in his later years, it seems he pushed the envelope a bit too far and his people groaned under the burden of Solomon's building programs. Solomon was a man of great reflection and observation and this included a lot of introspection. As in the book of Ecclesiastes, it seems that in his later years he also despaired at his inability to achieve lasting, constant excellence. It could be that in that mindset, and perhaps realizing the impact that his policies had in the later years of his reign, that his observations about leaders and followers were not included in his original collection.

Fast forward. Hezekiah became the king of Judah in 715BC and reigned until 686BC. Judah was a portion of Solomon's original kingdom and Hezekiah was a direct heir of Solomon. He had a leadership career that was marked by some serious ups and downs – gyrations might be a more accurate term - and the scriptures record that he experienced some personal revivals brought on by events and some severe personal reflection. It is Hezekiah's scribes that found Solomon's writings that now comprise chapters 25 through 29 of the book of Proverbs. I think this occurred because Hezekiah saw in them the truth that the *character* of a leader has a profound and unavoidable impact on his or her followers either for the good or the bad. And the key observation here if you read these verses carefully is that *synergy thrives under leaders of good character; synergy dies under leaders of bad character.* It really is as simple as that. Solomon observed and Hezekiah experienced the same dynamic that when leaders behave well, followers willingly give. When leaders behave badly, followers dig in, resist, and hide. Synergy either thrives or dies depending on the character of the leader.

Now if this scripturally based history lesson doesn't appeal to you, OK, then simply look around you and think through your own working career or the work experience of close family or friends. Look in your own life and think about the leaders you have been placed under and think about the response you have had to their leadership. Chances are you have experienced at least one leader who was so bad that all you really wanted to ever do was to avoid them at all costs, or perhaps even quit. I've had a couple that were so miserable and so toxic you couldn't dig a foxhole deep enough to get away from their awful conduct, accusations, and bile. People held back and minimized their efforts because they were either afraid of being condemned or rebuffed for something (the old adage "*No good deed goes unpunished*") or had become so resentful that there was no way they were going to give a single breath more than required, as if their employment was a form of some cruel tax levied daily.

On the other hand, I have experienced some great leaders at the helm of some of the companies and organizations I have been a part of in my lifetime and can tell you that some are so inspirational – that their character is so upright and positive – that it is a joy to work for them and the work and participation actually became fun. The result is as a follower you freely give everything you've got. *That* is synergy. The believability of the leader, driven by the evidence seen in the outward displays of character, is what *inspires* people, not high-powered, leveraged cheerleading.

Synergy is like bacteria in yogurt, or like a crop in the field, plants in a garden, or fish in an aquarium. Each require careful stewardship and cultivation of the living thing to make for a beautiful and fruitful existence. It takes creating the best possible environment and doing the best possible things in order to help those living things thrive. *Synergy thrives when cared for.* It dies when you act or behave in a way that is less than caring, less than stewardship focused, and less than considerate. The choice is yours, but remember, regardless of what you do, *there is ALWAYS a collateral effect.*

KEY TWEAKS TO GO

1)

2)

Chapter 16

The Progress Killers

"When the wicked come to power, people hide, but when they are destroyed, the righteous flourish."

Proverbs 28:28

Just as there are two sides to running an organization well, selfless leadership and proactive management, there are two sides that kill innovation and progress. Self*ish* Leadership and Thought*less* Processes will stifle, choke, and eventually kill any worthwhile organization and when it comes to volunteer organizations, I can't think of too many things in life that are more tragic. The really unfortunate part of this is that in many cases, those who are at fault know what they are doing. They have a plan and an agenda designed to keep or make things as they want them, the rest of us be damned. There is a singular quality to how they work, and often from the shadows or at least not out in the open. They work the political pathways, maneuver, plot, scheme, or will arrange things to either protect themselves, their territory, or their agenda and, as I said, the rest of us be damned. Quite frequently, these are the very people who will try to stop every effort to fix an ailing ORG. It is the individual opposer and the toxic culture that hurts and kills others and the organization itself.

No, I'm not describing an "evil empire" and do not intend to sound as if I'm cueing up the Darth Vader theme, but the fact of the matter is that, if you work in volunteer organizations and leadership long enough, you will run into someone at some point who is driven by their own agenda and have convinced themselves that their agenda is superior to the ORG's agenda. By "agenda" I mean vision, mission, and goals. The problem here is not that someone dreams up a way to improve an ORG's vision, mission, and goals – it's that they decide that theirs is superior and needs to be put in place regardless of what everyone else in the ORG says or thinks. Evolution in an ORG is fine, so long as it comes from and is approved by the *collective will of the membership. No single individual or group* has the right to hijack the vision, mission, and goals of an ORG without the consent of everyone else. It is selfish, prideful and cowardly, because if personal agenda was really as good as the perpetrators think it is, they would be able to get the consent of the entire group and act as real servant leaders out in the open and not work in the shadows or in a duplicitous fashion.

Quite honestly, this is the kind of foolishness that drives me crazy. I simply can't tolerate it. Those who know me well - family, friends, and those who I've worked with closely - know that if they want to see the bear in me come out, start leaning on these kinds of buttons. I have very little use for someone who is choosing to protect their own turf over the common good. There is *no place* for that kind of conduct in volunteer organizations and it doesn't belong in *community.* Perhaps I feel so strongly about this because of my faith and my cultural upbringing, but I have also been around the organizational block enough times to know that these are the things that ruin a good thing for a lot of people and it's a travesty. While this may seem slightly foreign to our politicized and polarized culture, there are cultures that feel much the same as I do, perhaps even more strongly.

The Lenni-Lenape are the Native Americans who originally lived in and around what is now Manhattan, Long Island, New Jersey and eastern Pennsylvania. Also known as the Delawares, part of the Lenni-Lenape cultural heritage is the legend of the Stone Roller Goblins. These mythical beings were believed to work against travelers as they walked the paths and trails across the Lenape nation by rolling stones and boulders into paths, planting thickets and thorns in the trails, and generally making serious mischief all designed to block the progress of an individual and keep him or her from their errand or goal. This was seen not as essentially harmless pranking, but as a serious violation of someone's *right to excel* or the *right to do right*. This blocking behavior was so accursed by the Lenape that someone who behaved that way towards other members of the tribe was considered to be a stone roller goblin. In a nation where the common good held such high esteem and was so essential to the survival of the entire community, it should come as no surprise that behaving like a stone roller goblin was one of the nation's few *capital* offenses – you could be condemned to *death* for it. Kill someone for good reason and there was no punishment. Continually act against the progress of others and you could be burned at the stake. That's how serious the Lenape took this kind of behavior.

Even if this is just legend, think for a moment how different – and perhaps how much better – our culture might be if we employed that same kind of mindset. Imagine how different our politics would be and what impact it would have on our communities. Our American culture believes so much in personal freedom, yet the one thing we often overlook is the obligation we have towards each other to allow our neighbor to do as they see fit and live in peace, and help them to excel and achieve their endeavors. Instead, we often greedily hoard our own interests and impose our will on others. *This* I believe is at the core of almost every ailment that eventually chokes the life out of our ORGs or turns them into haggard shadows of what they really should and could be. So if in the paragraphs that follow I seem to come down pretty hard on some of these counterproductive behaviors, please understand: *I'm holding back*.

Please also understand that this part of the chapter is not something I looked forward to writing. It is simply painful to write about this or to even have to go into this, but the simple fact of the matter is that as bad as things might be in your ORG, you may find that some of your members may be at the heart of the problem and *not* in an accidental kind of way. For one greedy or self-centered reason or another, they have made making a mess of things or gumming up the works their particular mission in life, and usually it has something to do with a twisted perspective on how to be in charge – an ugly way, though they may not fully understand that.

Bad Characters

The list of crazy characters you will run into is both long and distressing. I could write an entire book alone on the awful individuals ORGs have been forced to endure after allowing these monsters a chance to take root, but I think it may be more productive to simply mention some of the more common ones in order to give you an idea of what to watch for. In doing so, a pattern should emerge that will become easier to see once you become more aware of what progress killers look like. They have several common characteristics that override the sense of common good and community that is the hallmark of good servant leaders. In fact, the easiest way to see the flaws is to look for behaviors that are *counter* to servant leadership. So here are some of the common ones you will run into:

- **The Collector** – One of the more common counterproductive characters you will run into in organizations is what I call, "The Collector." This person usually finds their way into a position of power and begins to do a good job of getting some things done. They are usually pretty good administrators and, at least at first, do a solid job of running some small area. Then they start to accumulate. A task here, a responsibility there, and pretty soon you have a person who has collected several different job titles and responsibilities. They start pulling in more and more – but that doesn't translate into more and more getting accomplished. What separates them from good *leaders* or even good managers is that they have real difficulty *genuinely* sharing, delegating, and instructing others in the tasks and responsibilities they have accumulated.

I've seen this most often in churches. In one church I considered joining when I moved to Arizona, I ran headlong into a Collector who, among other things, was the lady in charge of greeting new attendees and potential members. She was perpetually busy and we had some difficulty connecting either by phone or in person. When we finally did connect, she was distracted and a bit too self-important – which should have been a dead giveaway to someone at the church that the task of potential member cultivation belonged elsewhere. When I casually mentioned that she seemed very busy, she rattled off all the responsibilities she had. "Isn't there anyone else in the church that can help ease your workload?" I asked. "No," she said, "No one can really do these things as well as I can," and she meant it. As prideful as that was, she really believed it, yet was blind to the fact that someone with half the talent and a little more attentiveness and time would have won me as a new member.

When I didn't join and stopped attending, I got a call from the new pastor who had just been assigned to the church. "What happened," he asked. "Why did you stop coming?" I told him what had happened and there was a long moment of silence on the other end of the phone. I suggested that he had a problem and that he had a "Collector" on his hands. He admitted that he had become aware of it over several conversations like ours but wasn't sure what to do. I told him to thank her for her hard service and assign several jobs to new people to lighten her load and break up the monopoly. "But we might lose her,"

251

he protested. I didn't say anything, and a long moment later he admitted that losing her might be the best solution to a host of ORG problems he was beginning to see.

- **The Centralizer** – If you think that is bad, this one may actually be worse. In another organization I belonged to, we had an administrator who slowly accumulated a vast empire of responsibilities to the point that she made herself irreplaceable. That was the real strategy, a form of insuring her job would never be threatened and the ORG could never afford to lose her. Yet, she became such a huge barrier to progress, using all kinds of strategies to inhibit initiatives that she didn't want to see happen, or blocking people she didn't care for. In a similar fashion, I ran into another leader – a true Boat Anchor – in the same place who, would starve, kill, beat, or dismantle any good idea that came his way unless he thought of it. If it didn't come from him, it never had a chance.

    These behaviors are not self*less*, but self*ish*. They are not behaviors of servant leaders or managers. They are not the best behaviors found in volunteer organizations, but rank among the ugly behaviors that really have no legitimate place in volunteer ORGs.

- **The Dictator** – This culprit is one of the most common. Their leadership style is anything but a servant leadership style and then tend to ride roughshod over their members. They don't listen to others well and rely heavily on their own force of personality in order to force their will on others. They are *not* collaborative leaders. As such, you can expect them to dispense with the organization's vision, mission, and goals whenever it suits them.

- **The Enforcer** – The Enforcer usually is not the top dog in the organization, but enjoys a position of empowerment where they enforce rules or the will of others on the rest of the membership. These folks eventually evolve into the keepers of the rulebook and will fiercely defend the rules even when it is obvious changes need or should be made.

- **The Centerpiece** – This one is the play actor that is more concerned with status and appearances than with reality or actually doing something. You can expect them to make promises and then make excuses or chuck others under the bus when things don't happen.

- **The Keeper of the Sacred** – This one often acts like a chameleon and appears to be a protector of good things. Often, though, they have an agenda of their own and will block the natural growth and evolution that every organization needs to go through. This can also become a culture within a group that can eventually kill the organization. The Barbershop Harmony Society went through something like this when they became entrenched in a rigid set of rules that constrained what was considered "real" Barbershop harmony. Eventually cooler (and newer) heads prevailed and the society has been through a renaissance in recent years, but keeping the sacred nearly killed them.

- **The Titlist** – Like the centerpiece, this one is more interested in authority than for what or how the

253

authority should be used. Their weakness shows when they get into organizational stress situations and they don't really know what to do.

- **The Gatekeeper** – Boy, if you want to gum up an operation, get yourself one of these. Having a leader *appoint* a gatekeeper to help control the flow of administrative things their way is one thing. But when someone on their own decides to act as gatekeeper and does so without the consent or knowledge of the leader, it has the effect of restricting the leader's effectiveness. The leader practicing MBWA, or Managing by Walking About, can rectify this in time, but leaders and managers cannot afford to default the flow of information through someone else without specific instructions and   clear   boundaries.

- **The Puppet Master** – This is one of the more prideful and foolish monsters you can run into. Anyone who thinks that they can control others, what they do and what they think, is a real danger to everyone around them. *Manipulation* is their art and craft – and has *NO* place in a community or volunteer organization. Beware of them. They tend to hide in the   weeds   like   the   snakes   they   are.

- **The Edifice** - The old guy or girl that won't move on; won't quit but needs to step aside. Enough said.

- **The "Owners"** (or the **"In" Gang**) – Even worse than the Edifice, when a clique environment prevails, genuine community does not and cannot thrive. Again, this behavior has *NO* place in community or volunteer organizations. They will ask others for all kinds of help and then just as quickly disrespect the efforts of others or cast you aside as unnecessary. It's one thing to take ownership and act as a good steward. It's another to think of a group as your personal play toy.

- **The Boat Anchor** – I *really hate* this behavior. This is the leader or manager that will publically support you, smile at you, *love* your idea and then choke the life out of it by quietly not supporting it behind the scenes. If *they* don't think of it or can't get the credit, they will insure no one else does. Those well-practiced at it will simply let your idea starve to death or bury it in ways that kill it off, kill your progress, or dampen your initiative. I like the old tradition of burning stone roller goblins at the stake – they deserve it!

- **The Bully** – Leaders that act like bullies need to go, period. 'Enough said.

- **The Sole Worker** – This one thinks they are the only one who can do *anything* or do it well enough to get things done. They are a wet blanket on the initiative within an organization because they keep others from contributing. This can eventually cause an organization to go into a stasis where no one can do or will do anything. Why bother? And the ORG falls asleep like Sleeping Beauty as a result. Then they complain that no one else will do any work. Communities share responsibility.

- **The Foreman in Charge** – Again, this is not the person at the top, but the one who has been allowed to step in and take charge by default. Unlike the Enforcer who acts as an extension of a bad leader, the Foreman in Charge often hijacks a weak leader's authority and can sew all kinds of unrest. They too usually function using their force of personality, but will eventually start exercising *their* will over those that are duly elected or in charge.

Two additional progress killers need to be mentioned. These two qualify as leader wannabes, but because they behave in a dysfunctional manner, they only succeed in gumming up the works and making life miserable for everyone   else.

- **The Malcontent** – Some folks look at what others do and just pick and pick and pick. In many cases the issue they pick at, or at least where they start, may have some grain of truth but gets blown way out of proportion. As the situation festers and grows worse, the focus of the problem may become some individual the Malcontent has decided not to like or is the reason why life in general is so bad. They tie the issue to a person. If you dig down far enough, there is usually some issue of jealousy or some slight that has provoked the problem, but it is also tied directly to the Malcontent's inability to address the problem or show leadership within the established chain of command or social structure of the group, or an inability to really solve the problem. So instead of providing solutions, the Malcontent takes a few other folks with him who are willing to believe the Malcontent's version of reality or join in demonizing

- **The Faulty Diplomat** – This one *thinks* they are providing a valued service to the group, but frequently their efforts are misguided. It is one thing to act as a diplomatic go-between when things are approached without any kind of dysfunction. However, often times the Faulty Diplomat uses others, or the illusion that there are others, who feel a particular way about an issue and they feel compelled to bring it to the leadership's attention by this quiet back door. In reality, they are probably afraid to raise the issue publically, knowing there might not be the right support for it, or that they don't feel secure or strong enough for the forum of full public scrutiny. Beware of secret messages that come via back channels. Other agendas may be in play and the leader needs to insist on transparency as well as diplomacy and to practice proper confidentiality.

How to Handle Progress Killers

Solving or getting rid of progress killers is not easy. Each situation is going to be as unique as the progress killers themselves and each one will require something different. However, there are some guidelines that may help you resolve the problem in a way that is most productive and the most helpful to your organization and this comes in two parts: the way to *approach* the problem and the way to *handle* the problem.

Dealing with these kinds of issues are the real acid test of good leadership and management because it hits you at the personal level of how you conduct yourself under pressure and in the face of (sometimes aggressive) resistance, while forcing you to have the backbone and skill to prevail in a battle that is very likely to get ugly. Progress killers rarely go quietly into the night.

Your Side

On your side of the equation, this is where ethics and character really have to anchor what you do and each move has to be well considered. You have to possess a healthy amount of **emotional intelligence** – that combined quality of maturity, calmness, and wisdom that keeps you focused and calm in the middle of a storm. Winning battles like these is *not* about who can yell the loudest, who can issue viler threats, or who can display more machismo. It's about finding the way back to the vision, mission, and goals of *the group* and making sure they don't get hijacked or supplanted by someone else's personal agenda. You have to stay focused on the bigger picture as calmly and as objectively as possible. Be patient.

You also have to have **a clear sense of timing**. Only fools rush in. Custer and his entire command perished from a lack of complete intelligence all in the name of rushing – don't make the same mistake. Try to get a complete picture – a *really* complete picture of what is actually going on and *who* is involved. Progress killers usually have minions, so watch for them. Frequently who you *think* is the progress killer may only be a puppet for someone lurking in the background. This is not the stuff of melodrama, but reality. Make sure you fully know as best as possible what you are dealing with. Be patient.

Then **make a plan** that is well considered, well thought out, and has a clear set of goals in mind. Consider how far you are willing to go and what the ramifications may be if change is not possible or fails. Avoid going it alone. **Make sure you have support** and that your support will stand with you. I once walked into a campfire circle at a camporee one time because the group was being so unruly that they were disturbing other campers in the park. As I headed for the campfire where all the leaders were gathered I had nearly a dozen others with me who were just as seemingly angry as me. But as I stepped boldly into the

258

center of the firelight and turned to address these leaders I suddenly became aware that *I was the only one there*. I thought, "Oh nuts," and immediately launched into an impassioned plea for the leaders to get their charges under control and how bad this looked for their organization. It was a doozy of a speech concluded with an emphatic, "Act like leaders. Fix this now," as I beat a hasty, if not controlled, retreat to the darkness where upon I found my supporters hidden behind, around, and up in the surrounding trees. Thankfully that one worked out, but I've been in a few other firefights where things did not go so well. Making sure the opponents understand you are not a solitary voice, but represent a significant chunk of the will of the people can make all the difference between success and resounding defeat. Be patient.

Most of all, find *Kotter's Eight Steps of Change* and study it. John Kotter, a scholar and best-selling author, penned the eight steps and is a renowned expert on how to make change happen. Get to know his process and understand how it works before you attempt to overthrow any progress killer. Any change requires certain pieces of a puzzle to be in place and as I discussed earlier in the Triage section, be sure that in trying to save the patient you are not doing more harm than good. The bottom line here is this: Be clear that what you are trying to do is not just an exercise in your own pride or righteous indignation. If it is that latter, do nothing. If there is one thing worse than a progress killer, it's an unskilled individual thinking they are a superhero for all the wrong or semi-right reasons and not *really* knowing what to do. Be patient.

Their Side

Once you are fully prepared to deal with them, then you have to decide *how*. Charging in with guns blazing and a take-no-prisoners attitude may be the way many of us default to – the rest of the world sees this as our American Cowboy mindset and, if we're honest, there is a certain amount of truth to that. The modern idiom of, *"not suffering fools gladly,"* means to have no tolerance or patience for foolishness, and it has come to mean an almost harsh intolerance for anyone engaged in any form of folly, either knowingly or unknowingly, but regardless, it infers a *lack of patience.*

Are you starting to see a subtext here?

Be patient.

It may almost seem counter-intuitive, but being patient and controlled in situations such as this may be far better than rushing in and attempting to overthrow whatever problem there may be. Of course we want to solve any problems as quickly as we can and getting rid of any kind of progress killer as quickly as possible is always preferred, but you also need to see progress killers for what they really are – and that's a cancer that has come to live within your organization. Any doctor or cancer survivor will tell you, getting rid of any cancer is tricky business. Progress killers always manage to *intertwine* themselves with the ORGs operations in ways that their removal almost always creates some kind of pain. You never get away scot-free. The trick is to get rid of them in a way that makes it stick, restores the organization to health, and does as little damage as possible. So how exactly do you do that? In stages.

The best advice is to approach this as diplomatically and calmly as possible, and by progressively ratcheting up the severity of the steps being taken. By "progressively" I do not necessarily mean slowly, but I do mean in a measured, steady, and relentless set of steps.

First, simply ask for change. The answer to this is usually, "no," but it is only right to let the progress killer know that their behavior is not universally accepted. If they are willing to listen, great! If not, then take the next step by pressuring for change collectively and more and more

260

publicly. If the answer is still, "no," then it's time for more aggressive action.

If you are in a position of official authority, take action steps to break up the monopoly, reduce responsibilities, take away authority, or reassign responsibilities if at all possible. If you are not, press the issue collectively with others for that kind of change, but explain the good reasons why often. Always keep *why* out in front of what you are doing so that the issues remain clear and keep shining the light on what is wrong.

If they don't get the message that way, ***fire them***.

Yes, you *can* fire volunteers. This can be done progressively as well. I learned this from a dear friend back at my Scout Camp. I had a volunteer who was driving me absolutely crazy. The guy took nearly fiendish delight in giving me a hard time and challenging my authority. When I gave instructions, he could be counted on to find some public way to dis them either in statements, challenges, or outright disobedience. He would also play on the other volunteers, puffing up his importance, and even got to a point where he threatened to retire from his position, but felt obligated to stay because he was obviously needed so badly. When I finally reached my breaking point one morning, I was ready to charge out and confront the guy when my friend Charlie said, "Let me handle it for you Ranger Tim," and he had two other helpers go with him. Charlie had some authority in the Council as well and marched up to the guy in his campsite, extending his hand and greeting the culprit warmly. Making sure they were surrounded by a large number of witnesses, Charlie continued to pump his hand and thanked him profusely for his years of dedicated service and all he had done for the Council. Charlie then, in no uncertain terms, let him know that we would honor his "retirement" and were replacing him immediately with a new volunteer leader who had already agreed to take his place and would be announced at the next District Meeting. Charlie reportedly smiled at the guy – who stood there stunned – slapped him on the shoulder, turned and walked away. We didn't actually have a replacement, but I fixed that within the hour – and it stuck!

You can also simply call someone in and let them know they are done. I've had to do that too. It's far uglier, but if you follow the advice of carefully ratcheting up the pressure, by the time you get to this point everyone will know why it is happening and it will set the best possible cultural tone for the organization – that behavior *not* based on the common good will *not* be tolerated. Even if you don't have the official authority, you can always establish a campaign to vote them out if need be.

The final step is this, and I hesitate to suggest it because I don't want folks defaulting to this step automatically, but if you can't pry the cancer out, can't reset the culture, and restore the mission, vision, and goals of the organization, leave – and take every one like-minded with you. Establish a new group *without* the progress killers. Staying for an endless political struggle only detracts from your *real* purpose.

Conclusion

The real takeaway here is this: This kind of awful behavior, these kinds of bad leaders and managers exist and thrive because good people don't step up and fill the vacuum. We've touched on the agricultural analogy before and progress killers are the weeds in your organization's leadership garden. They take root because a vacuum of some sort existed allowing them to start to grow. Eventually they take firm root – any gardener will tell you the longer a weed has to grow, the harder it is to eradicate. And just as in gardening, if the weed is allowed to grow unchecked, it can eventually choke off everything else in the garden. I've been involved in lots of old structure renovations and the ones that are the most tragic are the beautiful old places that were abandoned and have become overgrown with weeds. ORGs can be like that too. ORGs need constant, care-filled attention to insure that the weeds never get a chance to take over the garden. Ordinary, good people need to see that, as little as they may feel they have to offer, a less talented *good* person with a servant's heart is *far* better to have involved in the running of an ORG than one of these weeds, even if the weed seemingly has more talent.

Do your part. Learn the ropes. Be willing to serve. Keep the weeds at bay. After all, it is *your* community – be willing to put back in what you have taken out in benefit.

KEY TWEAKS TO GO

1)

2)

3)

4)

Chapter 17

Crew Chiefs and Delegation

"He who does not trust enough will not be trusted."

Lao Tzu

Delegation

Delegating responsibility is one of those skills that leaders and managers need to develop and hone to a fine level if they are going to get their organizations moving at a high level of performance and keep from burning themselves out in the process. We all have suffered, at one point or another, in our careers from professional leaders who have had difficulty delegating or sharing responsibility, but the whole topic of delegation takes on an entirely different character in volunteer organizations. It seems to me that if you can master the craft of delegation and get a thorough understanding of it in volunteer environments, it is one of those things that can benefit your professional leadership exponentially.

In volunteer ORGs, the delegation problem actually manifests itself three different ways. First, leaders and managers tend to hesitate more in delegating responsibility to volunteers because they tend to perceive them as either unreliable or they are unsure of how much they can trust to their members. Second, there is some truth to the question of how committed the members actually are. This could potentially justify my first statement and we've already discussed the need to know just how committed your members actually are. But the one almost no one ever sees is the variation and variety of member types – especially those who you *can* trust. What you can do with them and how to get the most out of what they are is almost never perceived or considered.

Let's take each of these in turn.

At the volunteer level you have to use a lot more finesse and inspiration to keep tasks and people moving forward.

The Question of Reliability

There *is* a good deal of justification to *not* handing out responsibility like it is candy and then expecting that your volunteer members will automatically rise to the occasion. The same skills you use to evaluate personnel at the professional level still needs to be used in determining who has what ability. In a professional setting you can almost expect or demand performance because, ultimately, keeping your job depends on it whether you are the one delegating or being delegated to. Volunteer members on the other hand cannot be handled like that. You can try it and some may respond positively to it, but many will just reach some personal threshold of cooperation inside themselves and decide to do it or cooperate when it pleases them.

Does this make volunteer members less reliable? Yes, it can be seen that way, but I think it has more to do with how we manage or lead people. In corporate settings there are leverage points that make compliance mandatory. At the volunteer level you have to use a lot more finesse and inspiration to keep tasks and people moving forward. Any volunteer leader who has been at it for any length of time will tell you that vision casting, coaching, and cheerleading are what they do more than anything else and they have to do them in far greater quantities in volunteer ORGs than what they are used to doing at work. Volunteer members almost universally *need to see the need* more clearly and have better justification in order to do something that employees can be commanded to do with little justification at all. It doesn't make volunteers less reliable. It makes them more *discriminating*, and *that* is the key.

The solution then to the reliability issue is, as we have discussed before, get to know your people and get to know them well. Be engaged. It is the only way you can find out enough about folks to make intelligent decisions about what they are capable of and IF they are willing. If you really get to know your people well, you will find out things about their background and experiences that could end up being a Godsend. In fact, some of the best delegation experiences I have had have been the ones where I dug deep enough into my people and was able to assign tasks or responsibilities where they just took the ball and ran with it. Almost every time everyone else around them said something like, "Gee, I didn't know you could do that."

Keep in mind that volunteer members are involved in your organization to fulfill some kind of desire, learn something new, or be with others who share the same interests. They are there because they *want* to be. *That* is your leverage point. Find out what they want out of the experience and then find a way to fulfill that. Happy and fulfilled volunteers are *active* volunteers.

Level of Commitment
This one is the wild card and the bridge. While their personal desire to belong to your group may have been enough to get them in the door, as we've already discussed in Chapter 9, the level of commitment may vary wildly from simple, casual interest to being an over-the-top enthusiast. Not everyone who joins does so with the motivation to attend everything, participate in everything, and do everything they can. Many will be content to sit back and watch what is happening to get the lay of the land and see how others interact before they will commit on a deeper level. So again, *connecting* with people, providing a clear path to maturity as

a member, and getting them informed of how things work – having a good onboarding process – are all key to helping members deepen their commitment. And again, vision casting, coaching, and cheerleading are the things you can do to reassure them that they made the right decision by joining and then point them towards ways they can get involved. Just never forget that commitment in any organization is something you have to *cultivate.*

The Characters You Can Trust

Cultivating a member is important for several reasons. One reason is to help you identify who can become key players or leaders within the organization. You always need to be looking for ways to identify and train the next generation of leadership for your group. It's equally important to understand the *kinds* of characters you can really trust in volunteer organizations. Getting this right will keep you from expecting too much or the wrong things from certain people while on the other end of the spectrum you will have a good idea who you *can* expect or groom to rise to the top or jump in as key leaders.

Corner Stoners and Plank Owners

There is a fascinating dynamic within volunteer organizations where the longer lasting ones always have several individuals who seem to have a solid handle on how things work, what the group stands for, and how things are supposed to be done. They are not necessarily the main leaders of the group, but when it comes to finding someone who embodies the beliefs and methods of the group, these folks are it. I call them "Corner Stoners."

Corner Stoners are the protectors of the legacy, the vision, and the principles that the organization has grown to embody. They are the "Elders," the ones who keep things on track, and are bold enough to call other leaders or the entire group to account if they see it straying from its foundational beliefs. When they have the best possible attitude and act proactively and productively this is a great picture of how organizations stay true to their characters. But if they have an attitude, are combative, or work against established leadership, they can become the proverbial millstone around the neck of the group, threatening to drown the very organization they should be protecting.

As a leader, one of the first things you should do is make friends with the "old timers." Get to know them and get to know the organization *they* joined and why. That alone will tell you a great deal about how you have gotten to where you are – both good and bad. They also may have some valuable intel on what has been tried before, what has worked and what hasn't. It takes a good, solid conversation to get to the heart of some of these things and sometimes they can keep you from repeating mistakes that have been made before. They may also be able to give you feedback on why something didn't work and perhaps how it *could.*

Plank Owners are even better. In the Navy, crew members who have been a part of the original crew when a ship is commissioned are referred to as "plank owners." They were there when the ship was being put together and were there at the start. These members are highly valuable because they can tell you a lot of valuable stories about the start of the organization and some of the teething problems and trials they initially went through. This is important because there are always valuable concepts, ideas, even the original vision itself that can help an ailing ORG get back on its feet or help get an ORG back to its roots. It's a lot like using a compass to navigate.

Before the days of GPS when we didn't have a receiver that would tell you exactly where you were on the planet, you would use a compass to navigate from point to point. You had to have a starting point and then know the bearing or direction you needed to go in to get to your destination and this was measured in degrees on the compass. But you didn't just go toward that compass bearing. It was important to make sure you kept where you came from and where you were going lined up, otherwise you might not make it to your destination. It's the same thing with our modern GPS-based directions we get on our phones or navigation units. My wife and I had a navigation unit that kept stroking out and would suddenly change either the "from" or "to" locations without any provocation from us. A few crazy turns that didn't make sense was what it took to realize the thing had gone on the fritz again and we quickly retired it. But the point is this; you need to know where you came from to be sure you are going the best way possible to your destination.

In either case, handling these people from either group takes respect and an open mind. You have to be able to see things from their perspective – and *that* is the real gain here. Being able to understand the true genesis of an organization is worth its weight in gold, especially when looking for ways to inspire the current crop of members. Pride and understanding in what the founders hoped for in your ORG are valuable tools in the hands of skilled leaders and managers, so treat your legacy members with respect and use them as a great resource.

Honor Thy Lurps

One of my favorite plays is *1776*, the musical loosely based on the writing of the Declaration of Independence. Near the end of the play, Williams Daniels, who plays John Adams, stands alone in the candle light of Independence Hall and launches into a dramatic number that resonates with me in a way that almost nothing else does. "Is anybody there? Does anybody care? Does anybody see what I see?" Adams, responding to a desperate communiqué from George Washington. He gives voice to Washington's frustrations and his own, when visions get mired down in the muck of conflicting needs, special interests, and entrenched traditions. The powerful scene goes on to describe the forces that can drive a leader to quit, yet Adams declares, "I have crossed the Rubicon, let the bridge be burned behind me, come what may, come what might: Commitment!" – they are words very close to what the real John Adams voiced in letters to his cherished wife Abigail – sentiments many of us, who could be called "Lurps," voice when the same forces within our beloved organizations drive us to the edge of madness.

What's a "Lurp?" Actually, the term more correctly is LRRP, an acronym for Long Range Reconnaissance Patrol, the highly-skilled and gutsy, groups that first served in Vietnam and several conflicts since. In the military, to be a *LRRP* or Lurp, you had to have experience, be able to think outside the box, function well on your own, and never forget that your mission was to keep the rest of your forces informed and to gather intelligence. There are certainly parallels within any organization, one of which is how the Army or any organization handles the intelligence brought back by the faithful Lurps. Unfortunately, at the organizational level, intel from those on the edges is frequently ignored and even occasionally disparaged in ways that would make any Lurp, military or otherwise, scream, "Is anybody there? Does anybody care? Does anybody see what I see?"

Any other organization with a big mission and big vision is going to have some members who just seem to be really, well, *out there*. I'm not talking about the occasional, certifiable wacko, but the member who just seems to march to a different drummer or who has an intensity that mystifies those around them. The ones that always seem to be coming at ideas from a completely different direction. Those are the Lurps. They tend to have this really annoying habit of pointing at things and trying to get the attention of the masses to say, *"Hey! This thing over here REALLY needs to be looked at. There are NEEDS here!"* right in the middle of other important stuff like choir rehearsals, building programs, and planning other important activities. When confronted with someone who is a Lurp, the average organizational member frequently doesn't know how to react, often deciding that ignoring them is easier than dealing with them or having to listen to them.

It can really be frustrating when you are simply wired differently from everyone else around you and you see something important and everyone else either ignores you or labels you as the resident nut, and this is nothing new. Two thousand years ago Christ said, "I've sent you prophets and you've killed them all." With twenty centuries of progress, we no longer kill our prophets, we simply marginalize them to the point of driving them away. Those inconvenient messages and things they bring to light just don't fit in so well with our programs or agenda.

But Lurps are a really important and vital part of any organization worth its salt. The problem is threefold: most Lurps end up feeling like oddballs, most groups don't know what to do with Lurps or how to treat them, and most groups have no idea what to do with the information discovered or uncovered by these faithful watchers. Israel's response to Joshua and Caleb is a case in point. They literally were LRRPs, even in the military definition of the term, and they even had a mission spelled out by those who sent them – to explore the Promised Land and report back – and *still* their report was rejected.

Being Oddball is OK

Let's take a look at what the historic LRRP members were like. In order to become a member of these elite patrols, you had to be an experienced soldier who had specialized combat training. You also had to be "in country" for enough time that you not only had combat experience, but you had combat experience *where you were*. More than likely you were an NCO, or non-commissioned officer, such as a sergeant, and you had to have the right kind of mindset: able to think outside the box, adapt to crisis situations, and remain cool under fire. *Proficient,* not just meaning knowledgeable, but knowing the job inside and out so that you could do it in your sleep is essentially the one-word definition, but there is more. As valued as these soldiers were, they too garnered some unusual reactions from their peers. They tended to keep to themselves, could be viewed as critical or elitist, and had difficulty blending because they were so different. Being so knowledgeable and experienced left many frustrated when others would ignore the warnings or advice, often with fatal results. Does any of this sound familiar?

Being a Lurp in any church or volunteer organization can be astonishingly similar. In a perfect world, Lurps would be regarded as visionaries, vision casters, futurists, even apostles. But instead, organizations tend to sort those who are different *out* of the mainstream, leaving these experienced individuals feeling increasingly isolated. As they try to help by highlighting things *they* see, they are viewed as being critical, obnoxious, or even out of step when deep inside they know they are right. The conflict grows until, in absolute frustration, they either shut down or move on to something else – and that is a profound tragedy. But two things could avert this.

If you suspect after reading this that maybe *you* might be a Lurp, the good news is that there are a few techniques you can use to survive and contribute. The first is to understand and accept that you are different. God may just have wired you differently and *probably for a purpose*. Not everyone can be *a Lurp*. In fact, most people can't be. It takes someone very special to fill this unique role. Remember too that in a reconnaissance role, you will see some things *earlier* than almost everyone else, so cut yourself and them a break by letting them catch up. Don't expect that the average individual is going to get what you are trying to tell them on the first go around, especially if it isn't part of the norm. As a Lurp, half the job is seeing what is out there. The other half of the job is communicating it to others, and that just may be the hardest part. Learn patience with others and yourself.

Also, give yourself a "walk-away" if you have to.

Elijah didn't really take a "walk-away," he *ran* away when Jezebel threatened his life, but the principle is there in God's Word. Sometimes when those around you just aren't getting it, it doesn't do any good to keep pressing the message home. It may actually do more harm than good. Remember that *God* is ultimately in charge, even of the initiatives you may be seeing that others haven't caught onto yet. It's *His* timing. Taking a "time out" may do your soul some good and, if nothing else, allow you some time to confer with the Lord and make sure you have it right. Then be patient with both yourself and those around you.

On the other hand, as a congregation, if you happen to bump into someone who may be a Lurp, try something different than the all-too-casual norm – try a little respect, or at least *listen and test*. Not the kind of test that is designed to simply shut someone down, but test these observations looking for any validity at all. In doing so, you will have enough time for the really different spin on something to sink in.

This isn't anything new. I think if we honestly look at history, we would conclude that most of our trailblazers, creative geniuses, reformers, and reformation heroes were all Lurps.

Legacy members, like Corner Stoners and Plank Owners, are the eyes and heart that looks back on where you came from. Your Lurps are your eyes and ears of what may lie ahead. Next come those who will help you get the job at hand done in the here and now.

Crew Chiefs, Soloists, and Team Players

It's foolish to try and do every job all on your own, even if you are sure no one can do any of it as well as you can. In a volunteer organization, that *isn't* the point. ORGs like this are usually created to be a shared experience, one anchored in personal growth, therefore, it's actually counterintuitive and counterproductive to keep others from pitching in, helping, and learning the ropes. Dr. David

Jeremiah, head of Turning Point ministries, has said that some of the best leadership advice he ever received was that if Jeremiah ever found anyone who could do a job 75% as well as Jeremiah could, that he should assign that person to that task and make it *their* responsibility, allowing them to *grow into* the job as time went on. That is one of the best practical approaches to delegation I have ever heard. Yet, at the same time you have to gauge if the person you are delegating to is the right *kind* of person for the job. Are they a leader of others, or that one can take the responsibility but prefers to work independently, or are they a great ensemble player? Knowing that will save you a great deal of anguish

---

It's foolish to try and do every job all on your own, even if you are sure no one can do any of it as well as you can. In a volunteer organization, that isn't the point.

---

and frustration.

A great example of this very issue is what I ran into with my maintenance volunteers at Camp Acahela. As our efforts began to gain momentum I knew I could get a lot more done if I assembled small teams and entrusted certain projects or tasks to them. In doing so, I could multiply our efforts and get more things done. For the most part it worked pretty well, but the assumption I made at the start was that *every* volunteer could eventually be *groomed to lead*. It sounds reasonable enough and from a maturing standpoint it made all the sense in the world but when I actually tried to apply this it didn't work nearly as well as it should have.

In particular I had a guy who was one of my most talented volunteers. He could do everything and was an absolute workhorse. No one on my crew worked harder. He had a great personality, had a heart of gold, and was respected by almost everyone. The guy was an ideal candidate to act as my right hand, leading other teams. Heck, he could have been a Master Crew Chief and I would have willingly given him that responsibility. The only problem was that every time I put him in charge of a team of other volunteers, he balked. Not in a way that was obvious at first, but he always seemed to lose interest in a project, or was unable to get together with his crew, or found some reason or way to wiggle out of being at the head of a group. I was really puzzled and frustrated by this at first. He was a guy who was an ideal leader and I couldn't get him to *lead*. Instead, he would just show up and work by himself – and was very content to do so. If he worked with anyone else, it was with a very small and select group of people. But to team him up with others or broaden the impact that he could have? It just wasn't going to happen.

I puzzled over this for a long time until I observed something about orchestras that I had never noticed until watching a performance of a famous symphony on PBS. In that broadcast, the conductor and the first chair of each section were the obvious leaders in the orchestra. The soloists on the other hand were not only like guest stars, but they were different from their brethren in the way they acted *and* how they *interacted* with the rest of the orchestra. Both of those groups were different still from the members of the orchestra who made up the various sections. The more I thought about it, the more I realized that an orchestra is a good functional model of the interplay and dynamics of the different kinds of people who populated my maintenance group – I had Crew Chiefs or Section Leaders (first chairs), talented players, and I had a few soloists. The more I thought about it, the more I realized that some folks gravitate towards leading and mentoring others, bringing them along, and setting an example of excellence. Then there are the members who, at least in the moment, are very content to be great ensemble players while developing their skills and contributing what they can. Finally, there are the virtuosos who know how to do something at an extraordinary level, but they tend to practice that craft on their own. They aren't necessarily interested in leading a group or coaching others, but more interested in performing their craft at the highest possible level and tend to shun everything else in favor of practicing the craft.

I decided to test my theory by going through the list of volunteers I had at the time. I carefully considered each and identified who my section leaders were, who my ensemble players were, and who my soloists were. When I did that, I realized I had several soloists. I also realized that I had several who were mature enough to act as Master Chiefs or Master Section Leads who could head up several groups at once and I was also able to identify who among the ensemble could grow into good leaders and who might be headed for being a soloist. Armed with that set of hunches and information, I modified my approach to assigning tasks, and once I did that, some of the frustrations and hiccoughs we had been experiencing went away and things seemed to work better. This was not a thunderclap change – it was far subtler than that and, to be honest, I don't think anyone ever knew I did it. However, it gave me a far better understanding of my people and *I* had more confidence in who I selected to do what.

Practical Application

Crew Chiefs often have to be identified and then cultivated before you have a chance to use them. Some may jump right out and ask to be put to work, but in most volunteer scenarios you have to beg people to get involved. The reason for this is that your average member may participate, but doesn't have much knowledge (or confidence) in how to do a particular task, and if we're honest about it, most volunteer ORGs are lousy at *grooming* folks for tasks. We never really stop to think that all it takes is for a willing or semi-willing newcomer to shadow an experienced volunteer in order to show them the ropes.

One of the more complex operations we had at camp

was a model rocketry program we ran for our Cub Scouts. The whole operation included a wide variety of tasks such as building three types of models, prepping the models for launch, setting up the launch areas, and then a whole series of tasks when it came to conducting the launches. At first, I ran around like a chicken with my head cut off keeping all these balls in the air, but right from the start I identified who would be good at certain tasks, asked them if they might be interested, and then had them shadow me as I completed the tasks or ran that part of the operation. In every case we did it several times and gradually I would see the trainee *want* to step up and run that part of the show. At that point I would stay with them, but gradually step back and give them the full responsibility, staying nearby enough if they had questions or ran into problems.

One thing that helped anchor this way of teaching what needed to be done was to review how the task or operation went afterwards. Even if it was just a casual conversation after the fact, it gave us an opportunity to review what to do, what not to do, and ways improvements could be made or celebrate lessons learned. The more complicated the task or operation, the more we worked at shadowing. In most cases we were able to have them do the shadowing in an on-the-job fashion as the event was actually happening. But in other cases where the tasks were more complex, I would arrange rehearsals or complete training sessions. For example, when it came to running the launch range for the solid propellant rockets, I invited the entire crew along to launch some rockets I had built as demonstrators. In this informal setting I was able to demonstrate what should be done in order to keep folks safe and how the basic procedures actually unfolded. It was essentially a "play" session but it instructed *and* got the crew excited about what we were doing. After that "play" session, I conducted a more formal rehearsal and because of what we had done earlier, it went far easier that if we had done it cold. *Shadowing* paved the way for more formal training and the staff had more confidence in what they were doing.

Likewise, actually building the rocket kits was complex enough that running through their assembly was essential. This time I offered to meet in our dining hall in the evening with anyone who wanted to learn how to build a rocket model. Again, keeping it informal, we all put the same rocket kit together, chatting and talking about it as we went, but focusing on building each one for ourselves. From this enjoyable event we then had a building class rehearsal where I ran through how I would take a class through building the kits in a set amount of time. From there, the first couple of classes were led by me with my heirs watching closely and helping, and before we knew it, *they* were doing it as if they had been doing it all their lives. I knew the process had worked even better than expected when I caught some of the staff then teaching new staff the same way without any prompting from me. It really is all about *confidence in replication.*

So if you need greeters, have them shadow your best greeters. If you need folks to help run the raffle, have them shadow the folks running the raffle. Whatever you do, avoid just handing a responsibility to someone without running them through *exactly* what is expected. *Show* them, don't just *tell* them – something is bound to get lost in the translation that way. Make sure they have a pretty good grasp of what should be done, but also allow them the latitude to put their own stamp on it or bring their own unique style to the task or operation. Then be sure to always review afterwards to build further confidence and brainstorm how things could work better.

These rules and ideas work regardless of whether you are grooming a crew chief, an ensemble player, or a soloist. You don't necessarily need to tell them how to do their jobs, but making it clear what is expected makes the execution much easier.

One final thought: *Never* forget to say *"Thank You,"* even for the most insignificant of tasks. Be sure to celebrate individual efforts, especially when they are first jumping in, and then celebrate group efforts. This builds the team, solidifies the culture of the group, and insures a solid legacy for the future. Whatever you do, make sure the celebration is genuine, heartfelt, and well-considered on your part. A showboat slap on the back in front of a large crowd will do more damage if the recipient feels as if he or she is a pawn in a play than if you uttered a quiet, personal thank you and really meant it. Handing out ribbons and other pointless junk (and I mean the kind of stuff you might hand to a sixth-grader) like its Halloween candy *exponentially* diminishes that act of genuine thanks. The guiding rule should be that the recipient will remember the event as something with pride, not suspicion or sarcasm. If you are going to hand out a reward, make it good, memorable, thoughtful, and meaningful.

KEY TWEAKS TO GO

1)

2)

3)

PART V

Final Thoughts

"The world is a dangerous place, not because of those who do evil, but because of those who look on and do nothing."
Albert Einstein

In life there is a funny dynamic that seems to frequently bring us full circle. The place where we started is a place where we are likely to return or at least revisit once the journey is done. It is usually a time of reflection, of seeing how all the pieces fit together, what the journey entailed and what lessons were learned in the process.

These last chapters are in that spirit and we once again return to the theme of how incredibly important attitudes and mindsets are in leading, managing, and running volunteer ORGs. You may discover that what you have learned here about running *volunteer* organizations may be some of the best leadership and management lessons you will ever learn.

Chapter 18

Four Thoughts on The Art of Balance

"Happiness in not a matter of intensity, but of balance, order, rhythm, and harmony."

Thomas Merton

By now, if you haven't realized it before, it should be apparent that leadership, especially in volunteer scenarios involves a great deal of balance, like riding a bicycle. Balancing while standing still is *very* hard to do, but by moving forward you now have to balance *and* maintain enough control and give enough direction to keep from crashing. Trade-offs are an obvious part of the mix. Along those lines as I wrap up, I wanted to touch on four thoughts regarding the art of balance and how it relates to leading our ORGs. These are not hard-and-fast rules, but are more along the lines of things to consider or watch for as you move from situation to situation.

Change

The issue of change and how to lead change well is so complex it could be a book all on its own. There are hundreds of works on this topic and entire studies have been devoted to how to do it well. One of the reasons why I don't delve into it here or focus on it in this book is that one scholar in particular, John Kotter of Harvard, has made a career of making change so understandable and manageable that his *Eight Steps of Change* is regarded as the gold standard in leadership circles. Leaders and managers should take the time to read, digest, and then practice his principles and thoughts on the matter.

In essence, Kotter states that for any change to be instituted successfully (and to stick), eight things have to happen. They are:

1. Create a sense of urgency about the issue or matter.
2. Build a guiding coalition.
3. Form a strategic vision and initiatives.
4. Enlist support.
5. Enable action by removing barriers.
6. Generate short-term wins.
7. Sustain acceleration.
8. Institute change.

Big changes or small, the idea remains the same – each of these steps will happen as a change is implemented and put in place. The problem is that many people don't want to change and they *resist* it because it is unfamiliar or they can't see the real benefits of making any changes. We all have seen lots of situations where change seems to have occurred just for the sake of change or to give some boss a chance to exercise his or her will in the belief that things will be better. To overcome *all* of that, Kotter's change theory forces leaders and managers to think the process out carefully, then systematically implement the change. But even knowing all that, one common sense rule still applies and should be respected above all others: *If it ain't broke (or dangerously obsolete), don't fix it.*

Over Control versus Letting Go

One of the first things I learned in pilot training was if things got crazy and I had lost control of the plane, to simply let go. In most cases, the docile Cessnas I was learning to fly would settle down and correct themselves. Years later, I was reminded of this when a buddy loaned me the use of his Bobcat front loader to do some work at camp. "If things start to go wrong," Jim said leaning into the cockpit of the little Bobcat, "all you have to do is let go of the controls. Everything will go to neutral and everything will stop." "So if I get myself in any trouble," I reiterated back to Jim's affirming nods, "just let go and everything goes right back to neutral." That's a simple truth that often works if you get into something crazy while leading a group and things suddenly go haywire – step back, let go for a minute, get your bearings, and then proceed *gently*.

It is entirely possible to get yourself into a situation where you suddenly are over controlling everything. A firm grip on situations, especially in a crisis, is mandatory. When operations can go back to being routine, you have to relax your grip and allow the plant to grow as it wants. As we have discussed, synergy *does not* occur in highly directed situations. It needs maneuvering room and space to grow on its own, so be sure to relax your grip and check yourself to insure that you are not overdoing leadership or management. Keep in mind the lyrics of the classic rock tune, *Hold on Loosely, by 38 Special.* It applies here as well.

Middle Ground and Stability

On one occasion I watched our staff of young Scouts during a week of setting up summer camp and witnessed something I found to be very profound and have never forgotten.

We had a floating swimming dock that was simply drifting around the pond. It had been pushed off of the shore where it had sat during the previous winter and wasn't anchored in its position yet, so it was placidly floating and drifting around the pond – at least until a group of our staff members on break got to it.

The young teenagers swam to it like they were assaulting a beachhead in an amphibious landing from World War II and they all tried to board it from one side. This nearly capsized the floating platform and the staff beat a hasty retreat. Some of the older staff members really should have known better, but boys will be boys. The younger ones simply didn't have the experience to know that it was possible to upend a heavy, floating dock.

After regrouping in the water a few yards from the platform, they tried again, this time working together to mount the dock from all sides at once. The team effort succeeded and, with a minimum of fuss and instability, the dozen and a half of them were soon frolicking and having a good time on and around the platform.

As I watched I noticed that if they all stayed close to the center of the platform, they could rough-house and carry on like a bunch of dancing pagans with very little instability. But when any significant portion of their group got out towards the edges, the floating dock took on an entirely different personality. When out at the edges, all it took was one or two individuals out of 18 to act wildly and the platform would start to get *very* unstable. When everyone got out to the edges, things got downright wild at the slightest provocation. While this seemed to be fun for a few, the rest weren't so wild about the potentials of what might happen or, even more so, how uncomfortable the ride was getting.

It struck me how much this actually reflects how things can get in any of our organizations. When you get only a few members, dancing and carrying on out at the fringes, it can get a bit uncomfortable for the rest of the group who just happen to like the middle where things are stable and on an even keel. It's one thing if the instability is caused by carelessness or thoughtlessness on the part of a few, but it's another thing entirely when it is done deliberately with the intent of disrupting the rest of the group. If you find folks like that and all they want to be is *destructive*, weed them out.

Between the Horns of a Dilemma

One final thought in all this is something I see that is frequently needed, but rarely practiced. At the start of this book we discussed the principle of Ugly, Poor, Good, Better, Best and how we often have to work up the scale when trying to make things better. On occasion, the situation you are faced with may put you between a rock and a hard place where either choice isn't great, optimal, or even what you might hope for. It seems that all you have are two choices, and neither is what you want or problems will be created either way you go. W. Edgar Moore refers to this as the "horns of a dilemma." Either way you go you are very likely to end up skewered by one horn or the other. But as Moore suggests, there are two solutions.

The first choice is to *break* one or the other of the horns by proving that the consequences are not nearly as bad as you might think. We often just give up on something thinking that it is worse than it really is. There is no harm in testing to see if a situation is really as bad as you believe – you may discover some simple but previously overlooked solution in the process. The other solution is to *escape between the horns of the dilemma.*

In this scenario you find an alternative that defeats the two terrible alternatives by refusing to be limited by rotten and potentially terrifying alternatives with some creative thinking. Moore uses a real life illustration of a hotel fire in Atlanta where several people lost their lives because they felt compelled to try and escape the fire by fleeing into the halls or jumping out the windows of their rooms. In the halls, many met their demise by inhaling smoke and poison gases generated by the fire many floors below, while those who jumped died on impact from the fall. Going between the horns of the dilemma, some guests stuffed wet towels and newspaper in the cracks around their doors keeping the deadly gases and smoke out and then opened their windows to let fresh air in while calmly awaiting a rescue. No doubt that even this solution created a great deal of angst, yet it was a *survivable* solution nevertheless, and far better than jumping or attempting to survive the deadly smoke in the halls.

The crises we often face in organizations is often like that. If we focus on right/wrong or uncompromising solutions, we can quickly find ourselves stuck between the horns of an ugly dilemma. But if we have a more realistic view – Ugly, Poor, Good, Better, Best, and that life is a continuum of making choices that hopefully continue to improve the situations we are in. If we do that then we can avoid being skewered by the horns of the dilemmas we often create ourselves by limiting our thinking or by *un*creative thinking.

The success of your organization can in some ways be seen as a formula as simple as this: Like riding a bicycle, it's all about balance, forward motion, steering well, and knowing when to hit the brakes.

KEY TWEAKS TO GO

1)

2)

3)

Chapter 19

Conclusion – Be Who You Is and Heartworthy

"As I grow older, I pay less attention to what men say. I just watch what they do."

Andrew Carnegie

Be Who You Is

When I was a young student at Northeastern Bible College in Essex Fells, New Jersey, the President of our little college, Dr. Charles W. Anderson would preach a sermon in chapel about once a year built around the idea of being genuine and learning to use the gifts that you have instead of trying to be something you are not or aspiring to things that lead to pride and selfishness. It was a great and necessary message for young church leaders to hear, but over the years I've realized that it is a great message for anyone who dedicates themselves to managing or leading others to hear. It's a message that draws a line in the sand in today's culture where we need to constantly remind ourselves *who* we are really doing all this for – *our members* or for *ourselves*?

Our culture leans so hard in the direction of posturing that we do not even realize when we are doing it. I was constantly amazed and frequently amused by the lengths some of my classmates would go to in order to establish who was the classes' top performer or best student. I've seen business letters, resumes, and have had some stunning conversations with people that were all so packed with language all designed to impress that it was hard to get at what they actually wanted. Worse still is that this behavior has become so commonplace that some who try to practice it don't even realize how silly some of the posturing actually is. We live in a generation of overblown talkers, wild statement makers, and proud, entitled executives who have forgotten that the strongest and most powerful statement of how good they are as leaders and managers is *how willing their people are to follow them*, not how well they stake their territorial claim.

I could write an entire book on the evils of pride and how destructive it can be, but that isn't really the point I want to make here. Less obvious – and *this* is the point: In our quest to present ourselves as qualified leaders we sometimes get our priorities all tangled up and lose sight of what we are supposed to be doing and who we really are. A well-practiced and well-centered servant leader doesn't worry about the credit he or she may get in a particular situation. They stay focused on the task at hand and let the rewards come as they may. In fact, the intensity of being focused on doing the job well is so sharp that it becomes a zone of comfort and a shield to distractions. If you observe a really noteworthy leader, one of the qualities that eventually registers is that they are incredibly comfortable in what they do, the position they have, *and who they are*.

What made the message that Dr. Anderson preached so memorable to me was the lyrics that he quoted from. The line, "Be who you is, not who you ain't," and, "If you is the tail, don't try and wags the dog," stuck with me as both amusing and a reminder to keep things in proper perspective. For years I tried to find what I thought was the poem this came from and only recently discovered that it is actually a song from an early 20th century musical called *"Moonshine."* The song, *"Don't Be What You Ain't,"* is a light-hearted colloquial statement of keeping your pride in check and goes like this:

> De sunflower ain't de daisy,
> And de melon ain't de rose.

Why is dey all so crazy,
To be sumfin else dat grows?
Jess stick to de place you're planted
And do the best you knows;
Be de sunflower or de daisy,
De melon or de rose.

Refrain
Don't be what you ain't,
Jess yo' be what yo' is.
If you am not what you are,
Den you is not what you is;
If you're just a little tadpole,
Don't you try to be the frog.
If you are de tail, don't try to wag the dog.
Pass de plate if you can't exhort or preach;
If you're jess a little pebble,
Don't you try to be the beach.
When a man is what he isn't,
Den he isn't what he is.
And as sure as I'm a talkin'
He's a goin' to get his.

De Song Thrush ain't no Robin,
And de catbird ain't no Jay.
Why is dey all a throbbin' to outdo each other's lay?
Jess sing de song God gave you,
And let your heart be gay;
Be de Song Thrush or the Robin,
De catbird or de Jay.

These lyrics from 1905 stand in stark contrast to our cultural mindset today. Don't they? The warning about being prideful or trying to be something you really aren't hardly gets any play nowadays, yet it is a necessary message. I almost feel inclined to apologize for the lyrics or have a need to explain them, but the idea is so simple and applicable, to do so would only spoil the impact. So I will leave it as it is and let it speak to us all on its own. Instead, I'm going to tell you how several great leaders I know have employed their craft in ways that avoid pride altogether.

One of the most effective leaders I ever met, and one who taught me a *great* deal about the common sense that gives genuine leadership the kind of traction it needs, was one of my volunteer leaders on my maintenance staff at Camp Acahela. When I first met Charlie, he introduced himself as a guy who was willing to come on up to the camp and do some work around the place just because he had camped there as a kid and had often brought his own troop up to camp there. That sentiment was pretty commonplace and at first I didn't think anything of it. But the more I got to know Charlie, the more I realized that there was a lot more to this than what was readily apparent. In fact, the more I learned about *him,* the more I learned about a lot of stuff, *especially* leadership.

Looking back, it's actually kind of funny. He came off as laid back, easygoing, and exceptionally polite. By day, he was a janitor for one of the area's middle schools and then worked at his church as one of the sextons, but in either case it became apparent that he was responsible for far more that what either of those job descriptions entailed. He was one of our Council Commissioners and I quickly came to understand that this guy had teeth too. He very easily could read someone the riot act in a way that would leave the recipient both stunned *and* compliant. You may have heard it said that you can't really fire a volunteer – don't believe it! I saw Charlie handle a troublesome volunteer that was driving me crazy. I told the story earlier, but when the guy finally crossed a line that Charlie felt was out of bounds he went up to the guy and *retired* him on the spot. He left the guy with his jaw hanging open and had enough witnesses that the "retirement" stuck. Charlie almost never had to raise his voice – the *look* could be withering enough - and 90% of the time he never even needed to ratchet things up to *that* level – he just had this way about him that got stuff done, and he often did it in a way that left me wondering how the heck he did it.

Occasionally, I would mention something we needed or a problem I was having with something or someone, and the next thing I knew, it was somehow resolved. Then, on a visit one day to his home I saw a bunch of photos and plaques. There were photos of him with several of our Governors, Senators, and other dignitaries. Charlie actually knew a *ton* of people in Harrisburg and was incredibly well-connected. The guy was a real incarnation of Bruce Wayne and Batman. By day he was a mild mannered janitor. By night, he was the president of his local Teachers' Union. Most of the time he appeared to be an unassuming helper, when in reality he was a powerful and well-connected leader who got things done one way or another. What an *incredible* man. I think he actually delighted in leaving us all wondering how he did what he did.

The point is that for Charlie it was never *really* about the position, though he could play that role better than anyone I ever met. He could slide from helper in janitor clothes to leader in a tux with an ease that just blew me away. He knew it was about *getting things done,* and he found a way to be who he really was at heart and make it count. He was one of the best leadership mentors I ever had.

Heartworthy

There is a beautiful, wooded trail on the property of Camp Acahela that meanders through the pine and maple forest as it heads towards the Tobyhanna Creek. If you walk the trail, you will be struck by how pretty it is regardless of the time of year. The seasons and all their changes reflect well on the trail so that it is always beautiful, always a delight, always refreshing whether covered in snow, lush with the blooms of spring, or painted with the rich colors of autumn. It *isn't* an easy trail to navigate – it is steep in some places, takes some effort to walk, and at times, it seems to wander pointlessly as if there is no purpose or goal, like God in His infinite wisdom just reached down and doodled in the woods with His finger and carved out a maze leading to nowhere. Almost uniformly, hikers, especially the younger ones, will reach a spot on one of the steeper, downhill parts of the trail and start to grumble and curse wondering where they are and what the point might be to all of this is. It's a place where you can't see very far ahead. You can't see very far behind either. In fact, the forest is so thick at that point that you can't see much of anything except trees and their canopy of leaves. In all its beauty, it can be deeply disquieting – akin to being stuck behind a big trailer on the Interstate as you travel through a state like New Mexico; you may be surrounded by incredible beauty, but it's hard to see.

Then, just when you are ready to turn back, and give up because of the monotony of being unsure of where exactly you are, you take a few more steps forward and step out on to one of the most beautiful overlooks you will ever see. Sixty-five feet above the Tobyhanna Creek and directly across from the ski trails at Jack Frost Ski Resort, the sudden arrival at such a beautiful destination is stunning, not only for its beauty, but for its sudden and unexpected arrival. I always found it to be a place of peace and a place where I could always reflect and find some clarity regardless of what season it was or the mood of the weather. More than that though, the place and the journey there was and still is an illustration for me about a truth in life that I have shared often with others.

There are lots of times in our lives when the path we are on is anything but straight. Frequently it is hard to see the future. What lies ahead and even the recent past is obscure in the confounding swirl of confusion we may have just passed through. Sometimes it is frustratingly difficult to get our bearings, figure out where we are and know for certain that the next step leads to something productive. Even if our determination and faith are in high gear, the trail at times can be hard to navigate and gives little in the way of clues on our progress or location. It is times like these that you have to reach inside, lean on the hope that a divine hand has some greater purpose in mind by all this, and continue to carefully move forward.

On Acahela's trail, depending on the season, the difference between being on the difficult trail and then arriving at the beautiful overlook where everything becomes clear and the reward of the journey makes the trip all worthwhile can be a matter of two or three steps or a half dozen – the forest is so dense. So it is with many of the journeys we face in life including the ones involving leadership and management and working on the behalf of others or in some worthy cause. The difference between a seasoned traveler and a grumbling rookie is that the seasoned traveler knows that at some point everything will come into plain view and there will be a place of clarity where the claustrophobic canopy and hard work will all melt away. The rookie's heart often fails and asks, "Why am I doing this?" while the seasoned traveler presses on, arrives at the goal and says, "*This* is why I came." It's all a matter of heart and faith and experience.

We are at the end of our journey together through this book, but the many trails of leadership and management and what your organizations can achieve still lay ahead of you. I hope that this book has added a few tools you can take with you as you go and I hope that several of the recurring themes here have stuck and will come back to you as you need them.

Remember that life is often a complex set of contradictions making our existence one rife with compromise, not as a matter of choice, but as a matter of necessity. We all love to imagine ourselves as steadfast and uncompromising but it might be more realistic and useful to imagine ourselves as downhill slalom skiers steering for all we are worth through a series of winding gates. I hope that the lessons about your mindset, thinking creatively, and remaining positive in the face of adversity, all help and that approaching problems with a desire to work selflessly on the behalf of others as you work up the scale from Ugly to Poor to Good to Better and eventually, to Best become part of your regular routine and serve you well so that you will successfully navigate all the gates of that downhill slalom at an exhilarating speed, and when you finally dash across the finish line in a spray of snow and come to a stop that you will scream out, "Man, that was *great*! Let's do that again!"

Heartworthy: The best practices and skills and tools, the hints and tips, all the formulas give way to a character infused with all these things that now acts with a synergistic quality within the individual.

I hope I've convinced you that our volunteer organizations need good stewards that care for them in a way that benefits not only the leaders or the needs of the leaders, but remembers why the organization was created in the first place. To rediscover the worthy cause or worthwhile reasons why the organization exists, even if it is just for the purpose of friendship and fellowship. We don't need to save the world all the time. Making life better and more enjoyable for each other is a worthy enough and sometimes difficult goal itself. Good, solid leadership and management are best accomplished as acts of *stewardship*, and I hope this has helped provide the tools needed to do that job well.

If anything, I hope I have persuaded you that volunteer leadership and management are worthwhile investments of yourself and all the skills you have, but in a way that serves others *first*. Leaders and managers are a special breed, each with special skills. The good ones practice the craft well. The better ones practice the craft in a particularly trustworthy way. The best ones evolve trustworthiness to another transformational level. I have seen

296

this only a few times in my life, and strive for it myself. I hope I get there some day and I hope you do too. That transformational level is when all the pieces we've talked about come together and when they do it has a way of transforming the leader or manager in a way that I think is best described as *heartworthy*. The best practices and skills and tools, the hints and tips, all the formulas give way to a character infused with all these things that now acts with a synergistic quality within the individual. Like seeing the character of Lincoln in his eyes in one of those old photos, the ones who have become and practice being *heartworthy* have what folks used to refer to as a certain "carriage," they walk and talk and carry themselves in a way that makes it abundantly clear that this is who they are. I hope that, for both you and I, as we progress down this trail of service that we would find that core and source in our beings that would lead us to being something more than a simple collection of leadership skills but to becoming *heartworthy*.

In the Old Testament, Proverbs 4:23-27 says this: *"Above all else, **guard your heart**, for it affects everything you do. Avoid all perverse talk; stay far from corrupt speech. Look straight ahead, and fix your eyes on what lies before you. Mark out a straight path for your feet; then stick to the path and stay safe. Don't get sidetracked; keep your feet from following evil."*

Finally, I hope this for you: I hope you succeed in shaping your organization for the better, that in the end you will succeed in leaving your organization with a legacy of good health and vitality for years to come. In the process I also hope that the organization shapes you as well, making you the best leader and manager and member you can be and realize that you have become *heartworthy* along the way.

Finally, a *REAL* Handbook for the Volunteer Groups we belong to!

Volunteer Groups and their leaders *finally* have a practical and realistic handbook designed specifically for the congregations, leagues, clubs, troops, and fellowships that make up the backbone of our communities. *TWEAKS* is written by veteran how-to author Tim Bongard in his familiar, hands-on and folksy style that will give you an immediate handle and understanding of the complex issues and demands needed to lead your volunteer ORG to greater levels of performance regardless of the condition it may be in now. Complete overhaul, addressing serious problems, or just some fine tuning, *TWEAKS* will be a guide you will turn to again and again.

If your organization is in trouble, struggling or just needs a tune-up, *TWEAKS* can give you the tools and practical knowledge needed to reset the trajectory of your organization no matter how large or small it may be. *TWEAKS* can have a profound effect on how you lead your group so that it can deliver on the very reasons people volunteered to join in the first place.

If you have been looking for a guide to help your ORG where it actually lives and make you a better leader, *this is it!*

AUTHOR Tim Bongard is a retired Ranger and experienced corporate and volunteer leader. Active in numerous community groups and clubs, he is currently working on his doctorate in Leadership at Grand Canyon University.